Sticks and Stones

The Troublesome

Success

of Children's

Literature

from Slovenly Peter

to Harry Potter

Jack Zipes

ROUTLEDGE

New York and London

Published in 2002 by
Routledge
29 West 35th Street
New York, New York 10001

Published in Great Britain by
Routledge
11 New Fetter Lane
London EC4P 4EE

Routledge is an imprint of the Taylor & Francis Group.

10   9   8   7   6   5   4   3   2   1

Library of Congress Cataloging-in-Publication Data

Zipes, Jack David.
   Sticks and stones: the troublesome success of children's literature from Slovenly Peter to
Harry Potter / Jack Zipes.
      p. cm.
   Includes bibliographical references and index.
   ISBN 0-415-93880-5 (pbk)
   1. Children's literature–History and criticism. 2. Children's literature, American–
History and criticism. I. Title.

PN1009.A1 Z57 2000
809'.89282'09045–dc21   00-032318

To Carol and Hanna

With hope and joy
in the present

Contents

Preface   *ix*

1   The Cultural Homogenization of American Children   1

2   Do You Know What We Are Doing to Your Books?   24

3   Why Children's Literature Does Not Exist   39

4   The Value of Evaluating the Value of Children's Literature   61

5   Wanda Gág's Americanization of the Grimms' Fairy Tales   81

6   The Contamination of the Fairy Tale   99

7   The Wisdom and Folly of Storytelling   126

8   The Perverse Delight of *Shockheaded Peter*   147

9   The Phenomenon of Harry Potter, or Why All the Talk?   170

Bibliography   *191*

Index   *205*

Preface

The more we invest in children,

the more we destroy their future. There is no

way out of the paradox that we have created,

unless we reconsider our investment. For

twenty-five years I have been engaged in writing

about children's literature and culture. I have always written with the hope that childhood might be redeemed, not innocent childhood, but a childhood rich in adventure and opportunities for self-exploration and self-determination. Instead, I witness a growing regulation and standardization of children's lives that undermine the very sincere concern parents have for their young. It appears that my hope for greater freedom and creativity in children's lives will be disappointed. Yet I have not abandoned this hope. I have become more sober about changing how we socialize children, even though the way we do it is nothing short of barbaric.

This may be a shocking observation, but it isn't new. Theodor Adorno, whose works have continually inspired my thinking, began making the connection between civilization and barbarianism well over fifty years ago. Appalled by the totalitarian practices of Nazi Germany, Adorno came in 1939 to live in the United States, where he wrote his famous book *Dialectic of the Enlightenment* (1944) with Max Horkheimer. Instead of rejoicing in the freedom of America, he was horrified to find that there were totalitarian tendencies in all spheres of life that could lead to a degradation of culture and diminished autonomy for individuals. He continually wrote about the culture industry's sophisticated and subtle mechanisms to limit our critical thinking and warned that we had created myths about reason and democracy that blinded us to the untruths which we celebrated through rationalization and ethical posturing.

Not everything that Adorno predicted in his writings until his death in 1969 has come true. But he has certainly shed light on the contradictory way we treat our children, even though he never wrote about the particular situation of children within the culture industry. All we have to do is look at the vocal complaints about the mass media and children's culture to see the relevance of his theories. It may be a far cry to link Adorno with the gifted American entertainer Steve Allen, but I was reminded of how much they have in common when I read a full-page ad in the Minneapolis *Star Tribune* of February 21, 2000. "Parents . . . Grandparents . . . Families," Allen's ad began, "This is for you. TV is leading children down a moral sewer. Now you and I can stop it. Are you as disgusted as I am at the filth, vulgarity, sex, and violence TV is sending into our homes? . . . Are you as outraged as I am at how TV is undermining the morals of children . . . encouraging them to have pre-marital sex . . . encouraging lack of respect for authority and crime . . . and shaping our country down to the lowest standards of decency? Well now you and I can end it. Yes we can, actually and literally. We can do it by reaching the TV sponsors whose ad dollars make it possible."

Though Adorno would never have been caught dead in a million years playing an activist role in opposing the culture industry, he would have certainly grasped and supported Allen's rage. In contrast to Allen, he would not have asserted that family values could easily be restored by exercising pressure on TV sponsors. He would have tried to understand how barbaric conditions have continued to persist because of our faith in the myth of Enlightenment.

What is most disturbing today is that we use rational methods to cultivate the tastes and values of the young in all kinds of educational, religious, and cultural institutions that are predicated on corporate practices and goals. Everything we do to, with, and for our children is influenced by capitalist market conditions and the hegemonic interests of ruling corporate elites. In simple terms, we calculate what is best for our children by regarding them as investments and turning them into commodities. Such rationalized practices lead to irrational if not vicious behavior. Success and justice are thus based on irrational and commodified relations. Children are expected to sort out the contradictions that are inevitable and intolerable in our society, and our vested interests drive them forward into hysteria, violence, and bewilderment.

American society is a wilderness. The wilderness is not only a lonely and lovely place, but it is dangerous because wild things are out there, bent on survival and ready to devour you. People are wild because they are controlled too much, cooped up, even though they appear free to roam wherever they desire. But they do not know their desires. We do not know our desires. They are packaged for us and induced. This induction forms part of the civilizing process that paradoxically produces the wildness and bewilderment in us.

Total control of our natural and induced desires seems to offer hope. So it is no surprise to me to see totalizing tendencies in all aspects of society. The totalitarian nature of the former communist states in Eastern Europe and the Far East were vapid in comparison with the capitalist conglomerates that penetrate our lives constantly in the name of globalization. Today we operate on ourselves to improve our bodies and minds in keeping with totally new images of ideal societies based on degenerate utopias. We seek to improve our children's lives by getting rid of moral sewers and by constructing purification systems that confine them. We do not realize how much our purification systems actually produce the waste and turpitude that we complain about.

These sobering misgivings of mine have fortunately been offset by personal experiences of resistance to totalizing forces that I have had in North America and Europe. Human beings are devious. We know and feel the hypocrisy of compliance with irrational norms. We engage in all sorts of subversive practices in the home, on the streets, and at work. We desperately want to save our children from the future that we have planned for them. We engage social and political forces on the battlefield of children's bodies and minds.

During the past twenty years in America many diverse groups have formed to do battle with the culture industry and government on behalf of children, including teenagers. Interestingly, these groups span the spectrum from the religious right to the radical left. Since it is difficult to describe all their activities, I want to comment on general tendencies in two groups. The first group, whom I call the activists, believe that interference with the culture industry practices can bring about the necessary changes that will allow children to have a more spiritual and creative childhood. Here the media watch groups, family associations, religious institutions, and feminist organizations place pressure on the government and mass media to alter shows, images, and literature that they feel are destroying the moral health of our children. In their view children are innocent and passive victims and are at the mercy of outside forces. The second group, whom I call the realists, is made up largely of theorists influenced by the Birmingham School of cultural studies, who argue that children are much more creative and independent than we think. Resilient, they learn how to play with and use the mass media and other forms of children's culture to their own benefit. Given the power children have, although limited, the realists believe that children can be guided to employ all forms of culture in imaginative ways. Indeed, active children can transform the material objects of their culture to bring about greater choice and freedom in life.

My own position lies between these two large groups: I believe that they neglect both the manner in which children are inscribed in particular socialization processes, and how their thinking and behavior are influenced through their social class and ethnic group and through the language and literature they acquire and learn at an early age. The sociopsychological impact of reading materials, the spoken word, and images cannot be measured clearly or definitively by anyone, but I believe that we can analyze the framework, the institutions, families, and schools in which we interact with our children to grasp how we are "homogenizing" them. This is not to say that children are passive victims and are being turned out all the same way. They are indeed very active participants, but participants in processes and games that are rarely of their own making. The input they have may bring about limited changes in their socialization, but we adults ultimately shape and determine the children's private and public spheres. This is why the essays in my present book challenge many of our common assumptions of children, childhood, and children's literature. It is debatable whether we can draw clear lines between the cultural spheres of children and adults.

This book is a compilation from my own personal engagement in the so-called children's public sphere and cultural life. It consists of seven unpublished talks that I have delivered in the past four years, one published essay on *Struwwelpeter*, otherwise known as *Slovenly Peter*, and a final chapter on the Harry Potter books as a postscript. Since the essays are engagements, I have preferred to publish them in the style of active talk, words that intervene in debates about children's literature and culture, mainly in the United States. But what I have to say and how I engage myself I hope will have some bearing on debates in other parts of the world.

Given my tendency to rethink my critiques and perspectives, I have carefully revised all the original talks and lengthened them without altering the informal style. I spoke on "The Cultural Homogenization of American Children" at Mankato State University in Mankato, Minnesota, on February 4, 1997; "Do You Know What We Are Doing to Your Books?" at the Reading the World Conference, Center for Multicultural Literature, University of San Francisco, on February 15, 1998; "Why Children's Literature Does Not Exist" at the Reading the World II Conference at the University of San Francisco on February 14, 1999; "The Value of Evaluating the Value of Children's Literature," the keynote speech at The Children's Literature Association Conference, at the University of Calgary in Calgary, Canada, on July 4, 1999; "Wanda Gág's Americanization of the Grimms' Fairy Tales," at the seminar "Rereading Wanda Gág" organized by the Weisman Art Museum, University of Minnesota, on January 11, 1998; "The Contamination of the Fairy Tale" at the International Institute for Children's Literature in Osaka, Japan, on November 20, 1999; and "The Wisdom and Folly of Storytelling" at the Library for Children's Literature in Tokyo, Japan, on November 24, 1999. A slightly different version of "The Perverse Delight of *Shockheaded Peter*" was published in *Theater Magazine* in the spring of 2000 and is partially based on my essay "Struwwelpeter and the Comical Crucifixion of the Child" in Feral House's *Struwwelpeter: Fearful Stories & Vile Pictures to Instruct Good Little Folks*. "The Phenomenon of Harry Potter, or Why All the Talk?" was written exclusively for this book.

There are many people who helped inspire the writing of this book, and I should like to express my deep appreciation to Alma Flor Ada, Lella Gandini, Bev Hock, Herb Kohl, Rod McGillis, Erika Munk, Adam Parfrey, Louisa Smith, and Junko Yoshida. They have all challenged or helped me in one way or the other. In addition, I have especially benefited from the careful criticism of my wife, Carol Dines, whose insights have been most important for my work. Throughout the production process I have received valuable editorial guidance from Jennifer Hirshlag, and I am most grateful to Norma McLemore for the thorough copyediting of this book. Last but not least is Bill Germano, a great editor, who has relentlessly prodded and supported me in all my endeavors.

Jack Zipes
Minneapolis, January 2000

The Cultural Homogenization of American Children

1

Since I am going to talk about children and since I am probably going to say many unwise things with which some children might disagree, I would like to give children the first word and quote three wise statements from the January 1997 "Monthly Forum for Young Writers" in the Minneapolis *Star Tribune*. As you will then hear and see, I shall deviously twist the children's words and mold them into a critique of the systematic homogenization of American children that demands our immediate attention, for this "civilizing process" bespeaks the methodological manner in which we cultivate familial and institutional practices to make kids think and act in the same predictable ways. We prep them to respond to the demands of the markets so they will find their niche. Paradoxically, this disturbing homogenization is occurring at a time when we appear to have learned how to appreciate and honor multiculturalism and to provide children with more free choice in their lives. But let us first quickly listen to the children:

> I imagine I got my morals the same place everyone else got theirs: instilled in us by those who raised us (our parents and the TV).
>
> — Lloyd Zisla, age fourteen, grade nine,
> New Brighton, Irondale High School

> Invest your money wisely. In the world today, I've learned the world does not take kindly to people with no money.
>
> — Ryan Giannetti, age ten, grade five, Apple
> Valley, Westview Elementary School

> When I was born, the first thing my parents told me was 'Hi.' The next thing was probably, 'Rule number one. . . . '
>
> — Chris Chamblerlain, age eleven, grade six,
> Clontarf, Benson Elementary School[1]

These are wonderful, insightful statements, but they are also warnings and sad commentaries about our society. Does TV raise children as much as parents do? (Some critics might even argue that TV plays a more significant role than parents.) Is money the major factor in determining a person's worth? Are regulations more important than love? These are some of the questions that the children appear to be asking when they make their comments. I said "appear," but the sorry facts are that they have already realized that TV is as important as their parents; that they must sell themselves on the market to determine their worth; that conformity will be demanded early in their lives, rather than mutual respect. In other words, these children, who probably represent the views of many children, have realized (at the very latest by age ten) that their choices in life are circumscribed by their parents and TV and that their capacity to earn money will determine their self-esteem. Interestingly, they do not cite the community when they discuss values, nor do they reflect upon alternatives to their socialization.

Perhaps you will now expect me to lament that we have failed our children and to begin developing a moral critique of American society à la William Bennett calling for the return to the virtues of the Judeo-Christian tradition and the basic values of the family. But I do not want to preach about absolute or essential American values that we have lost and that may have never really existed in the first place. Nor do I want to pretend that there is an answer to the present predicament of cultural homogenization. What I should like to explore with you is how certain cultural practices play a role in homogenizing American children and send contradictory messages that are bound to undermine their capacity to develop a sense of morality and ethics and to recognize that their autonomy will be governed by prescribed market interests of corporations that have destroyed communities and the self-determination of communities.

In his important study *Out of the Garden: Toys and Children's Culture in the Age of TV Marketing*, Stephen Kline argues that "childhood is a condition defined by powerlessness and dependence upon the adult community's directives and guidance. Culture is, after all, as the repository of social learning and socialization, the means by which societies preserve and strengthen their position in the world. The forms of children's cultural expression are therefore intimately bound up with changing alignments that define a community's social beliefs and practices of cultural transmission."[2] This does not mean that children (and teenagers) lack social agency and are victims in American and Western societies whose practices have become geared toward making profits out of the young and enabling them to profit from a system that regards them more like commodities than human beings. Young people are constantly reacting against and defining themselves against a culture of institutionalized relations of production that foster sameness and conformity to corporate systematized beliefs and values. For instance, in her book *Sold Separately: Parents and Children in Consumer Culture*, Ellen Seiter argues that "children are creative in their appropriation of consumer goods and media, and the meanings they make with these materials are not necessarily and not completely in line with a materialist ethos. Children create their own meanings from the stories and symbols of consumer culture."[3] But the actions and agency of young people *and* adults who seek to resist commercialization and commodification are constantly compromised by the steady, subtle, and crass influences of mass-media conglomerates, bureaucratic demands of social institutions, and political hypocrisy of our so-called leaders, with the result that their struggle for freedom from cultural homogenization and their urges for more authenticity in life are turned against them. Paradoxically the freedom taken by young people and adults to question or to articulate their opposition to homogenization is often used and co-opted by a hegemonic culture industry to represent and rationalize a false freedom of choice, for all our choices are prescribed and dictated by market systems. We are free to consume and become part of a variety package of the same products, and children are predisposed to this homogenization through the toys, clothes, games, literature, and movies they receive from infancy through their teenage years.[4] To develop my critique of the homogenization processes in American society, I should like to begin by discussing two enlightening but disturbing essays about children's culture by the critics Tom Engelhardt and David Denby to explain what I mean by the cultural homogenization of American children that has ramifications for children throughout the world as American domination of the global media takes effect.[5]

Engelhardt, an editor at Pantheon for many years, is now a freelance writer and author of *The End of Victory: Cold War America and the Disillusioning of a Generation* (1995). He also wrote "Reading May Be Harmful to Your Kids: In the Nadirland of Today's Children's Books" in 1991,[6] and, as the recent debates about the cultural values of R. L. Stine's *Goosebumps* series and J. K. Rowling's *Harry Potter* books that concern proper reading and censorship reveal, this essay is still highly relevant today. Engelhardt points out it was not until the late 1970s that, for all sorts of social, economic, psychological, and demographic reasons, children's book publishing grew into a $1 billion business with four hundred specialized children's bookstores nationwide, five thousand titles published a year, and many authors and illustrators receiving hefty advances. However, this leap was not predicated on the improved quality of children's literature. In his study of the best-selling books of 1990, Engelhardt noted a "disturbing vision, one revealing the complex relationship between glut and deprivation in our age,"[7] because the books he read were mostly formulaic and predictable, guaranteeing young readers that whatever anxieties and chills they may experience, the end will always be the same. "All told," Engelhardt remarks, "whatever might be wondrous or inexplicable" to children:

> has simply been eliminated, and what energy these books hold seems borrowed from an adult world in the process of discovering its new power over children. During the 1980s—a decade when, by almost any statistical measure, the situation of children was worsening, globally and nationally—the middle-class American child's private space miraculously filled up with toys, tapes, technological gimmicks, even books, a flood of books. Many of the best-sellers I read, stripped down though they may be, celebrate this bounty by portraying children mainly as consumers and the mall as the site of their encounters with abundance. In a number of these books, shopping habits come to serve as a telling indicator of "character"—the positive characters being told they shop for themselves ("selfish'") or for parents, teachers, and siblings.[8]

Engelhardt argues that there has been a dramatic transformation in the content of the majority of best-selling children's books and the habit of reading that threatens to make children into simply consumers of "brands" of literature. As he explains it, there was a boom in children's publishing in the 1960s spurred by visions of the Great Society and New Frontier and funded by huge government support of libraries. One result of this support was that libraries had difficulty spending all the money they had for books. More important is that they indirectly stimulated many writers such as Virginia Hamilton, Robert Cormier, Rosa Guy, and others to write highly innovative novels of social realism, and many other imaginative forms of literature for the young were developed. The library was the institution fostering the new children's literature and creating social space in which children could explore and discuss books without being obliged to buy and own them. However, as funds for libraries were cut in the 1980s and children themselves had more money to spend, Engelhardt maintains, children's book publishing was rescued by the fast-growing chain bookstores to be found in malls throughout the United States and by upscale children's bookstores. This social space was different from the library in that the child or parent chose books without the advice or supervision of a librarian or teacher and without discussion of the books' merits. To attract children and adults as consumers of literature, the very nature of the book—its design and contents—began to change. Gradually, books began to be produced basically to sell and resell themselves and to make readers into consumers of brand names.

Of course, as Engelhardt makes clear, this second boom of children's literature, which we are still witnessing today, was ignited not simply by the commercial bookstores but also by a concern of parents that schools and governments were failing our children. American education was allegedly not as good as Japanese or European educations. Math and reading scores were dropping.

> It seemed, though, that even if we could do nothing about schools, government, or any other future-shaping institution, we could, at least, become better parents. Reading, then, was pushed hard both as royal road to success (the earlier mastered, the better) and as parental responsibility. What this offered children's book publishing was not just a business boom of unexpected proportions but a responsibility equal to it: to nurture in the young—increasingly vulnerable to screen culture, glued to Nintendo, and ready to make fashion statements at the local mall—a most crucial (yet imperiled) habit, the habit of reading. That habit was invoked with reverential seriousness by the people producing the flood of new books. To inculcate that habit in the young was, it seemed, not so much a vocation as a consummate challenge in a world where competitive distractions for children came ever thicker and faster. In fact, the issue was increasingly not so much what you read but that you read at all. Anything with words that attracted children (or parents) was seen as a good first step onto a lifelong path leading to that other, less popular adult "joy."[9]

In order to shape the choices and habits of the readers as consumers (young and old), a publishing house had to develop market strategies so that its books would be more distinctive and acceptable than another publisher's and stimulate "customers" to buy and re-buy its products not only in the form of a book but in spinoffs such as records, tapes, clothing, movies, and videos. When Engelhardt examined the best-selling books for children in 1990—and it is more or less the same today—they were *Teenage Mutant Ninja Turtles*, *New Kids on the Block*, *Mary Ann and Too Many Boys* (part of the *Baby-Sitters Club* series), *Where's Waldo*, *The Berenstain Bears*, *Charlotte's Web*, and *Where the Wild Things Are*. In all cases, even with the latter two books, the works have been transformed into products first and foremost. Rather than opening new worlds to children, they invite them to repeat certain predictable and comforting experiences that they can easily and affordably buy into. As Engelhardt puts it:

> For even the youngest readers, the "book" has, in a sense, been freed from the page and can now be encountered in an almost unending variety of audio, video, play, and fashion formats. In the same sense, the habits of reading, listening, viewing, playing, dressing, and buying have come more and more to resemble one another. That children, culture, and commercialism have long been wedded is undeniable. After all, John Newberry, the eighteenth-century publisher who first grasped the existence of a children's book market, worked his patent medicines right into his books. In *The History of Goody Twoshoes*, the heroine's father actually dies for lack of Newberry's "fever powder." Nonetheless, past commercial book ventures for children—even those of a few decades ago—seem quaint and limited, matters of momentary opportunism, when set against the ongoing rhythms of the present entertainment environment, which involves not just the blurring of bookish boundaries but the changing nature of childhood itself.[10]

Children's books are formulaic and banal, distinguishable from another only by their brand labels. Yet book publishers argue that as long as these books *get children to read*, this is a good in itself. In other words, the habit of reading (one habit among others, like watching TV or going to malls) is a virtue unto itself. Publishers do not explain, however, that they are no longer, as in the good old days, simply small firms with good editors that just produce books. Most publishing houses—and this is something that Engelhardt does not mention— are now part of huge conglomerates and are directed by business managers. Decisions to design and publish books are more often than not made by the marketing people in the firm. Editors are expected to acquire and shape good products in keeping with corporate guidelines. These days a publishing house will more than likely have ties to a food or toy company or will be part of a vast conglomerate that will expect the book company to meet rigorous financial goals. In my daughter's former elementary school, for instance, Scholastic Inc. induced her teacher through benefits to recruit children into the Scholastic Book Club, which obligated children to buy a certain number of books per month. Children could even join without parental permission. The ends at stake for book publishers are not the welfare of children, their education, and acquisition of knowledge and good habits, but the publishers' own pocketbooks. As Engelhardt states succinctly toward the end of his essay:

> What is at issue here is not whether a child will somehow be damaged by a book, any book, or whether there aren't wonderful children's books amidst the thousands of new titles churned out yearly. . . . What is at issue is the *mass itself*, and whether the habit of reading in the context of such a mass may not represent something other than the simple development of a wonderful lifelong practice. Certainly, the entry into children's time of a full-blown commercial apparatus and an ever-larger cast of adults bent on selling Product to the child has also meant the entry into childhood of a new dependency. Previously, it was assumed that dependency on parents would end in some form of independence at adulthood. In this newer world of commercial planning for children, however, early brand loyalty means a lifetime adventure in dependence. This, it seems to me, is what the "habit" of reading is coming to mean in children's books— and the only exit increasingly being offered from such a world is into infantilized best-selling genres for adults.[11]

This prognosis is, of course, quite pessimistic, and I shall explore whether there are some alternatives to the commercialized habit of reading that Engelhardt has described. The important point to bear in mind is that Engelhardt is arguing that literacy is not functional, or put another way, literacy is to function within the framework of market dictates, that what is offensive about such books as the *Goosebumps* series is not their horrific content but that the purchase and reading of such books can lead to an addiction whereby the young, curious reader is transformed into a homogenized reader, dependent on certain expectations and codes that make it appear the world is manageable and comforting. Though the book publishing industry is anything but manageable and homogeneous and though there is no plot to make children into "reading addicts," the glut of books produced in the United States reflects a calculated way of looking at children as consumers with a common denominator, and many of the products represent a dumbing down of children rather than a challenge to their creativity.

In this regard the title of David Denby's essay "Buried Alive: Our Children and the Avalanche of Crud" speaks volumes. A film critic for various New York magazines and author of *Great Books: My Adventures with Homer, Rousseau, Woolf, and Other Indestructible Writers of the Western World* (1996), a recent important study of canonical literature at American universities, Denby is not an enemy of the mass media. But with two small children to raise, he has critically reflected on the predicament that he and all parents in America confront with regard to the violence and junk that the mass media offer the young, or perhaps I should say with which the mass media inundate the young. As Denby puts it:

> The danger is not mere exposure to occasional violent or prurient images but the acceptance of a degraded environment that devalues everything—a shadow world in which our kids are breathing an awful lot of poison without knowing that there's clean air and sunshine elsewhere. They are shaped by the media as consumers before they've had a chance to develop their souls.[12]

Denby asks: How can we control what our children breathe? But he is really asking how we can minimize the potential damage of television and movies, given that our children (and we ourselves) are totally immersed in a mass-mediated society that even infects computers and the Internet with violence, advertising, crime, and pornography. He makes it clear that his two sons are not totally addicted to TV and that they are not completely consumed by pop culture. Nevertheless, he is concerned about their habits:

> In the nineties a great deal more than horror comics is jabbing at children, but we can agree with [the cultural critic Robert] Warshow that kids stay interested in nothing very long. The computer games and the TV shows, for instance, mark and cut the path of their own extinction, quickly creating a restlessness that causes the child to turn against the games and the shows themselves. Children go from one craving to another, discarding—I don't know—"Looney Tunes" for "Superman," and "Superman" for "MacGyver," and "MacGyver" for "The Wonder

Years," and "The Wonder Years" for Wolfenstein, and Wolfenstein for Sim City, and Sim City for Myst, and Myst for Doom, and Doom for Doom II. Nothing lasts. The restlessness produced by each station on this Via Dolorosa annihilates any chance for real devotion and the child passes on. Finally the child passes *out*: he emerges at the other end of the media tunnel—though perhaps still ungratified.[13]

There have been many scientific tests, surveys, and books about the harmful effects of the mass media, but Denby angrily asserts, "no social scientist need prove a direct effect on children's behavior for some of us to hate *the bullying, conformist shabbiness* [my emphasis] of the worst pop and the way it consumes our children. If children are living in pop culture, and a good part of it is ugly and stupid, that is effect enough; the sheer cruddiness is an affront."[14] The general accumulative effect of this pop culture is to make consumers out of children, not responsible citizens concerned about the quality of their social life. Like many parents, Denby is offended by his boys' vulgarity and disrespect, which he can clearly trace to the shows they watch on TV, but he does not want to ban TV and also knows that the same "attitude" is all-pervasive—in the malls, stores, schools, radios, advertisements. "Aided by armies of psychologists and market researchers," Denby states, "the culture industries reach my children at every stage of their desires and their inevitable discontent."

> What's lost is the old dream that parents and teachers will nurture the organic development of the child's own interests, the child's own nature. That dream is largely dead. In this country, people possessed solely by the desire to sell have become far more powerful than parents tortuously working out the contradictions of authority, freedom, education, and soul-making.[15]

Denby blames both conservatives and liberals for contributing to the present situation in which parents have little control over the cultural socialization of their children. He maintains that the conservatives' promotion of deregulation has led to a society that is controlled by market interests. Paradoxically, the free market has limited the choice of children and parents when toys, movies, books, and television shows are all devoted to the same product and marketed by the same company. In the case of liberals, Denby asserts that the absolute emphasis on freedom of expression has led to a confusing relativism of values, so that the right of artists to use deplorable sex and violence in their words is defended.

Denby ends his essay with a passionate cry to do battle with the culture industries that have practically taken over the acculturation of our children:

> Choice! It has to mean more for parents than an endless opening to the market. An active and engaged liberalism, while rejecting censorship, would encourage the breaking up of such vertically integrated culture monoliths as Disney, Sony, and Time Warner. It would ask for more regulation. (The V-chip is only the beginning.) It would, for instance, support the attempt of Reed Hundt, the reform-minded F.C.C. chairman, to require broadcasters to put on three hours of educational television a week. (Which might mean three fewer hours of trash.) And it would go far beyond the mere celebration of choice. It would insist on discrimination—not in the racial sense but in the cultural arena, where liberals, so eager to appreciate everyone's point of view, are often milky and weak. If parents are not to feel defeated by the media and pop culture, they must get over their reluctance to make choices that are based on clear assertions of moral values. They cannot leave to the "virtuecrats" [William Bennett and his followers] the defense of religion, high culture, the meritocracy, the Western literary classics, or anything else that implies a hierarchy of taste. They have to join the discourse and make it aesthetically and morally alive.[16]

Both Denby and Engelhardt reflect on the manner in which our society has cultivated reading and viewing habits that prey upon and exploit the desires and needs of the young to make it appear that virtue is constituted by one's ability to buy and consume whatever one chooses, and that the more one consumes of product names, the more one is identified with the successful, omnipotent product. Such consumption, they argue, while seeming to be free, is actually determined by mass-marketing techniques and technologies that have a profound effect on our culture. This critique has recently been echoed by Jean Kilbourne in her book *Deadly Persuasion: Why Women and Girls Must Fight the Addictive Power of Advertising*, a powerful indictment of the toxic cultural environment in which girls in particular but also boys are raised. As she notes, "Advertising creates a worldview that is based upon cynicism, dissatisfaction, and craving. The advertisers aren't evil. They are just doing their job, which is to sell a product, but the consequences, usually unintended, are often destructive to individuals, to cultures, and to the planet."[17]

Generally speaking, the formation of culture depends on the capacity of a group of people to transmit customary beliefs, social forms, and material characteristics from one generation to the next. Acculturation, or what we can also call the civilizing process, has always been determined by the elite within a given society and the institutions that represent the intellectual and moral standards which evolve in a dynamic process of exploration and struggle between social classes. The family, schools, and religious organizations have been the nodal points of socialization and acculturation, but their authority—here I am talking about authority in a positive sense and constituted by local and communal leadership and guidance—has yielded and been undercut by the force of the mass-mediated market. Whatever healthy differences in perspective and identities that are fostered by the family, school, or church in heterogeneous communities are leveled by homogeneous market forces that confuse the issue of freedom and choice and equate the power to buy with the power to determine one's identity and destiny. Denby and Engelhardt have shown how children are cultivated through the mass-mediated transformation of reading and viewing popular culture to develop the same tastes and attitudes toward the world. Difference and otherness, rebellion and nonconformity have become commodities that children are encouraged to acquire because they can use them to defy parents and the community while furthering the same profit-oriented interests of corporate America. What is fascinating here—and frightening—is how the same prevailing consumer attitude in children is passed on as free choice and is embedded in all our daily cultural practices. In one of his most prophetic essays, "Free Time," Theodor Adorno remarked:

> The naturalness of the question of what hobby you have, harbours
> the assumption that you must have one, or better still, that you
> should have a range of different hobbies, in accordance with what the
> "leisure industry" can supply. Organized freedom is compulsory. Woe
> betide you if you have no hobby, no pastime. . . . The industry alone
> could not have forced people to purchase its tents and dormobiles,
> plus huge quantities of extra equipment, if there had not already been
> some longing in people themselves; but their own need for freedom

gets functionalized, extended and reproduced by business; what they want is forced upon them once again. Hence the ease with which the free time is integrated; people are unaware of how utterly unfree they are, even when they feel most at liberty, because the rule of such freedom has been abstracted from them.[18]

Adorno was somewhat optimistic at the end of his essay and believed that individuals could resist the total integration of consciousness and free time into the culture industry. But he wrote his essay in 1969, and if anything, the rationalization of free or leisure time has led to a prolongation and extension of corporate organization and thinking into entertainment and educational institutions. Here I should like briefly to demonstrate how our free time is no longer free but regulated by culture industries that have a vast impact on our schools. Bluntly speaking, our activities in the movie theaters, sports, and schools are all governed by the same prevailing corporate interests.

Movies

What actually occurs when we decide to go to a movie? Let us imagine that parents and a seven-year-old child are involved. Generally speaking, this family would be subjected to a huge advance publicity campaign of a month or two that would influence their choice. In the case of the recent live-action *101 Dalmatians*, a repeat of an animated film that had already made millions, there were previews at movie theaters intended to lure children; books published by the Disney Corporation; stuffed dogs and other products on sale in chain stores and bookstores; and ads on TV and in the papers. Before the film's premiere, it was practically impossible for most Americans not to associate a Dalmatian with the film. Knowing that the film would be harmless, parents would heartily agree that this is a desirable film for their children, just as the videotape would later be regarded as an acceptable commodity. Of course, the child would have long been seduced to see the film. He or she would be nobody unless the film were seen. This becoming somebody like others would be verified by the packed movie theater. But before going into the theater, popcorn, candy, and drinks will have to be bought. Depending on the theater, Dalmatian articles might be available for sale. In the theater itself, there are advertisements on the screen, and also special ticket deals are offered to encourage you and the family to see more films at a cheaper price. The noise level is high. There are several previews designed to lure the children to see other films. Since the story is well known to everyone—and most plots for children's films are simplistic—there are no surprises. It is the event itself that counts, the habit of consuming and watching what others think you should want.

Do children learn anything from the film? Do they learn anything about animals or Dalmatians? Do they learn why Glenn Close as Cruella De Vil loves furs and wants to kill animals? Do they learn about animal rights? Is the humor of the film any different from the hundreds of sitcoms they have already seen on television? For the producers of the film and the owners of movie theaters, all these questions are irrelevant. What counts for them is that the habit of going to see a movie is reinforced by the ritual of buying and subscribing to something that appears worthwhile and fun. Children are not to see different things differently, but to envision the world as the same story with perhaps slight variations depending on the category of the film.

According to Cary Bazalgette and Terry Staples, the great "accomplishment" of the American film industry was not to have created children's films from a child's perspective but to create the family film that drew in a larger family and focused on the problems of coping with kids. The family films are intended to lure greater audiences, largely mothers with their children, into the theater, and they depict conflicts from the viewpoint of adults, even when it seems that they endow children with more power than they have. This is, more than anything else, a blatant appeal to young viewers to create a youth culture that assumes its identity and revolves around the commodity production of the present-day corporate conglomerates. Whether the film be a digital animated feature like *Toy Story* and *Toy Story 2* or a live feature like *Hook* and other adaptations of children's literature like *Huckleberry Finn* or *Little Women*, the quality of the film is incidental to the routine of attendance and production of consumptive desires based on ideological sameness. Bazalgette and Staples are clear about this:

> Arguments in favour of family films have always stressed their "universality" of appeal, although from a mixture of motives. Ideologies of

"childhood" stress that children are all the same, and are all the same the world over. There are certain themes and character types that are, it is assumed, "guaranteed" to appeal to children. This idea is not exclusive to right-wing or romantic notions about the purity and innocence of childhood; the idea that children can transcend or ignore national, ethnic and religious boundaries has an obvious appeal to anyone wanting to prove that such boundaries are unnatural constructs. But whatever its ideological bent, the "universal appeal" theme coincides happily with the needs of the American distributor seeking wider markets.[19]

Sports

Most of us both participate in sports or are vicarious spectators. Children do both, but they do it more and more on adult terms. As all parents know, most sports are highly organized and cost a fair amount of money and time. In the 1999 feature article of *Time* magazine on the crazy culture of kids sports, Andrew Ferguson reported, "Some estimates put the number of American youths participating in various organized sports at 40 million. . . . But it is not just the number of American youths playing an organized sport that's unprecedented. It's the way they're playing it—or, to be more precise, the way their parents are arranging for them to play."[20] In Minneapolis, to join a team means spending money on a coach, uniforms, membership, and gas. Depending on the parents and the coach, there may be two practices a week along with a game and some tournaments. And again, depending on the coach and the parents, the emphasis may be heavily on winning, with a great deal of pressure placed on the boys and girls to become number one. In many of the leagues that I have observed, coaches and parents are not interested in exploring how the sport can lead to developing cooperation among children, the sharing and developing of skills, and the pure enjoyment of learning how to master a game. The coaches and parents determine everything—I don't think that the notion of a pickup game has ever occurred to the children. Today, all sports for children, beginning at age five, are highly organized and regulated by adults who imitate the professional world and gear the activities to professionalize their children as athletes and to market their abilities. Uniforms, training, special summer camps demand that parents invest in their children, and they want a return on their investment. The adults determine that competition is the essence of sports and that all training and learning should be directed toward defeating opponents, achieving fame, and becoming number one in the world. Some parents even impart to their children the grand notion that sports will help them financially in the future. Sports then becomes a means to selling oneself. Sports is connected to self-advertising as well as advertising for the businesses that sponsor them, for the uniforms that the kids wear transform them often into walking advertisements for a firm.

If a child does not experience this commercialism in his or her participation in sports, the child certainly learns about it through the media or by attending a basketball, football, or baseball game or hockey and tennis matches. Going to a professional basketball game is almost like going to a circus spectacle. Before entering the arena, a child will encounter all sorts of hawkers selling sports articles with the insignia of teams and all sorts of refreshments. The selling continues into the arena, where there is a huge television screen dangling from the roof that also advertises all sorts of commodities. Of course, there are the decorative female cheerleaders who strut their stuff to urge the team on and an insipid mascot who hops about the court in a ridiculous animal outfit. When the show finally begins, the stars, whom we all know because they have been made into products and have been advertised by the media and their sponsors, play a game that is largely controlled by their coaches, who are also stars in their own right. That is, the game is not free play and inventive but highly rationalized and predictable because it has been made into a product that is to fit into TV's schedule and the business schedule of our everyday lives. We must know more or less how we are to spend our time and we are conditioned to follow a certain scenario. Many spectators follow the game by watching the big screen. Though the outcome of the game is not entirely predictable, the way it is packaged and sold is. Spectatorship, like reading, is a habit that has been socially constructed, and the manner in which we view an activity also influences and stimulates desire and creativity. If basketball players (tennis players, hockey players, runners, or skiers) wear athletic shoes, jackets, hats, and even underwear with certain logos while playing, and if the same players appear in the mass media endorsing these products, they are basically displaying how to sell oneself and a product at the same time. They are perfect examples of how most cultural habits are commodified and developed to further the business interests of our society.

Schools

Naturally, our schools have not been untouched by this commodification process. In his highly significant book, *Giving Kids the Business: The Commercialization of America's Schools*, Alex Molnar comments:

> Listen closely to the language that already fills discussions about school reform. It is the language of commerce applied to human relationships. Children are defined as "future customers," "future workers," and "future taxpayers." There is little talk of the value of children in their own right—right now. There is lots of talk about "tough love" but little mention of any other kind of love. Costs are put in terms of the "bottom line," not what justice demands. When the logic of the market is allowed to dominate society, relationships are inevitably turned into commodities to be bought and sold. And every person can be assigned a material value, either great or small. The antithesis is the democratic ideal that all people are created equal.[21]

Molnar traces the efforts by different political groups and corporations to bring about schools for profit, private school vouchers, and charter schools. Beginning with the publication of the *Nation of Risk* report commissioned by Reagan administration secretary of education Terrel Bell in 1983, there has been a concerted effort on the part of conservatives to place the blame for economic crises and the putative backwardness of the economy on the failure of our education system to train our children for the future. However, as Molnar clearly points out, this report and many other doomsday pronouncements about our education system are largely unproved and have served as a smokescreen to allow corporations to take over and infiltrate schools to serve their own commercial interests. By defeating measures that would enable more tax dollars from corporate America and the wealthy segments of society to help reduce class sizes, renovate inadequate buildings, and address social inequalities, corporations and their political allies have pretended to provide technology and aid to schools that basically enhance their hold over children. To quote Molnar again:

> Business efforts to gain access to public schools in order to sell products and establish name recognition, as well as to propagandize for corporate social and economic points of view, have been common for most of this century. However, in the 1980s, a Rubicon of sorts was crossed. Not only did the volume of advertising reach new levels of intrusiveness, marketing efforts were also often unashamedly characterized as legitimate contributions to curriculum content, as helpful teaching aids, and as a good way of promoting school-business cooperation. As a result, in homes across America, parents have since discovered that their sons and daughters are given "Gushers" fruit snacks in class, told to burst them between their teeth, and asked by their teachers to compare the sensation to a geothermal eruption (compliments of General Mills); that their sons are being taught the history of the potato chip (compliments of the Potato Board and the Snack Food Association); or that their daughters are discussing "good hair days" and "bad hair days" in class (compliments of Revlon). Tootsie Roll has provided a lesson on "the sweet taste of success," and Exxon has distributed a videotape to help teachers reassure students that the *Valdez* oil spill wasn't so bad after all.[22]

Some schools in the Minneapolis area have business partners that obligate the schools to fulfill their programs if the schools are to receive financial help. Thus television sets and computers have been donated to schools with the provision that children must watch certain programs that advertise the products of the donors, who then take a tax write-off for their altruism. Perhaps the most controversial invasion of advertising has come through Channel One. As Stephen Manning reports:

> Channel One offers schools a sweet deal: it provides each school with free TVS, VCRs, and satellite dishes as long as the school agrees to air the network's daily 12 minutes of news broadcast and two minutes of commercial advertisements to 80% of its students on 90% of school days. Channel One is beamed daily to 12,000 middle and high schools and is watched by 40% of American teenagers. According to the network, the show is broadcast in 48 states, with its strongest base in the south.[23]

Though this television station has endeavored to improve its programming, its main purpose is to convey advertising and to present news determined by its own interests. The partnership set up with schools always places the schools and children at a disadvantage.

In my daughter's former Kenwood School, Burger King offered a corporate partnership which amounted to offering a free "Happy Meal" for any student on the night of Kenwood's open house for parents. But this meant that the parents would have to buy their own meals if they took their children to Burger King. The business world is fully aware that the schools are understaffed and desperate for equipment, food, space, and renovations, but corporations are unwilling to support changes in the tax base that would enable schools to obtain funds and develop programs that are based on the children's needs and that would give the schools themselves unconditional control of the financial help. In fact, corporations are making certain that their vested interests help shape the lives of the students and reform schools (and universities) in their image.

In addition to companies like Burger King, General Mills, Exxon, Microsoft, IBM, and Apple, publishing houses like Scholastic, as I have already mentioned, have set up book clubs and magazines that not only prompt children to buy their books, such as the *Goosebumps* series and the Harry Potter books, but also advertise numerous products by other companies like Apple, Coca-Cola, Johnson Wax, and Discover Card. No matter what altruistic claims these publishing houses make, their primary aim is to make consumers out of the children and to cut a profit at the same time. Their reading materials and interactive technology, some of which are quite good, are incidental to their primary goals—to cultivate buying habits and to hook children into identifying labels and brands. Critical reading and creativity are low on their lists of priorities, and certainly, freedom of choice is something that is foreign to their vocabulary.

Clearly, within schools, within the domains of sports, movies, and the mass media, we homogenize children so that they will respond to the market interests of mass corporations in the interests of business. Whether we do this critically or uncritically, we prep them systematically to fit into institutions, teams, clubs, companies, associations, and corporations to succeed according to standards set by these hegemonic groups. This process does not mean that our children are being mass-produced and are being transformed into automatons. Anyone who has worked with children knows that it is practically impossible to make children conform completely to standards and regulations that will determine their behavior as adults. On the other hand, we do know from fascist and totalitarian societies that governments, business, educational institutions, and religious groups can have a profound effect on the belief systems and comportment of children. We also know today that there are more subtle psychological and sophisticated mass-mediated techniques that can determine how children think and behave. In the United States, we socialize children according to the consumer factor: from the day they are born, in America children are prompted to buy and sell themselves according to explicit and implicit market criteria that in turn have a profound effect on our moral and ethical values. No matter how different and free our children seem to be, their actions, thoughts, and sensibilities are governed by an intricate market system that has pervaded if not invaded families and all our cultural institutions.

Does this mean that we are living in some new kind of totalitarian state that may in fact be connected to capitalist globalization? Does this mean that business, government, and cultural institutions are so completely propelled by the profit motive and consumer interests that they cannot change and will "infect" our children with a virus called CB—the consumption bug? Is there no cure for this virus that may be more deadly than AIDS?

I want to suggest that there have always been and are alternatives to the cultural homogenization of children that we are experiencing today. Here are some thoughts on how we can keep these alternatives alive and viable.

Let's begin with the premise that the cultural homogenization of children—their conditioning to become indiscriminate consumers of masses of fashionable commodities—will, like any virus, never be completely cured, but that there are forms of a more humane life that we can develop to protect ourselves. This very recognition itself will foster the type of critical thinking and responsible behavior that we can impart to our children throughout our daily activities. There are thousands of teachers, librarians, and small educational groups (the

Reggio Emilia preschool movement, unions, alternative educational organizations, antiviolence societies), socially concerned religious and community-based groups, consumer protection organizations, child-defense organizations, media watch groups, and numerous other nonprofit societies that, in one way or another, mitigate the effects of our society's tendency to treat our children primarily as consumers and investments in the interests of corporate America.[24]

The most important battleground right now for all these groups is our public educational system from K through graduate school. Since the communist systems have collapsed and have left their socioeconomic systems open to capitalism (otherwise known euphemistically as the globalization of the world), businesses and corporations can no longer count on making great profits from producing weapons and military technology. Therefore, they have gradually turned away from the production of arms to the production of the appropriate workers and consumers for their products as their markets have "peacefully" expanded to Eastern Europe and China. To accomplish their goals, American businesses need individuals who will comply with their standards of work and thinking and who will function in a dependable manner. This is in part why the reformation and privatization of our schools and universities have become the major goals of corporate capitalism, and this is the front where concerned citizens must do battle with all those cultural and commercial forces that appear to have the interests of children at heart while merely seeking to make profit off them and setting up an elitist educational system that will widen the gap between poor and rich in the United States.

To put "children first," as Penelope Leach has argued in her superb book about the socialization of our children, means that we must constantly challenge all the efforts to privatize our schools, to make them into profit machines, and to transform cultural practices into consumer addictions. It means that local communities must work together to control and develop day-care centers, preschools, and early schooling and alter economic priorities so that there is mutual support of all children and families to offset socioeconomic inequalities. Here the emphasis cannot be placed on functional literacy, tests, and canonical learning. Rather, we must seek to cultivate pedagogical, social, and cultural practices that enable children to think for themselves and to develop sensitivities that make them aware of their fellow creatures as humans and not as competitors and consumers.

Here I should like the children to have the last word: "I imagine that I got my morals the same place everyone else got theirs: instilled in us by those who raised us (our parents and the TV)." "Invest your money wisely. In the world today, I've learned the world does not take kindly to people with no money." "When I was born, the first thing my parents told me was 'Hi.' The next thing was probably. 'Rule number one. . . . ' " I stated at the beginning that these statements were warnings and sad commentaries about our society. But they can also be read as words of hope. Children see and recognize very early how we are indoctrinating them and caring for them. Soon after they are born they feel and sense what value we place on their lives, and it is this personal and social placement of value that will influence their development of values and difference. In this regard, it is a good sign that the children whose words I quoted recognize the cultural homogenization with which they are confronted. The difficulty is that they will not be able to resist the constant pressure to conform to market demands and to retain their critical and creative perspectives if we ourselves do not keep alive alternatives and change our daily cultural practices. Let us imagine what would happen if children were truly to come first in American society and we did not have to worry about how cultural homogenization was turning them into commodities. Let us imagine what the children would say.

NOTES

1. These quotations appeared as part of Misti Snow's article "The Value of Virtue," *Star Tribune*, January 9, 1997, E1–2.

2. Stephen Kline, *Out of the Garden: Toys and Children's Culture in the Age of Marketing* (London: Verso, 1993), 44.

3. Ellen Seiter, *Sold Separately: Parents and Children in Consumer Culture* (New Brunswick, NJ: Rutgers University Press, 1995), 10.

4. Aside from Kline's study, several recent, important studies draw connections between the commodification of children through toys and other cultural artifacts. See Ellen Seiter, *Sold Separately: Children and Parents in Consumer Society*; Gary Cross, *Kids' Stuff: Toys and the Changing World of American Childhood* (Cambridge, MA: Harvard University Press, 1997); G. Wayne Miller, *Toy Wars: The Epic Struggle between G. I. Joe, Barbie, and the Companies That Make Them* (Holbrook, MA: Adams Media, 1998); and Beverley Lyon Clark and Margaret Higonnet, eds., *Girls, Boys, Books, Toys:*

Gender in Children's Literature and Culture (Baltimore: Johns Hopkins University Press, 1999).

5. See the chapter "The Media System Goes Global" in Robert W. McChesney, *Rich Media, Poor Democracy: Communication Politics in Dubious Times* (Urbana: University of Illinois Press, 1999), 78–118. Also interesting is Heather Hendershot, "Sesame Street: Cognition and Communications Imperialism," in *Kids' Media Culture*, ed. Marsha Kinder (Durham, NC: Duke University Press, 1999), 139–76.

6. Tom Engelhardt, "Reading May Be Harmful to Your Kids: In the Nadirland of Today's Children's Books," *Harper's Magazine*, June 1991, 55–62.

7. *Ibid.*, 56.

8. *Ibid.*

9. *Ibid.*, 57–58.

10. *Ibid.*, 58.

11. *Ibid.*, 62.

12. David Denby, "Buried Alive: Our Children and the Avalanche of Crud," *The New Yorker,* July 15, 1996, 48.

13. *Ibid.*, 51.

14. *Ibid.*

15. *Ibid.*, 52.

16. *Ibid.*, 58.

17. Jean Kilbourne, *Deadly Persuasion: Why Women and Girls Must Fight the Addictive Power of Advertising* (New York: The Free Press, 1999), 75.

18. Theodor Adorno, "Free Time," in *The Culture Industry: Selected Essays on Mass Culture*, ed. J. M. Bernstein (London: Routledge, 1991), 164–65.

19. Cary Bazalgette and Terry Staples, "Unshrinking the Kids: Children's Cinema and the Family Film," in *In Front of the Children: Screen Entertainment and Young Audiences*, ed. Cary Bazalgette and David Buckingham (London: British Film Institute, 1995), 96.

20. Andrew Ferguson, "Inside the Crazy Culture of Kids Sports," *Time,* July 12, 1999, 54.

21. Alex Molnar, *Giving Kids the Business: The Commercialization of America's Schools* (Boulder, CO: Westview, 1996), 184.

22. *Ibid.*, 17.

23. Steven Manning, "Channel One Enters the Media Literacy Movement," *Rethinking Schools* (Winter 1999/2000): 17.

24. One new way that many of these groups inform each other about each other's work and form links is through the Internet. A good example is Jean Kilbourne's Website (www.jeankilbourne.com/resources), one portion of which is devoted to "Resources for Change." She has an extensive list of groups under such categories as "National Organizations for Equality," "Media Advocacy and Media Literacy Organizations," "Public Health and Prevention Organizations," "Government Action and Agencies," "Corporate Action," and publications on sexism, racism, and the image of women in the media, on advertising and corporate power, and subliminal advertising.

Do You Know What We Are Doing to Your Books?

2

Three years ago I attended a conference on fairy tales in Richmond, Virginia, and I was sitting onstage with three gifted writers and illustrators of children's books, one of the foremost professors of education, and a professor of library science, when a woman, evidently a teacher, raised her hand to ask all of us a question: "Do you actually know what we are doing with your books?" Then she repeated herself with a slight shift in emphasis: "Do you actually have any idea what we are doing *to* your books?"

There was silence. We, not known for our reticence, were all flabbergasted. I was hoping that she would let us give her a multiple-choice answer sheet in response, and she could check one of the following answers for us to discuss:

a) we eat them;
b) we use them for scrap paper;
c) we read them to the children who can't read;
d) we don't have time to read, and the children don't have time to read, but we leave them on the shelves for all to see;
e) we can't buy your expensive books or have any books because we have no money for books in our budget;
f) all of the above, or none of the above.

Fortunately, while we were all desperately trying to think of how we could respond to the questioner, she volunteered an answer and informed us that she took apart the books sentence by sentence and talked about the grammar, syntax, and structure, while some of her colleagues did other things such as composing worksheets with questions about the contents, or retelling the story. And as she went on, I began to wonder to myself whether anyone knows, really knows, what we do to and with children's literature. And who is this *we* anyway? Is it the teachers? The teachers with children? What ages are the children? Is it the parents? Parents with children? Is it the publishers and editors? Is it the critics and educators? What constitutes this *we*, and are all the "we's" connected in some way?

I want to reflect upon the "we" I know—university academics—and the development of literary criticism of children's literature in the past twenty-five years, primarily in the United States. My reflections will be broad and sweeping and will commemorate and celebrate certain accomplishments in the field, but they will also place them and my own reflections in question. And one way I want to try to do this is by interspersing parts of a recent *New Yorker* essay by William Finnegan that makes me wonder not only about what *we* are doing to children's literature, but what thousands of "unwanted" youngsters—unwanted in the sense of neglected, abandoned, and abused—are doing with their everyday lives in American society. So I want to start with Finnegan's essay about Antelope Valley, California, which is among the fastest growing areas in the States.

Finnegan reports:

> There was a street war raging in Lancaster [a community in Antelope Valley] between a white-supremacist skinhead gang known as the Nazi Low Riders and a rival gang of antiracist skinheads who called themselves Sharps. This obscure, semi-doctrinal conflict fascinated me long before it escalated to homicide, as it eventually did. And yet no adult, I discovered, could shed any real light on it. I needed a native guide, and I found one in Mindy Turner, who, at seventeen, was already well embarked on a kind of casually terrifying existence I was starting to regard as common.[1]

Ever since Francelia Butler, who was the prime force behind the establishment of the Children's Literature Association, founded the journal *The Great Excluded* in 1972, later renamed *Children's Literature*, the field and the criticism have undergone immense changes. After a wobbly start, the ChLA has become the major supporter of university scholars in the United States specializing in children's literature. Not only does it hold an annual conference at which various awards for scholarship are presented and seminars and workshops are held, but it also publishes the fine journal *Children's Literature Association Quarterly* and a small book series. In addition, ChLA has close ties to other associations such as the International Research Society of Children's Literature, and these ties have enabled North American scholars to develop projects and collaborate with colleagues throughout the world. Thanks to the interest and activities of members in the ChLA, other scholarly journals such as *Children's Literature*, *The Lion and the Unicorn*, *Canadian Children's Literature*, *Children's Literature in Education*, *Signal*, and even the traditional *The Horn Book* have made progress by exploring all types of theoretical approaches to children's literature. New book series such as the one I edit for Garland (*Children's Literature and Culture*) are now in place, and major university presses such as Yale, Georgia, California, Johns Hopkins, Chicago, Oxford, and Pennsylvania as well as commercial companies like Greenwood, Twayne, and Routledge have published significant studies of children's literature and culture. There are also a growing number of studies on children's toys, videos, films, and games, such as Stephen Kline's *Out of the Garden: Toys and Children's Culture in the Age of TV Marketing* (1993) and Ellen Seiter's *Sold Separately: Parents & Children in Consumer Culture* (1995), as well as important collections of essays such as Henry Jenkins's *The Children's Culture Reader* (1998), in which children's literature is treated from an interdisciplinary perspective. One could easily assert that the kiddie-lit profession has finally come of age and has become mature and respectable.[2]

This claim may, however, be an exaggeration, and the actual growth and expansion of activities on the academic level during the last twenty-five years may not be as great as many of us had hoped, for many of the leading universities in the country still do not have courses in children's literature, and I cannot think of anyone teaching children's literature courses at "elite" Ivy League universities with the possible exception of Alison Lurie at Cornell and U. C. Knoepflmacher at Princeton. Even at the University of Texas at Arlington, a more "typical" university, the situation is no better, complains Tim Morris:

> I teach in a university English department in which adults, children, and culture are strongly linked. The nature of the connections, however, is frequently ignored. We require our majors to take a course in children's literature if they are seeking teacher certification. Our children's literature courses are always full, but always taught by adjunct faculty. Children's literature is neglected in hiring plans and curriculum discussions, even though its study accounts for a large percentage of our undergraduate enrollment. We offer no graduate courses in children's literature, have no lecture series or other activities devoted to it. Our library holdings in children's books consist of a few hundred ragged volumes of school texts closeted off in an airless room. These signs of neglect are no accident; they are part of a larger power relation.[3]

In a highly significant essay entitled "Disdain or Ignorance? Literary Theory and the Absence of Children's Literature," Deborah Thacker argues:

Children's literature still remains beyond the range of most literary studies, and . . . the distance that now exists will persist, given both the absence of a consideration of those particular texts and multiple, socially constructed readers. The transformation of critical theory over the last few decades has meant that theory *needs* children's literature. As theorists move from a textual emphasis toward the interplay and between reader and text and the social and political forces that mediate those interactions, so the part played by texts written primarily for children and the ways of reading available to children, within a web of discourses that both encourage and control interactions with fictional texts, need to be included and examined.[4]

Unfortunately, there are few signs that this need will soon be fulfilled, nor does it seem that the connections to the daily lives and reading habits of children are being made on the university level. Children's literature is still being relegated to schools of education and library science if they are being relegated at all. And yet the qualitative transformation of the scholarship at the university level among academicians in the field of children's literature has exceeded expectations.

Mindy had always been a good student, earning B's, but had slipped academically in junior high (as a disturbingly high number of American girls do). In the seventh and eighth grades, she became first a "hesher"—into heavy-metal music and smoking marijuana—and then a "hippie," into reggae and smoking marijuana. She also became sexually active. Her lovers were mostly older; some were much older. . . . Mindy's Nazi period had various sources. Spike Lee had helped her into it, she said. She and a friend had gone to see *Malcolm X*. They found they were the only whites in the audience, and a black guy had asked them sarcastically if they were in the right theatre. "That's why I hate Spike Lee," she told me. "Because he's a racist. And that's when I started thinking. If the black kids can wear 'X' caps, and Malcolm is calling us all 'white devils,' what's wrong with being down with white power?" (63)

Gone are the well-meaning descriptive works of Paul Hazard (*Books, Children and Men*, 1944), Isabelle Jan (*On Children's Literature*,

1973), Lillian H. Smith (*The Unreluctant Years*, 1953), May Hill Arbuthnot (*Children's Books Too Good to Miss*, 1948), Cornelia Meigs (*A Critical History of Children's Literature*, 1953), and others. These were the pioneers of children's literature who fought for "good" books, the recognition of the importance of children's literature, and felt they knew what good children and good children's literature were. There are now highly sophisticated studies of children's literature that draw on theorists such as Freud, Winnicott, Klein, Bakhtin, Barthes, Lacan, Foucault, and Derrida, to name but a few representatives of such schools of thought as feminism, critical theory, Marxism, reception theory, new history, poststructuralism, and semiotics. These works challenge and explore questionable definitions of children, childhood, and children's literature. Just a glance at the titles of some of the more significant studies published in the United States, Great Britain, and Australia during the last ten years will give you an idea of how broad and varied criticism has become in children's literature: Perry Nodelman, *The Pleasures of Children's Literature* (1990), Peter Hunt, *Criticism, Theory, and Children's Literature* (1991), Jerome Griswold, *Audacious Kids: Coming of Age in America's Classic Children's Books* (1992), John Stephens, *Language and Ideology in Children's Fiction* (1992), Lois Kuznets, *When Toys Come Alive: Narratives of Animation, Metamorphosis, and Development* (1994), Gillian Avery, *Behold the Child: American Children and their Books 1621-1922* (1994), Karín Lesnik-Oberstein, *Children's Literature: Criticism and the Fictional Child* (1994), Maria Nikolejeva, *Children's Literature Comes of Age: Toward a New Aesthetics* (1995), Rod McGillis, *The Nimble Reader: Literary Theory and Children's Literature* (1996), Murray Knowles and Kirsten Malmkjaer, *Language and Control in Children's Literature* (1996), Beverly Clark, *Regendering the School Story: Sassy Sissies and Tattling Tomboys* (1997), and Robyn McCallum, *Ideologies of Identity in Adolescent Fiction* (1999).

These are just a few of the critical studies that have made a mark in the field. I could also mention numerous important monographs on single authors and the publication of important essay collections such as Claudia Nelson and Lynne Vallone's *The Girl's Own: Cultural Histories of the Anglo-American Girl, 1830–1915* (1994) and Sandra Beckett's *Reflections of Change: Children's Literature Since 1945* (1997) and *Transcending Boundaries: Writing for a Dual Audience of*

Children and Adults (1999) as well as informative reference works such as Anita Silvey's *Children's Books and Their Creators* (1995), Daphne Kutzer's *Writers of Multicultural Fiction for Young Adults* (1996), and Peter Hunt's *International Companion Encyclopedia of Children's Literature* (1996). In the latter book, Margaret Meek summarizes the trends and accomplishments in the field:

> In the 1980s and 1990s, critics of children's literature have experimented with the take-over of the whole baggage of critical theory derived from adult literature and tried it for its fit. Most now agree that reading is sex-coded and gender inflected, that writers and artists have become aware that an array of audiences beyond the traditional literary elite are becoming readers of all kinds of texts. Moreover, before they leave school, children can learn to interrogate texts, to read "against" them so that their literacy is more critical than conformist. Some theoretical positions are shown to have more explanatory power than others: intertextuality is a condition of much writing in English; metafiction is a game which even very young readers play skillfully. There are also experimental procedures, as yet untagged, which show artists and writers making the most of the innocence of beginning readers to engage them in new reading games.[5]

She also warns that:

> there will be no escape, however, from learning how children read their world, the great variety of texts beyond print and pictures. Interactions of children and books will go on outside the academy, as has ever been the case, in the story-telling of young minds operating on society "at the very edge of the forest," inventing, imagining, hypothesising, all in the future tense.[6]

But there are many questions that Meek leaves unaddressed: Which children are reading? What do they learn to read? What are they doing with our books and knowledge? Does children's literature as we conceive it really matter to children? Even if teenagers learn to read, are they influenced by the literature? Does the literature enable them to grow and narrate their own worlds?

Her real political inspiration, though, was methamphetamine, which is also known as crank, crystal, ice, or simply speed. The leading illegal drug in the Valley, methampheta-

mine is a powerful addictive stimulant whose longtime consumers tend to suffer from paranoia, depression,
hallucinations, and violent rages. The Nazi Low Riders were
one of Mindy's speed connections. . . . [Later when she had
to be hospitalized and began a period of detoxing] Mindy
seemed to snap out of her gang-girl trance. "I just realized I
didn't hate black people," she told me. "Also I'm totally
infatuated with Alicia Silverstone, and she's Jewish. I've seen
Clueless like eleven times. So how could I be a Nazi?" (63)

The richer and more tolerant children's literature has become, both in criticism and in the writing for children, the poorer children and adolescents are becoming in their material and social conditions. Moreover, the racial and class divide does not seem to have diminished. Let me state here that I do not want to join the doomsday critics who complain about the lack of virtues in our families, the miserable teaching in our inadequate schools, the persistent racism, and the violence perpetrated on the young by film and television. To be sure, there is something to be said for their vocal complaints, something about mass hysteria over problems that camouflage special interest groups and minimize problems that affect the majority of children. But I am here more interested in the disparity between the criticism in our profession and the actual conditions under which children learn to read texts today, define themselves, and react to and against the corporate culture industry.

Let me begin with a brief anecdote. A couple of years ago I did a storytelling session with thirty sixth-graders in the Bryn Mawr Elementary School in Minneapolis. It involved creative drama, drawing, and reading. One girl in particular impressed me because she was so imaginative and articulate. When I commented about this to her teacher at the end of the session, she told me that the girl could barely read and that she very rarely participated in classroom activities with enthusiasm. She went on to add that most of her students were reading at second-grade level. The teacher was very committed to her school, and the school was an average one in the Minneapolis school system, rated one of the best in the country. Clearly, literacy, both functional and critical, is a major problem in the United States if not in the world. A recent Associated Press report stated that most children in public schools read below their grade level and "problems with such basic chores as reading bus schedules or newspapers hamper nearly half of U.S. adults." Adults in other Western nations share similar difficulties. "Depending on the nation, between one quarter and three-quarters of people ages 16 to 65 who were surveyed failed to attain a suitable minimum skill level for coping with the demands of modern life and work."[7]

> Mindy's own "beliefs," as she called them, were eclectic. Her brave and principled rejection of racism, even her devotion to Alicia Silverstone, did not mean she had embraced enlightened liberalism in all matters. She still had a soft spot for Adolf Hitler—she claimed she was the only N.L.R. [Nazi Low Riders member] to actually study *Mein Kampf*—and her all-time favorite "leader" was still Charles Manson. "My mom thinks I'm sick, but I think he's cute," she told me. "In a weird, gross way, I think he's attractive. He has the real fuck-you blood. He acts as his own lawyer. He talks for himself." (64)

But it is not only literacy, functional and critical, that is of serious concern when we regard the future of children in the States. In his book *Children in Jeopardy: Can We Break the Cycle of Poverty?* Irving Harris points to following problems in the broad picture:

1. The feminization of poverty: comparing 1960 with 1993, the Census Bureau (1961, 1994) reports that the number of children in black, female-headed families living in poverty has more than doubled, from 1.5 million to 4.1 million.

2. The National Center for Education Statistics sponsored a national test in 1992 on literacy levels. The results showed that only 17 percent of black seventeen-year-olds could locate, understand, summarize, and explain relatively complicated literary and informational material, as opposed to more than 50 percent of white seventeen-year-olds.

3. Most inner-city schools are poorly funded, and teachers work without sufficient support and materials.

4. Fifty to 70 percent of inner-city children drop out of high school.

5. Approximately 50 percent of minority young m̲
ployed.

6. Violence in the subways of New York is paralleled in ma̲

7. Murder in inner-city projects across America is a daily̲
rence.

8. There were more than 3.1 million cases of child abuse and neglect̲
reported in the United States.

Now, these statistics have varied since 1993, but the problems persist, and it is in conformity with and rebellion against the problematic background of growing up in America that cultural proclivities and tastes are formed. To deal with literature on any level means that we must analyze the conditions under which children come into contact with material culture of all kinds and how their daily lives are circumscribed by family, school, and community relations. Class and race continue to matter very much in learning behaviors and in the formation of taste, though the mass media and advertising operate on principles of homogenization and profit. Too often it is the inability to articulate an effective response to homogenization that leads to self-destructive acts and lifestyles.

> Mindy was by no means the only girl I had met in the Valley who had a prisoner boyfriend. I asked her what it was about guys in jail. "It's sick, I guess," she said. "But I just find it really attractive. I guess it means they're capable of doing something really spontaneous, without regard for the consequences." "Like shooting somebody." "Yeah. They're adventurous. And they're tough, usually." (64)

In *Kinderculture: The Corporate Construction of Childhood*, Shirley Steinberg and Joel L. Kincheloe have gathered together provocative essays that examine the artificial nature of childhood in North America. In their introduction they argue:

Cultural pedagogy is structured by commercial dynamics, forces that impose themselves into all aspects of our own and our children's private lives. Patterns of consumption shaped by corporate advertising empower commercial institutions as the teachers of the new millennium. Corporate cultural pedagogy has "done its homework"—it has

en are unem-
ny cities.
occur-

orms that are wildly successful when judged
pitalist intent. Replacing traditional classroom
with dolls with a history, magic kingdoms,
eractive videos, virtual realities, kick-boxing TV
orror books, and an entire array of entertain-
stensibly for adults but eagerly consumed by
erica has revolutionized childhood.[8]

Marsha Kinder, Ellen Seiter, and Henry Jenk-
ins argue that the corporate influence on children through the mass
media is not as devastating as most people think. Children, they claim,
are not victims, and they have an unusual capacity to play with the
commodities that surround them and create their own meanings. Ultimately, they claim, the young define their own culture. Certainly there
is a great deal of truth to this claim. Nevertheless, children—and I
include teenagers here—must still operate in toxic environments in
which their "found objects" and material products are heavily satu-
rated with messages and meanings that suit the overall tastes of adults
and the tendencies of consumerism. Since all consumerism is ideologically coded and fosters stereotypical thinking, even the rebellion
against it or play with it promotes one-dimensional thinking within an
alleged market of opportunities. There is no such thing as a children's
culture or children's realm. There are many kinds of realms in which
the young interact, and they are not innocent victims of the mass
media. But all these realms, whether the young create some of them
themselves, can be comprehended only if we realize that they are
marked by divisive political and social struggles and the impositions of
their parents that leave many young people without a sense of place,
tradition, and community.

Martha Wengert, a sociologist at Antelope Valley College,
said, "This area has grown so fast that neighborhoods are
not yet communities. Kids are left with this intense longing
for identification." Gangs, race nationalism, and all manner
of "beliefs" arose from this longing. I thought of Debbie
Turner's inability to comprehend [her daughter] Mindy's
enthusiasm for the likes of Charles Manson and Adolf
Hitler. "The kids reach out to these historical figures," Dr.
Wengert said. "But it's through TV, through comic books,

through word-of-mouth. There are no books at home, no
ideas, no sense of history." One thing the Valley's young
people knew, however, Dr. Wengert said, was that the economic downturn of the nineteen-nineties was not cyclical,
that the Cold War was over and the aerospace and defense
jobs were not coming back. (78)

Clearly, the majority of children in the United States are not reading what the experts in children's literature are reading, and they
may not be reading much at all because of lack of reading habits and
lack of money to buy books. Even if they have money, the young tend
not to buy books. Young Americans are, nevertheless, reading many
other "texts" through television, video games, computers, film, and
advertising. It is not that they have stopped reading, it is that their
reading habits have changed, and their habits are based very much on
their home life, immediate surroundings, and peer pressure.

No matter how much we try to deny it or repress it, class and race
differences in American society and the pauperization of children and
women appear to be increasing, and the sociocultural conditions for
learning how to read and reading any kind of text, from corporeal
bodies to printed bodies of texts, have become both commercialized
and specialized. It is practically impossible to talk about the average
reader in K–12 when a large percentage of this group has difficulty
reading and when books are too expensive to buy. Though there is a
striking number of gifted and concerned writers who write about the
conditions that produce the Mindy Turners of our society—I am
thinking of Robert Cormier, Virginia Hamilton, Rosa Guy, Norma
Fox Mazier, Brock Cole, Bruce Brooks, Francesca Block, Jerry
Spinelli, Chris Crutcher, Anne Fine, and Michael Rosen—their books
are rarely read by the young people depicted in them. Certainly, the
major readers, or should I say consumers, of children's literature and
so-called young adult literature, are white, middle-class children,
their parents, teachers, university students, and professionals in the
field, even when the books are multicultural and diverse—and this is
not to argue that other ethnic groups are not reading.

The consumers are us, the professional academics, and, though we
do not often realize it or articulate it, we are also connected to Mindy
Turner, who represents the marginalized work of professionals and is

at the core of our work. We have difficulty drawing connections to young people like Mindy Turner because of our class and institutional adherence and because the public spheres in which we move are separate. The institutionalization of our work, class division and division of labor, and the encroachment of corporate culture into all aspects of childhood doom what we in our highly sophisticated criticism do to children's literature to being ignored by children and having little effect on teachers and parents, just as the reverse may be true. We tend to go our separate ways. It is also doubtful that publishers of children's literature care very much about our criticism because they rely less on us than on the book reviewers of local newspapers, the *New York Times Book Review*, or trade publications. Moreover, their major concern is having their books appear prominently in Barnes and Noble, Borders, and other chain bookstores or used in classrooms and libraries. For the most part, academic critics of children's literature— and probably many editors and writers—are in a quandary because we want to influence this literature but are at odds with the corporate publishing world and the culture industry that produce it and shape it.

As critics of children's literature, we need to stop talking about how children's literature crosses boundaries and should be treated similarly to adult literature. The fact is that children's literature has done this from its very inception. More important, we critics and scholars of children's literature need to be crossing if not violating boundaries and forming links with critics in other disciplines in our theoretical and pedagogical work. This is not to say that we have not already begun to do this (as indicated in Marcel Danesi's *Cool: The Signs and Meanings of Adolescence* [1994], Grace Palladino's *Teenagers: An American History* [1996], and Kay E. Vandergrift's *Ways of Knowing: Literature and the Intellectual Life of Children* [1996]), but that we must go further and make theoretical and concrete connections concerned with what we and others do to children's literature and to children. These connections include:

1) exploring the class, race, gender, and regional differences of young readers in the past and present and being more specific when we talk about children as readers and consumers of cultural products;

2) being more cognizant of the role that adults as parents, teachers, and university students play in purchasing and reading literature for

the young, for they may constitute the major audience of what we call children's and young adult's literature;

3) examining the construct of childhood and adolescence from a sociohistorical perspective and investigating the conditions of reading at homes, schools, libraries, and bookstores throughout the different historical periods in relation to changing familial and societal relations;

4) reflecting critically on postmodern and poststructuralist theories that are in vogue and are connected to the institution of the academy, for the theories are conditioned by professional determinants, career considerations, and cultural wars.

5) focusing on children's literature as an institution with corporative, educational, social, and familial determinants that keep shifting, depending on the subject of study and historical period;

6) forging greater ties between educators in different disciplines and in the schools to improve the quality of our research and the effectiveness of our critical teaching.

7) making more careful use of terms like "multicultural" and focusing on the clash of cultures or conflicting cultures in an effort to grasp differences and contradictions in our society and not gloss over them with token acknowledgment of different ethnic, class, and regional backgrounds.

Finally, we must reflect theoretically and critically about the *unwanted status* of thousands if not hundreds of thousands of young people like Mindy Turner and about how her predecessors have been neglected in our writing about children's literature. And then we must come to an understanding, clear and unambiguous, of why we shall not be able to develop our criticism further if Mindy Turner is not linked to us and to what we do to and with children's literature.

NOTES

1. William Finnegan, "The Unwanted," *The New Yorker*, December 1, 1997, 62. All page references in the text are to this article.

2. Sue Gannon provides a useful summary of some of the recent work in children's literature and childhood studies in "Children's Literature Studies in a New Century," *Signal* 91 (January 2000): 25–40. She remarks: "The scholarly profession of 'Children's Literature', which once focused on a territory

that could be clearly bounded and mapped, is evolving into an informational ecosystem composed of differentiated yet interactive and interdependent clusters of scholars linked in ever-shifting relationships as they pursue their studies within or across 'disciplines'" (27).

3. Tim Morris, *You're Only Young Twice: Children's Literature and Film* (Urbana: University of Illinois Press, 2000), 1.

4. Deborah Thacker, "Disdain or Ignorance? Literary Theory and the Absence of Children's Literature," *The Lion and the Unicorn* 24 (January 2000): 1.

5. Margaret Meek, "Introduction," *International Companion Encyclopedia of Children's Literature*, ed. Peter Hunt (London: Routledge, 1996), 11–12.

6. *Ibid.*, 12.

7. "Survey Finds Low Levels of Literacy," *Star Tribune*, December 11, 1997, A6.

8. Shirley R. Steinberg and Joel L. Kincheloe, introduction to *Kinderculture: The Corporate Construction of Childhood* (Boulder, CO: Westview Press, 1997), 4.

Why Children's Literature Does Not Exist

3

I am not being coy—children's literature does not exist. If we take the genitive case literally and seriously, and if we assume ownership and possession are involved when we say "children's literature" or the literature of children, then there is no such thing as children's literature, or for that matter, children. As we all know, children cannot easily be lumped together in one amorphous category. As Philippe Ariès revealed some time ago in *Centuries of Childhood* (1973) and as many other significant studies have demonstrated,[1] "children" and "childhood" are social constructs that have been determined by socioeconomic conditions and have different meanings for different cultures.[2] Thus the concept of a children's literature is also imaginary, referring to what specific groups composed largely of adults construct as their referential system. Within that system children do not own their literature or want to own up to their putative literature. They do not particularly want to possess what we adults, especially those of us who specialize in children's literature, mean when we use the term *children's literature*, which, if anything, is used to distinguish or cast distinction on adults who take privileged positions in determining the value of a literature for young readers. In fact, most of the readers, writers, agents, editors, critics, and publishers of children's literature are adults, as are the distributors and owners of bookstores.

There never has been a literature conceived *by* children *for* children, a literature that belongs to children, and there never will be. This is not to say that children do not produce their own cultural artifacts that include literary works. There are now even children's magazines and Websites established and produced by children, and children, which includes teenagers and young adults, have produced their own literary products, journals, newspapers, cartoons, comics, plays, and videos. But the institution of children's literature is not of their making, nor is the literature that they are encouraged to read, digest, and incorporate into their cultural experience and heritage. Certainly they participate in children's literature and the process of making it what it is, but children's literature *per se* does not exist. More important for understanding what we arbitrarily call children's literature is the institution of children's literature, which, I claim, paradoxically undermines the quality products for children, that is, the "great" fiction, poetry, and artwork that it purportedly wants to disseminate and use to socialize and develop future humanist thinkers. This is because the institution of children's literature must operate more and more within the confines of the culture industry in which the prevailing consumerism and commercialism continue to minimize and marginalize the value of critical and creative thinking, and with it, the worth of an individual human being.

What, then, is the institution of children's literature? How did it originate? How has it evolved? Why is it necessary to grasp the structure of the institution of children's literature in order to evaluate and grasp the limited role children's literature plays in our society and how that has changed?

Before looking at the institution of children's literature—and I shall be using the category of children's literature to include books for teenagers and young adults—I want to consider the writer of so-called children's books. I shall make some speculative assumptions that, I hope, will challenge traditional conceptions of the writer for children and young adults. My focus will be mainly on American and British writers of children's books of fiction, for the conditions of writing for children from toddlers to teenagers differ from country to country and even from region to region in those countries, and these cultural differences determine the nature of writing for children and young adults.

A few anecdotes to set the stage for a definition:

Ever since the boom years of the 1970s, when children's literature became a big business and many writers and illustrators actually began making a lot of money by producing books for children, workshops have developed throughout the States to cater to aspiring artists. These workshops draw mainly women, though many men are also interested in the so-called profession. They often think it is easy (or should be easy) to write or produce children's books, and they want—and there are books on this subject—to know the formula, step by step, to manufacture a successful children's book, how to find an agent, and how to market the work. At a recent meeting of one of the chapters of the Society for Children's Literature, many of the writers complained of inadequate distribution of their books and their profits and wanted to learn about marketing gimmicks. Others claimed that they had not achieved the fame and celebrity they deserved and sought to learn how they might network more effectively. In fact, the commercial aspects are very much at the forefront of the Society for Children's Literature and other organizations for writers of children's literature throughout the United States. Certainly, many children authors or prospective authors think like the heroes of the Nike ads: Just do it! Success will come. Perhaps celebrity. Perhaps even money.

One publisher who entered the children's book business in the 1990s and was looking for a way to expand his horizons and his pocketbook caught wind that "feminist" fairy-tale books were somewhat profitable. So he hired some writers to write tales with strong female protagonists, and he himself created some feminist tales and got children to write comments and choose the tales they liked best. Riding the wave of political correctness, he has published several volumes of tales to market himself and his company.

One gifted writer, part Native American, wrote an autobiographical book about how he valiantly raised two adopted children who had fetal alcohol syndrome, but he did not reveal that he abused the children. He also created some fine books for children, based on Native American issues, perhaps out of a desperate need to work through the problems that eventually caused him to commit suicide. Indeed, some writers exhibit sadistic-masochistic tendencies in their works that, as in the case of Hans Christian Andersen, are played out in extraordinary narrative strategies.

One very competent illustrator I met in Richmond was so hungry for commissions that, he told me, he would illustrate anything that comes his way.

A teacher who read one of the volumes in R. L. Stine's *Goosebumps* series thought that she could write books according to a formula like Stine's and make a lot of money. She quit teaching after she published a few trite books, but she has yet to make big bucks.

Another teacher discovered that she had a gift for improvising stories with her fourth-grade class. She had so much fun inventing stories with them that she began writing them down. Eventually, on a lark, she sent the tales to a small publisher, and before she knew it, her tales were published, but she has not stopped teaching and is not particularly keen on publishing many more books because of all the changes she had been forced to make by the publisher.

A famous British writer never told her publishers whether she was writing for children or for adults; nor would she categorize her work when she wrote a tale or a book. Her publishers were the ones who decided whether her work would be marketed for children or adults. She wrote.

An American writer I knew wrote a book a year—one year for adults, the next year for children. She confessed that she wanted to legitimize herself as a writer for adults because she was not getting the recognition she wanted. So she switched gears and pushed a button to change her mind-set every year.

A gifted academic was tempted to write for children, but he ended up withdrawing a story he submitted because an editor changed the language and the contents, saying they were not proper for children.

Another accomplished American writer wrote three wonderful scripts for a TV series, but they were rejected because they were too sophisticated, original, and challenging for the audience that the producers wanted to create. She refused to dumb down her scripts, and the producers have not pursued her.

In reporting about the successful rise of Michael Lynton to the position of chief executive officer of Penguin Books, Robert Boynton commented on Lynton's interest in the film *The Prince of Egypt*:

> For all Lynton's aesthetic appreciation of *The Prince of Egypt*—a cartoon that turns the story of Moses and the Ten Commandments into a buddy movie about the Hebrew prophet and the Pharaoh Ramses— his real interest in the movie was economic. According to his calculations, *The Prince of Egypt* will spawn a dozen children's books; already, one of the most celebrated authors in the field, Madeleine L'Engle, had been signed to write the lead title. One of the first deals Lynton concluded when he became chairman and C.E.O. of the Penguin Group, a year ago, was to publish books based on Dream Works' upcoming movies. As he reminded his audience, selling books the Hollywood way can be enormously lucrative.[3]

Enough anecdotes for now. Clearly there is no easily defined category as *the* children's literature writer, yet hundreds of writers for children face common problems within the institution of children's literature governed by market conditions and educational systems. Though a risky affair, let me try to define what I perceive to be a writer or illustrator of a children's book.

Like all writers, authors of children's books write primarily to conceptualize and materialize, through symbols and signs, experiences and psychic fantasies, what their existence is and why, and whether it is meaningful. In fact, it is through the writing down of experiences and mental representations that the writer endows life with meaning within the codes and symbolic referential framework of a culture and language. This is a shared activity because we write to communicate, to make public our innermost feelings and ideas, even though we may not totally understand them ourselves. There is always an implied audience or audiences, and the implied audiences of a children's book are constituted first and foremost by an editor/agent/publisher, then by a teacher/librarian/parent, and finally by children of a particular age group. Only rarely does an author write expressly for a child or for children, and even then, the writing is likely done on behalf of children, that is, for their welfare, or what the author conceives of as a children's audience or childhood. What distinguishes a children's book from literature intended primarily for an adult audience is the fact that the writer must take into account many more audiences and censorship than a writer of a work intended for adults does. In this regard, it is much more difficult to write a publishable work intended for children, certainly much more complicated, especially if the writer is concerned about finding a narrative voice or images to which children might respond. The necessity and decision to find a narrative mode to which children might relate is what distinguishes the creative process that the children's book writer must undertake. In this process the writer conceptualizes what the child as implied reader is—the age, the background, the culture. The writer conceptualizes childhood, perhaps seeks to recapture childhood or the child in herself, or wants to define what childhood should be. The figure of the child and an ideal of childhood undergird the narrative plot and are used by the writer to rationalize her position regarding the amusement and socialization of children. The writer works through the child in herself to grasp past experiences and to project the possibility of redressing certain problems or to project alternatives and different notions of childhood.

The intention of the author, as we know, may never be clear and certainly may never be accomplished in the manner that the author hopes it might be. In describing the three works that he wrote for teenagers, Peter Hunt, who is also one of the foremost critics of children's literature, wrote that they were all:

> designed broadly for fluent, intelligent readers, and centered on children. They are all experimental, designed to confront rather than confirm expectations. The first two attempt to do something original with the camping/fantasy genres, the third with the detective story. In all three, I have used a dense, elliptical style, based on three beliefs:

first, that the child-reader is capable of highly sophisticated understanding of texts (which is, after all, no more than writers would have
us believe, and no more than educators have proved); second, that if
the book is to survive in the face of highly sophisticated alternative
media, it cannot afford to be simple-minded, but must use all the
resources available to it; and third, that the form of the classical-real-
ist novel, for all its dominance, should be challenged.[4]

What is fascinating about Hunt's statements is not just his clear
intention, but also how much he is invested in his work, how concerned he is to use narrative strategies and concepts of childhood to
work through problems for himself. He also frankly admits that he
has very little control over his final product despite the fact that he
cares more than many about the effects of his work. Yet many writers
of children's books simply want to make money and do not take their
putative profession seriously. Some merely want to amuse themselves and their audiences. Others have a religious or political
doctrine that they want to disseminate. All these intentions are to a
certain degree obvious in the form and contents of the book or story,
but there is always more buried in a narrative than the author
thinks. Moreover, the work itself is embedded within a vast institution of children's literature that may undercut or reinforce the
author's intentions. His role in the work is largely finished when it
leaves his hands. The distributor and the market will determine the
reception of the book within the institution of children's literature. In
fact, the institution of children's literature can heighten, embellish,
diminish, or destroy the existence of the person who writes a book for
children. In effect, the author's highly personal mental representations that materialize in a book depend totally on the position it
assumes within the institution of children's literature if the author
wants to connect with audiences or to be guaranteed that form of
communication in the public realm.

The institution of children's literature as it presently exists is
mammoth and very complex, and it has undergone vast changes in
the last thirty years. Though literature for children was produced on
a minor scale during the Middle Ages and Renaissance—we must
remember that 95 percent of children in Europe could not read up to
the eighteenth century, and those who could were mainly boys—the
institution of children's literature did not come into play in full force

until the eighteenth century. Then it had three major components: production, distribution, and reception. At that time printing technology and commercial distribution improved and became more efficient, and bookstores began to include more books for children. This was also the period when the literacy rate of children gradually began rising along with emergence of the middle classes, and the establishment of public school systems fostered more reading. One of the results of increased education and literacy was that publishers realized there was a market for children's books that included more fiction than ever before. The impetus behind book publishing for children at this time was not entirely making profits. Rather, certain publishers considered it their civic duty to print books for children that would improve their morals, instruct them about given subjects, and delight them so that their spirits would be uplifted. Religious and educational societies and associations would pay to have books printed for children. Thus most of the books produced for children from the eighteenth century up through the middle of the nineteenth century tended to be overtly religious, didactic, and serious. The reading audience was constituted mainly by children of the aristocratic and middle classes. Books were expensive. Children rarely bought books. They were given them as gifts on special occasions. When not reading the Bible, their major reading, or some other book borrowed from their parents' library, they read the books selected for them, or someone else read books aloud to them.

For a children's book to be recognized as a book *for* children, a system had to be in place. That is, a process of production, distribution, and reception had to be instituted within which places were assigned to different groups of people. Gender, age, and social class played roles. Indeed, it was not possible for a broad range of books to be approved and to reach children in specific ways until the system of production, distribution, and reception was instituted and became focused on how to socialize children through reading. Children's needs were not necessarily taken into consideration. It was and still is the need of the socioeconomic order that dictates how children will be formed and what forms are or are not acceptable. Each genre or type of literature for children, including the primer, the ABC book, the Bible, legends, fables, fairy tales, nursery rhymes, chapbooks, poetry, toybooks, didactic stories, penny novels, picture books, romances, and comics, were institutionalized in very specific modes in North America and Great Britain. The institution of children's literature served a function in acculturating the child and molding his or her reading habits in light of specific socioeconomic needs. In fact, reading in the eighteenth century was to be controlled and governed in a rational way; otherwise there was a danger, some educators and churchmen thought, that it could be a pleasurable activity, and too much of this reading could result in masturbation.

But reading could not be totally controlled, nor could pleasure, and as more and more children were educated during the nineteenth century and literacy grew, the institution of children's literature kept changing and modifying its form and functions in response to the experiences of children and adults at home and in the schools. It's important to bear in mind that the capacity to read was to be a measure of one's status in society, and the capacity to read and determine what was proper or appropriate for a civilized person and for children was indicative of one's cultural standing. The design and appearance of the book became increasingly important because, as a commodity, the book signified something about the character of the person using it. Also, as the market for children's books expanded greatly by the end of the nineteenth century, publishers cleverly sought to attract children and adults by covers and illustrations to purchase books as magical items that might open children up to new worlds.

The allure of the book has always been negative *and* positive, for the texts and pictures between the covers have helped many young readers to discover and grasp the world around them in a pleasurable and meaningful way. But the allure has also enabled authors and publishers to prey upon young readers' dispositions and desires and to sell them a menu that turns out to be junk food. The texts and pictures titillate children or reinforce certain formulaic patterns of thinking that reduce the possibility for the child to develop his or her own creative and critical talents.

But the book for children in today's highly commercialized and computerized world of learning has an entirely different function from only a few decades ago. As Boynton makes clear in his article "The Hollywood Way," "In big publishing, books are increasingly being regarded less as discrete properties than as one vital link in a media food chain that begins with an idea, takes early shape as a magazine article, gets fleshed out between book covers, gains bigger life on a movie or TV screen, and enters the hereafter as a videocassette or the inspiration for a toy."[5] In the case of children's literature, this trend would seem likely to have become dominant for the majority of buyers. If so, children's literature would surely become irrelevant or entirely commercialized.

But this is not the case. Although production and sale of children's books are dominated by large corporations, which produce books largely intended to lure adults and children to buy their trademark, and although the books themselves take second place to movies, TV shows, and even commercials, the institution of children's literature is seeing a flowering of innovative books and illustrations for readers from two to sixteen that are not simply economic ventures. Children's literature needs and thrives on the work of fine writers and artists and fosters experimentation and challenges to the market. Unfortunately, the corporate structure will appropriate the new, sometimes highly unique children's books to quantify and rationalize these works according to their market needs and calculations. That is, they will be made into commonplace phenomenal best-sellers to reduce their originality. At the same time, this corporate structure that thrives on homogenization and convention will always demand change, originality, uniqueness, and variety to keep readers and consumers interested in corporate products. The question remains open—narrowly open—as to whether some kind of quality literature will survive the global capitalization of the institution of children's literature, and whether recreational reading will become more and more commercial and functional, dictated by fashions and trends in the culture industry.

Short of producing a long—very long—book-length study of the institution of children's literature today, I can't explain fully the intricate mechanisms of this institution. However, I can lay here the basis for such a study to show how it has a bearing on our evaluation of children's literature. Since the major components of the institution—production, distribution, and reception—have remained intact, I shall use them, but only to elaborate on how and why they have altered in light of enormous changes in the publishing and marketing of books for children.

Production

The producers of a book for young readers are the writer, the literary agent, the editor, the marketing director, the artist (if there are illustrations), the designer, and the publishing house. I have already endeavored to demonstrate how no writer simply writes for children or should be classified as a children's writer. Some people decide to write a book that might be marketed to young readers, and in the process, the writer works through and promotes her interests and needs in some kind of narrative form. For example, numerous books are now being written by sports stars, often with the help of a so-called ghostwriter and intended for teenage readers, that are basically intended to celebrate the star's life, which is often a rags-to-riches exemplary story. Or there are illustrated books with simple texts that indulge the fantasy of the artist-writer and are intended to awaken and delight a child between three and five. Whatever the psychological and economic motives of the writer may be, he is always using language to represent himself to the world. If the writer decides to produce a book for young readers of a specific age group, then he will next take into consideration the literary agent and the market for such a book. Peter Hunt remarks:

> Before authors begin to write, they make adjustments within the genre in which they are working. Dubrow quotes E. D. Hirsch that "A genre is less like a game than like a code of behaviour," and the code of behaviour relating to children's books has structural and stylistic axes based on a far more personally nostalgic and publicly didactic sense of text than that of any other type of book. Just as we read children's books in several ways simultaneously, so the writer, consciously or unconsciously, has to consider the generic, socio-cultural, and didactic implications of writing children's books. We might also add, or distinguish, the influence of landscape and place, both on the personal and on the cultural level.[6]

The literary agent has become a fixture in the book publishing world, and it is now very difficult for a writer to gain access to a publishing house without the assistance of an agent, who often gives editorial advice about producing the book and serves as the intermediary between an editor at a publishing house and the writer. Once the literary agent is successful in selling a book, the editor may suggest or demand changes that are enormous or small. These changes are often predicated on internal discussions with production and marketing editors. Finally, once the book is ready for production, a designer will be involved as well as the marketing people, who have assumed more powerful positions in the publishing industry than ever before. Many times the author will not be consulted about the cover or illustrations for a book, although there is generally some courtesy shown to the author, especially if the book is heavily illustrated.

Some writers who care about their product will have a clause included in their contract that they have final approval of the cover and the illustrations for the book. These are the exception, the writers with clout. With very few exceptions, writers of books for young readers cannot make a living from their writing. They hold all kinds of jobs: teachers, lawyers, janitors, guards, professors, homemakers, athletes, professional journalists, waitresses, bartenders, actors, and more. Some have a low opinion of what they do, especially those hack writers who ghostwrite series books or patch together fairy tales that have been in the public domain. Some writers believe they are on a mission to convert children to a special way of seeing and feeling the world. Many are gifted writers who are not concerned so much about how children react to their works but are dedicated to their art and are pleased when their works are well received by parents and children. Some successful artists and writers travel throughout the States and give readings and work with children and try to learn from them so that they can establish a more "genuine" rapport with young readers in their works. Also, a growing number of writers teach children's literature or are academics trying their hand at creative writing for children. Other writers attack adult society and even the merchandising of books for children through their controversial and provocative books. All these diverse writers make for a wonderfully diverse literature, but the diversity is quite often bracketed and categorized by the demands and needs of the publishers. What appears at first to be diverse is sooner or later homogenized or suppressed if it does not accommodate itself to publishing and the institutions of education.

Whatever the writer intends and decides to do in the production phase will ultimately depend on the publisher and publishing industry in general. In 1997, *The Nation* published a special issue on "The

Crushing Power of Big Publishing" in which Mark Miller pointed out:

> Aside from Norton and Houghton Mifflin (the last two major independents), some university presses and a good number of embattled minors, America's trade publishers today belong to eight huge media conglomerates. In only one of them—Holtzbrinck—does management seem to care (for now) what people read. As to the rest, books are, literally, the least of their concerns. For Hearst, Time Warner, Rupert Murdoch's News Corporation, the British giant Pearson, the German giant Bertelsmann, Summner Redstone's Viacom and S. I. Newhouse's Advance, books count much less than the traffic of newsstands, TV, the multiplex: industries that were always dominated by a few, whereas book publishing was, once upon a time, a different story.[7]

Indeed, although there are numerous editors dedicated to quality children's books published by the firms within the big eight media conglomerate, the tendency is to find and produce as many marketable books for young readers as possible and to meet quotas necessary to maintain a steady flow of attractive products. It is almost incidental whether a book will hit or miss with the public because so many are produced each year that they cannot all be great successes. If a few manage to attract attention for whatever reason, the publisher will capitalize on the success. Sometimes a publishing house, however, will not pursue the success of a book because the staff is overworked, the budget is too little, and there are too many forthcoming titles. Besides, most of the publicity money nowadays is spent on children's books based on TV programs and movies or vice versa. The blockbuster books are often written by corporate writers who may have been involved in the movie or TV production.

The large publishing houses, certainly the reputable ones, generally produce a very marketable product, and care is taken to guarantee that the book looks attractive. But once it is produced, there is a certain indifference about its fate because there are so many more to come that it is not necessary to cherish and cultivate the final product. Smaller publishers of books for young readers—and there are now many throughout the United States—are much more concerned about the final product and tend to shape it with tender loving care. Again, there are so many differences among these small independent publishers—representing feminist perspectives, the alternative scene, New Age, ethnic minorities, and religious organizations—that generalizations are dangerous. But to survive, unless the publisher is endowed by some nonprofit group or a rich foundation, the small independent must collaborate closely with the writer, editor, and marketing people and carefully seek to manufacture a book that will be a success in the target area.

Distribution

Even if a book for young readers is exceptional, it will not necessarily be read, reviewed, or receive significant attention unless it is advertised and distributed properly. For the megacorporation publishers, this is not a problem because they have national and international networks that enable their books to be placed in the bookstores of their choice. They also exercise a certain influence on reviewers because publishers will not advertise in newspapers or magazines if their books are not sufficiently reviewed. In addition, the megacorporations have large budgets for advertising and for publishing attractive catalogues which are sent to readers throughout the States. In some cases, publishers have regional representatives who visit the bookstores and make sure that the books are being prominently displayed, and the publicity editor will arrange for readings, if the author is well known or has a chance to become well known. Books are also sent to conferences where the author may be speaking or doing some kind of presentation.

Although most major cities in the United States, and some small cities, have bookstores that specialize in children's books, many of these independents are being forced out of business (as the reactionary film *You've Got Mail* shows and apparently approves) by big chains such as Barnes & Noble, Borders, Waldenbooks, and large discount stores. In some instances, the Barnes & Noble corporation has influenced the design and title of a book and can decide whether a book will have a minimum amount of success. Many of the giant chains now have spaces for children and their parents to read, sit down, and have refreshments. These spaces, though apparently cozy for reading and choosing a book, are designed to make buying more pleasurable and often resemble small libraries. Often parents and children will ask for advice about which book is good and appropriate reading, and the clerk (mainly in chain bookstores), who is often unversed in the field of children's literature and has rarely taught children, will be regarded as an expert. In bookstores that specialize in children's literature, the helper often *is* an expert. The owners and clerks will be walking bibliographies and will have devoted a good deal of time to studying or teaching children's literature.

Since hardcover and picture books are prohibitively expensive for most American families, they are generally bought by libraries, well-to-do families, and adult collectors of children's books. The paperback reprints have more of a chance to reach a broader audience than the first editions, but the hot-selling items tend to be the Disney books, series like the Golden Books, books based on popular characters from television, and cheaply produced ABC books, imitations of popular classics such as the Beatrice Potter bunny books, Margaret Wise Brown's *Goodnight Moon*, fairy-tale books, fables, and nursery rhymes. These books sell in the hundreds of thousands, as do comics, cartoon books, magazines, and reading material attached to compact discs, cassettes, and video films.

Most small publishers of children's books find it difficult to distribute their books on a national scale and to guarantee that bookstores will display their books in an attractive space or promote them. Many small publishers are satisfied with a good regional service, and they use catalogues effectively in a mail service distribution. Today, however, the rise of the Internet has opened up new possibilities. Aside from the fact that Amazon Books and Barnes & Noble have changed the scope of distribution and advertising through the Web, most publishers now have their own Websites to sell and distribute their own books. And numerous children's book authors promote themselves on their own Websites. Some even set up their Websites so they can chat with their readers. Finally, bookstores themselves have their own sites to compete with publishers and distributors that are undercutting them while at the same time expecting bookstores to continue to distribute their wares. In the case of Barnes & Noble and Borders, there is no real competition because their corporate structure encompasses production and distribution.

As we all know, the Internet and the computer have changed the way we read and communicate with one another and will continue to do so into the twenty-first century. Some texts, especially classical texts, are produced in their entirety and distributed through the Web.

Like television, the Web can be used freely by children and adults to surf for reading and viewing material that appeals to them.

Reception

Given the vast choice and enormous production of reading material for children, it is almost impossible to assess what children are reading and how they read and absorb the literature determined for their eyes. Certainly, they do not read what we hope they will read or want them to read, and my guess is that the largest reading audience of children's books in the United States and England is constituted by those students at the college and university level who take courses in children's literature along with teachers, librarians, and writers, who eagerly and discriminatingly read vast numbers of books for children. I want to speculate about the audience for children's books. Whether my hypotheses are right or wrong, they address certain problems in the assumptions that we make about children's literature, what it is, and how it is read.

Although not all of the two thousand or more colleges and universities in the United States offer courses in children's literature on a regular basis, the majority will certainly include some course that touches on children's literature. In fact, children's literature as a field has grown immensely during the past twenty-five years, supported by the American Association of Librarians, Children's Literature Association, the Modern Language Association, and the National Council of Teachers of English. There are also numerous important journals and reviews such as *Children's Literature Quarterly*, *The Lion and the Unicorn*, *The Horn Book*, *The Bulletin of the Center for Children's Books*, *Canadian Children's Literature*, *The Five Owls*, *Children's Literature*, *Book List*, *Children's Literature in Education*, and *Signal*. Though all these publications differ in their editorial philosophy and purpose, they publish highly sophisticated and insightful essays dealing with all aspects of children's literature from the medieval period to the present. Many are now on the Web, and there are even private Websites that review books for children, some maintained by young readers. In addition, some offer reviews of contemporary works and scholarly publications.

The growth of the academic audience, including professors, teachers, librarians, and students, has led to the formation of a large reading audience that takes children's literature more seriously than ever before in the history of the university or education system. Not only are there courses that deal with the literature *per se* but also programs that focus on this history of childhood, children and the mass media, the psychology of the child, multiculturalism and children's literature, adolescent culture, and more. Thousands of American and British students are exposed each year to a literature written for children that they never read when they were children. Certainly they may have read some of the titles, but they undoubtedly did not read and discuss most of the classical literature for children, and certainly they will not have covered the wide range of contemporary books that a professor may ask them to read during a semester. These students will be mainly female, white, and from the middle or lower-middle class. Many will go on to become teachers or librarians of mass media centers. Many take the course for their own pleasure because they heard it was enjoyable, easy, or exciting. Some are baffled and disturbed if the professor analyzes a book from a deconstructionist, Freudian, Jungian, feminist, Bakhtinian, or Marxist perspective. But these kinds of analyses have become almost standard in the profession of children's literature, which receives and studies contemporary and classical works in enterprising ways, often based on exhaustive historical research and demanding interdisciplinary approaches.

About 90 percent of the professors in the field of children's literature are female,[8] which may parallel the percentage of women in children's book publishing, and for many years children's literature had been (and perhaps still is) associated with women and looked down on at the academy as "kiddie lit," a viewpoint that ironically reveals the ignorance and arrogance of many male colleagues in English departments who have rarely studied children's literature and probably still don't. But the intricacies of the reception of children's literature at the academy do not concern me except to say that the audience of students and professors has in recent years increased, and constitutes the primary public for children's literature. And it is from this public that teachers, librarians, educators, and journalists are born, so to speak, and they constitute the second key audience of children's books.

Teachers and librarians are, of course, the most voracious, rabid, and demanding readers of children's books on the face of the earth. Not only do they continually look for, read, and discuss the new books that are printed every month, but they also continually reread their favorites, develop curricula that include important works of the past, take part in pedagogical experiments to improve literacy, and explore new approaches to the teaching of reading. Given the amount of freedom that teachers and librarians have in choosing books for their courses, it is difficult to determine what their preferences are and how they evaluate books. They are helped somewhat by professional reviewers and magazines that judge books and award prizes such as the Caldecott and the Newberry. Depending on their workload, they are involved in all kinds of reading projects, meetings, and associations that concern children's literature. As key readers and users of children's literature who received their primary exposure to the field at the university, teachers and librarians are distributors of these books: they decide which books will be purchased and used at the school, and they, along with parents at home, disseminate ideas about the literature and influence reading habits.

Parents are also great readers of children's literature, mainly mothers, although some fathers in recent years read to their children and sometimes buy books for them. For the most part, however, mothers are the ones who take an active interest in the literature that their children read and will go with their children to bookstores or go by themselves to determine what they want their children to read or view. This process begins with alphabet books and picture books for toddlers and does not stop, for if there are grandchildren, you can be sure that a grandmother will continue to be interested in the reading habits of the grandchildren. Of course, the social class and ethnic background of the family will play a role in the reception of literature in the home. Given the great social divide in America, with growing poverty especially in single-parent homes, many families do not have money to purchase books for children, and if anything is to be bought, it will generally be a television and video player along with a radio that has a CD player or tape deck. Books are a luxury for many poor families and middle-class families alike. They are not a priority. In addition, the sales of popular books such as the *Berenstain Bears*, *Where's Waldo?*, Disney books based on *Beauty and the Beast*, *Aladdin*, *Pocahontas*, fairy-tale books, fables, and so on indicate that there is a certain tendency to purchase what the culture industry highlights and makes affordable. It is at school and at the library that children have a better chance to be exposed to a greater diversity of books than through their parents or through a bookstore. Too often parents rely on reviews in local newspapers or the windows and display of a bookstore, or the advice of a bookseller who is not well versed in children's literature.

I do not mean to slight the reviewers of children's books in local newspapers or in the popular press, but I have rarely read a negative review of a children's book or a book for young adults. It appears that everything and anything is good for children's minds and eyes. Good is rarely defined, though the reviewer may appear to have a firm grasp on what is appropriate literature for children and is a discriminating reader. On the other hand, children from two to sixteen tend to be indiscriminate readers. This is not to slight their intelligence or taste, but they rarely voice complaints. They read and view what they like, and unless prompted or forced, they are reluctant to state their critical views except to say they like or dislike something because it's cool or uncool. They will read and look at anything placed in front of them including books, comics, fashion and sports magazines, newspapers, advertisements, dictionaries, textbooks, address books, mail, posters, and signs. They form their tastes and reading habits within their immediate environment, consisting of the apartment or house, the school, the neighborhood, the television, and the movies. They grow and develop their capacity to read, absorb what they read, make sense out of it, and form predilections based on their experiences and taste. They will confront a vast amount of reading material that resembles a battlefield or bombardment of signs and symbols which seek to entice, seduce, govern, elicit, titillate, provoke, convert, instruct, dictate, implore, warn, and delight them. We call this the civilizing process. We call this acculturation. The children are expected to adjust to the signs and symbols, learn how to use linguistic codes, so that they can become perfect citizens. It is through the instruction of linguistic skills and the mastering of them that social status is achieved in every country; this is why great battles are so often fought over what language is to be used in schools and public offices and how the language is to be taught, and what books are to be used with children. This is why it is impossible to talk about the existence of a children's literature, especially a body of children's literature that can be clearly defined, and why it is of utmost importance to discuss instead the institution of children's literature.

Of course, one might argue that whatever materials children read constitute a *kind* of children's literature, but this is not the children's literature that we commonly assume when we use the expression. But if we focus on what children actually appropriate as their own or even produce, the reading matter to which they are most exposed, *this* children's literature would seem to consist of cartoons, the texts of sports cards, stories that accompany dolls (ranging from the New American Dolls to the famous Barbie dolls), board games, gum wrappers, comic books, leaflets and booklets that accompany tapes and CDs, cheaply produced picture books, fashion and sports magazines, series books like *Sweet Valley Twins* or *Goosebumps*, greeting cards, window displays, posters, primers, instructions for various machines, video games including games for the computer, texts and stories on the Web, television advertisements, graffiti, signs of all kinds, letters, autobiographies by sports heroes and actors, dog and cat stories, and examination texts. I am sure that I may have missed some important items, but my main point is that a child is less apt to read a poem, story, or novel by a noted writer or illustrator than any of the above.

This is not a deplorable situation—unless you indeed consider our culture deplorable. The fact is that there are marvelous works by talented and serious writers and artists along with all this other reading material, all competing for the attention of the children. They constitute the cultural reading process of children and adults alike, and instead of irresponsibly arguing for a canon of preferred literary texts to which all children should be exposed, as William Bennett and Edward Hirsch, among others, have sought to do, we should assume the responsibility for all the different kinds of texts which we help produce, promote, and disseminate and to which children are exposed. A child can learn to read and appreciate critically any text so long as a teacher or parent is patient in guiding the child and also learns to read and see what children are actually reading and confronting. As Geoffrey Williams has asserted, "Offering children some access to semiotic tools which enable them to describe visual and verbal patterning in literary text may have some potential to develop a different reading pedagogy, remaking it to include the possibility of children delighting intelligently and critically in the nature of a text's composition without excluding their enjoyment of the constructed story."[9] What I am suggesting is that we take into consideration the intertextual nature of the reading habits of our children and study all kinds of children's literature with them so that they (and we) can learn and use the linguistic codes in reading for their and own pleasure and growth. In the process, children will learn to discriminate and make value judgments and to contend critically and imaginatively with the socioeconomic forces that are acting on them and forming and informing them. They will also learn perhaps to set and demand high standards of production with the adults that may further the production of quality fiction and poetry for young readers. Unless children and adults become critically aware of how all reading matter is part of the institution of children's literature that functions within the larger culture industry, reading and enjoying literature will be nothing more than acts of consumerism that further consumption for the sake of consumption. The existence of children's literature depends on this kind of awareness. Otherwise it does not exist.

NOTES

1. See A. James and A. Prout, eds. *Constructing and Reconstructing Childhood: Contemporary Issues in the Construction of Childhood* (London: Falmer Press, 1997); Karín Lesnik-Oberstein, *Children's Literature: Criticism and the Fictional Child* (Oxford: Clarendon Press, 1994) and "Essentials: What Is Children's Literature? What Is Childhood?" in *Understanding Children's Literature*, ed. Peter Hunt (London: Routledge, 1999), 15–29; Rex and Wendy Stainton Rogers, *Stories of Childhood: Shifting Agendas of Child Concern* (London: Harvester Wheatsheaf, 1992).

2. For one of the most sober and informative approaches toward defining children and childhood, see Hugh Cunningham, *Children and Childhood in Western Society since 1500* (London: Longman, 1995).

3. Robert Boynton, "The Hollywood Way," *The New Yorker*, March 30, 1998: 48.

4. Peter Hunt, *Criticism, Theory, and Children's Literature* (London: Blackwell, 1991), 163.

5. Boynton, "The Hollywood Way," 48.

6. Hunt, *Criticism, Theory, and Children's Literature,* 157.

7. Mark Crispin Miller, "The Crushing Power of Big Publishing," *The Nation*, March 17, 1997, 11.

8. See Betsy Hearne, "Research in Children's Literature in the U.S. and

Canada: Problems and Possibilities," in *Children's Literature Research*, ed. International Youth Library (Munich: K. G. Saur, 1991), 111. Hearne says that of specialists in children's literature in American colleges and universities at the beginning of the 1990s, "about 92% are women; about 50% are assistant professors; about 40% are associate professors and only 5% are professors."

9. Geoffrey Williams, "Children Becoming Readers: Readers and Literacy," in *Understanding Children's Literature*, 161.

The Value of Evaluating the Value of Children's Literature

4

In the fall of 1994, I was on a sabbatical year in Paris with my wife and daughter, Hanna, who was ten years old at that time. It was a troublesome year for Hanna, who was obliged to study in a French public school, and though she spoke some French, it was extremely difficult for her to articulate herself the way she desired. At first she did not make friends very easily. But Hanna did know how to express her feelings at home, and she directed her anger at my wife and at me with pouting and mood swings. At one point—I don't recall exactly how or why this happened—she received a box of twenty paperbacks of the *Sweet Valley Twins* series from her grandmother, who thought she needed some enjoyable reading material in English. To our horror, Hanna began reading these books over and over, sequestering herself from us with the books both in protest against our expectations and standards of "good reading" and in evident pleasure and appreciation of the contents of the books. The value she placed on *Sweet Valley Twins* books was evidently in direct contradiction of the value I placed on these works and challenged many other values I held with regard to children's literature. I felt as though I were living with subversive agents in the house, just as I did when my sister gave Hanna her first Barbie doll (with many to follow) at age four. How could my daughter read such trash? Where had my wife and I failed her? What values had we instilled in her? Were we helpless against corporate America and the culture industry, my favorite targets of criticism?

When I reflect back on that situation in Paris, I realize that my behavior and thinking were symptomatic of the contradictory manner in which I and many others evaluate the value of children's literature and perhaps of the false notions we have about the value of children's literature. Instead of endeavoring to appreciate the value my daughter placed on the *Sweet Valley Twins* books and determining with her what significance the books held for her immediate experiences as well as mine, I dismissed the stories as trash, closing my eyes to the arbitrary value system I was using to judge this literature. I suspect that I am not alone in doing this: children's opinions, judgments, notions, desires, needs, conceptions, views, and tastes are probably the last consideration when critics are reviewing and evaluating a book produced for an audience of young readers (even though some critics, including myself, use a rhetoric that would like to convince us that they or we know what is good for children and have children's interests at heart). The problem of evaluating children's literature is, of course, complicated by the accepted notion that there is such a homogenous thing as children's literature: that is, that adults write expressly for children, that their works can have a particular effect on the sensibilities of children, and that we can detect, determine, and alter their values. All of this is nonsense.

It is nonsense because children's literature is produced primarily by and for adults, and the evaluative processes established by critics, parents, the press, institutions, authors, and illustrators of what is "good" children's literature exclude, for the most part, the opinions of young people, while they engage this literature, appreciate, and judge it (or do not read or engage it and find no value or pleasure in it) in a manner that we analyze, examine, critique, question, and sometimes approve. Implicit in all the evaluative processes generally controlled by adults is a notion of an absolute value, that we can determine what a good or bad book for children is, that some books possess universal moral and ethical values that distinguish themselves from other immoral and pernicious literature that may damage the health and minds of our young. Yet we rarely question how we come to evaluate children's literature and form the values and standards that we employ unhesitatingly as though they were second nature to us and as though there were standards of objectivity and uncontroversial methods that could prove the correctness of our judgments.

In her highly stimulating book *Contingencies of Value: Alternative Perspectives for Critical Theory*, Barbara Herrnstein Smith maintains that "works of art and literature bear the marks of their own evaluational history, signs of value that acquire their force by virtue of various social and cultural practices and, in this case, certain highly specialized and elaborated institutions."[1] Within the North American academy we have developed special mechanisms to maintain distinct groups of students and associates in other institutions and related fields whom we train to share and appreciate literature and works of art as we instruct. Or, as Herrnstein puts it: "That is, by providing them with 'necessary backgrounds,' teaching them 'appropriate skills,' 'cultivating their interests,' and generally 'developing their tastes,' the academy produces generation after generation of subjects for whom the objects and texts thus labeled do indeed perform the functions thus privileged, thereby ensuring the continuity of mutually defining canonical works, canonical functions, and canonical audiences."[2]

Now, it is not my intention to open up what has almost become the "canonical" can-of-worms debate about how we have formed exclusive canons in children's literature. In any evaluative process canons are necessary, and it is also necessary to question and critique them. I am more interested in exploring what changes have occurred in the production of value in children's literature and how we in academic institutions from preschool through graduate school participate in the evaluative process in an intense, somewhat desperate struggle to guard, shield, dominate, control, manipulate, animate, and cultivate young people and to distinguish ourselves.

Since there have been radical changes in the way we discuss and evaluate children's literature in our academic institutions and in publishing houses during the past fifty years that will have great ramifications for all of us (children and adults) in the twenty-first century, I should like to reflect upon some of our critical practices of evaluation first by exploring what the value of children's literature is and how I see its value changing in relation to what Pierre Bourdieu calls the *habitus*, which he defines as "necessity internalized and converted into a disposition that generates meaningful practices and meaning-giving perceptions; it is a general, transposable disposition which carries out a systematic, universal application—beyond the limits of what has been directly learnt—of the necessity inherent in the learning conditions."[3] Bourdieu argues that, out of necessity, we must learn to position ourselves and internalize sets of tastes, codes, and values if we want to assume a particular role or function in a social institution, class, or group. We must dispose ourselves to take on a position. We adjust our customs and lifestyles to accord with the systematic practices of larger associations, and we form a *habitus* that identifies us just as much as we try to identify ourselves. This habitus is constituted by our acts, speech, choices, and tastes in our daily interaction with other people, and it distinguishes us from others. I shall return to elaborate on Bourdieu's definition of *habitus* later, but his major point will serve as the underlying motif in my analysis of how we evaluate the value of children's literature: we comport ourselves as agents to distinguish ourselves in power relations and to make a certain subject distinct in systematic practices in which we use our accumulated knowledge of children's literature as cultural capital. As Bourdieu remarks, "The dialectic of conditions and habitus is the basis of an alchemy which transforms the distribution of capital, the balance-sheet of a power relation, into a system of perceived differences, distinctive properties, that is, a distribution of symbolic capital, legitimate capital, whose objective truth is misrecognized."[4]

We distinguish and misrecognize children's literature in its form of exchange value, as commodity. It is inevitable that we do this because its symbolic value in our institutional practices necessitates this. Just the very manner in which we think we are distinguishing children's literature from so-called adult literature belies the objective fact that there is no such thing as children's literature. On the other hand, there is a commodity that takes the form of a book, textbook, comic book, drawing book, religious book, gift book, and so on, that we use and children use and we use with children. There is nothing inherently or essentially "childish," "childlike," or "appropriate for children" in a book. There is nothing definitive about a text or a book that automatically demands that it be classified as a children's book. As Peter Hunt has remarked, "Children's literature is an amorphous, ambiguous creature; its relationship to its audience is difficult."[5] What indeed do we mean by the audience of children, if children really are the main audience? Are we speaking about the ages four to twelve, or two to ten, or five to sixteen? Are we talking mainly about white, middle-class children, integrated audiences, or separate religious and ethnic groups? Perhaps we are "kidding" ourselves by pretending there is such an audience as children or literature produced expressly for children. Citing the work of Jacqueline Rose (*The Case of Peter Pan; or The Impossibility of Children's Fiction*) and Karín Lesnik-Oberstein (*Children's Literature: Criticism and the Fictional Child*), Rod McGillis has provocatively remarked, "What we call children's literature is an invention of adults who need to have something to write about, something to play with, something to help them construct a vision of the way things are and ought to be so that the present generation and more importantly, the next generation will behave according to standards those adults who write children's books and publish them feel comfortable with."[6] In addition, ever since the highly significant work of Philippe Ariès in *Centuries of Childhood* (1973) that has caused enormous meaningful debates up through Hugh Cunningham's *Children and Childhood in Western Society since 1500* (1995),[7] we are all aware of the ambivalent and changing categories of childhood and children, and we are all aware of the changing historical conditions that have produced multiple definitions and conceptions of children's literature. Underlying all the definitions is the exchange value of this literature as commodity. From the very beginning, if we date the institutional rise of children's literature to the eighteenth century, various books intended for children of the upper class were produced as commodities to provide pleasure and instruction. The exchange value of these books depended on the publishers, parents, educators, religious groups, and vendors and the uses to which they put the books within various social institutions such as the family, school, church, library, and university. In the eighteenth, nineteenth, and early twentieth centuries the value of books intended for the young was contingent on the setting in which the book was read and absorbed and on the personal background of the reader. For instance, a primer or collection of stories used in an elementary school in a lower-class neighborhood in New York at the beginning of the twentieth century could enhance the literacy of the children, could provide them with hope to change their social situation, could make them aware of social codes, or could reinforce a particular ideology. The value of the particular book or story was contingent on the teacher's pedagogical and ideological disposition, the reading situation, the contents of the book, the social class of the family, and the dominant ideological educational and social practices. Indeed, numerous studies about the racist, imperialist, and sexist contents and ideologies in books intended for the young and in reading and teaching practices reveal how the books as commodities had a particular acculturative value for the dominant classes of Western societies throughout the early part of the twentieth century. Whether they had or can have the intended effect is a matter of dispute, but books for the young, perhaps even more than books intended for older readers, have always been used as weapons or instruments to train and cultivate taste, to help children to see distinctions and distinguish themselves. The value of these specific uses has been examined, appreciated, and appropriated especially by teachers in group settings, but there are also a multitude of private and individual uses that young readers have made of books that involve identification with the characters, empathy with their situation, regeneration of hope, re-creation of the self, learning about the world, and so on. It is almost impossible to predict the value that a person, young or old, will place on a book as commodity without knowing and analyzing the sociohistorical context and the shifting positions that social and educational groups take in evaluating the books and establishing dispositions toward literature read and used by the young. Nevertheless, the contingent value of children's literature and books for the young can always be somewhat assessed, and bearing this in mind I want to look at some key factors in the changing world of children's literature since 1945.

In the period between 1945 and 2000, the overall general value of books for young readers as commodities has increased in both quantitative and qualitative terms. The books have more multiple uses and meanings, and the increase in diversity has been determined by shifting institutional practices within the educational system and social practices within the family and culture industry. A few examples: The money made by publishing houses through the sale of books targeted at young readers far exceeds that made by any other category of literature. Millions of dollars are spent each year on the publicity and marketing of children's books and associated products as valuable commodities. Given the extraordinary sums that publishing houses, large and small, can potentially make by manufacturing books for young readers, and given the reduction in costs of production, particularly in the last fifteen years, the publishers have swamped bookstores, supermarkets, department stories, malls, airports, drugstores, and newspaper stands with a huge assortment of cheap and expensive books that range from the banal to the sublime. The value placed on children's books in the chains and other bookstores can be gauged by simply assessing the amount of space, generally a prime location, allotted to the children's book section. With the rise in the estimation of children's books by publishers has come a rise in the number of writers and illustrators of books for the young whose value has increased as their market value increases, depending on how highly their books are regarded and on what types of books they write. Their value will often depend on how they market themselves or how their agents and publishers market them. Not only is the book a commodity; so is the author/illustrator, whose name must become distinguished and distinct for his or her work to be recognized and evaluated by particular institutions and audiences. Although the economic situation of the libraries in North America has deteriorated in recent years, the libraries fostered and continue to foster a great demand for the purchase and dissemination of books for the young. Libraries and schools account for a huge market for textbooks and primers that publishing houses produce by evaluating the market potential and audience tastes in given regions and states of North America. Universities and, in particular, schools of education and library schools are also key markets for books for young readers, which are read by college students in classes that deal with all types of children's literature and related subjects. The value of these books is determined by professors, librarians, and students in courses established to determine their worth. Of course, the worth of a book produced for children may be a very simple thing for some people like parents or adults who want to purchase a cheap or expensive book for a child in a bookstore. The story or meaning of a story will not count much. But the price and design of the book will. Sometimes the book will be stamped with a value and bear the imprint as the winner of a Newberry, Caldecott, Carnegie, or Greenway prize, or it will have blurbs from leading newspapers or critics. There are also many situations in which the value of a book is decided in discussion with a clerk in charge of the section for children's literature in a bookstore. The act of purchasing a children's book as a commodity is, in my opinion, a privileged act of endowing value on a book or showing a sign of agreement with the value already placed on the book. It is a privileged act because many families cannot afford them or because the parents do not think it necessary or valuable to have books in the house, especially if there is a television. It is a privileged act because many families do not participate in or have been excluded from the discussions and debates about the issues pertaining to books produced for young readers. These discussions and debates often take place in specialized journals, magazines, newspapers, educational pamphlets, and now on the Web to which they do not have access or want to have access. In other words, the value accorded a particular book produced for young readers is established through a process of selection by a select group of people.

Now, some critics might argue that this select group of people has become larger and more democratic since 1945, as has the selection process. There is a good deal of truth to this argument. For instance, until 1945, the process of selection of good and appropriate reading matter for the young in most institutions, including publishing, schools, libraries, and universities, was in the hands of educated, white, middle-class women—a social history that has yet to be written. Today, for better or for worse, many more men are involved in the process, as are many more people from different ethnic groups and social classes, though the status of education and membership in a particular educated group still sets the cutting edge in evaluating books for the young, and women are still the dominant force in the field. But while the selection process may be somewhat more democratic and broader, reflecting the rise of multicultural interests, and while there are more prizes for all kinds of writing and types of books, there has also been a growing commercialization of the process and of taste, and the marketing divisions of publishing houses increasingly are the dominant influences on how books produced for young readers get evaluated. To a certain extent, books and reading material for the young are no different today from other products packaged and marketed for the young: baseball cards, computer games, doll sets, toys, T-shirts with logos, skateboards, running shoes, CDs, posters.

And yet this reading material is different because of the way we use the book as cultural capital and evaluate it as such. When I speak of *we*, I am now talking about *us*, primarily about professors, teachers and librarians, who are in the business/profession of teaching and evaluating children's literature at higher institutions of learning. When we say that we teach "children's literature," or when we speak of "children's literature," we mean something vastly different from what the ordinary man, woman, and child on the street thinks of children's literature and something vastly different from most of the children's books that are currently being marketed and sold as commodities. For us, children's literature is a *field*—it's *our field*, and many things have grown on our field, and we have planted and continue to plant many things that we call subjects. These subjects have roots, many deep roots, and we call them genres or types of children's literature that we cultivate and continue to cultivate. Often we pluck their flowers as examples of how well we cultivate, and sometimes we let them outside of our hothouses and nurseries to be disseminated by people with true appreciation of our work that comes from our field. Occasionally we will turn to products that have not been produced in our field, and we may appropriate them and splice them to grow in our field, but we are careful not to contaminate our products or our work. We read and cultivate what we think the young should read, critique and discard what we consider contaminated, while they read or don't read what the markets offer them, materials often not consistent with what we cultivate and teach. For us, children's literature is a vast historical complex. For the young and their families, children's literature does not exist, but the single commodities exist for a moment of pleasurable or compulsive reading.

It would seem from this brief, exaggerated description of our field and our relationship to our field that we have little effect on the production of reading materials for the young and how they receive and use these materials. But this is not at all the case. Our seemingly restricted systematic practices in our field have ramifications way beyond what we see because we do not and cannot see, or are unwilling to recognize what lies beyond our sphere of activity, or we simply misrecognize what we are doing. As Bourdieu states:

> While it must be reasserted, against all forms of mechanism, that ordinary experience of the social world is a cognition, it is equally important to realize—contrary to the illusion of the spontaneous generation of consciousness which so many theories of the "awakening of class consciousness" (*prise de conscience*) amount to—that primary cognition is misrecognition, recognition of an order which is also established in the mind. Life-styles are thus the systematic products of habitus, which, perceived in their mutual relations through the schemes of the habitus, become sign systems that are socially qualified (as "distinguished," "vulgar," etc.).[8]

Bourdieu maintains that we live in a world of signs that generate misrecognition unless we learn to read the signs critically and actively seek to bring about recognition of their values and meanings with other individuals or agents. The difficulty is that the sign systems have become like second nature and contribute to a habitus that we regard as natural. Ironically, it is through misrecognition that we distinguish ourselves and our work and establish hegemonic models of cultural practices from which we benefit and derive our living. Most important in our evaluative work in our field of children's literature is that we *engender taste*, and taste, as Bourdieu defines it:

> the propensity and capacity to appropriate (materially or symbolically) a given class of classified, classifying objects or practices, is the gen-

erative formula of life-style, a unitary set of distinctive preferences which express the same expressive intention in the specific logic of each of the symbolic sub-spaces, furniture, clothing, language or body hexis. Each dimension of life-style "symbolizes with" the others, in Leibniz's phrase, and symbolizes them.[9]

Taste is acquired through family training and education, and this acquisition of taste is dependent on proving oneself within systematic rules and regulations. One's position in society is linked to taste and to the disposition toward fulfilling the requirements of a caste. Taste is thus an indicator of a person's distinctive position within a group or class of people that distinguishes itself by the power it wields in a particular field.

Of course, there is no one dominant taste in the field of children's literature. In any field there are contentious positions and debates that engender conflicting and contingent values and alter the structure and the nature of the field itself. As Bourdieu states:

The field of cultural production is the site of struggles in which what is at stake is the power to impose the dominant definition of the writer and therefore to delimit the population of those entitled to take part in the struggle to define the writer. . . . In short, the fundamental stake in literary struggles is the monopoly of literary legitimacy, i.e., *inter alia*, the monopoly of the power to say with authority who are authorized to call themselves writers; or, to put it another way, it is the monopoly of the power to consecrate producers or products (we are dealing with a world of belief and the consecrated writer is the one who has the power to consecrate and to win assent when he or she consecrates an author or a work—with a preface, a favourable review, a prize, etc.).[10]

However, as a result of the struggles, there are consensual practices and accepted methods through which we produce taste and value that enable us to distinguish ourselves as authorities. What are some of these select and evaluative practices? What have they come to mean? Here my focus will be on the North American universities, largely on departments of English and schools of education, a small part of the field of children's literature. The field of children's literature must include the interrelationships between children, teachers, librarians, parents, publishers, bookstore owners, vendors, business corporations, the mass media, and their various practices of producing and consuming books intended for the young as commodities. Yet university professors and librarians are pivotal in the field, especially when it comes to determining evaluative processes in associated fields and institutions.

The field of children's literature in North American universities has a curious history that sets it apart from most other academic fields. Until the post-1945 period, the study of children's literature was relegated to higher schools of education and schools of library science or libraries and schools; the teaching of children's literature was stigmatized as a feminine occupation, the domain of women, and was given little value within the hierarchy of the university and only token value in the mass media. Few Ph.D.s in children's literature were offered by universities, and the press did not review many children's books. There weren't special sections in *The New York Times Book Review* and daily newspapers as there are today. Needless to say, there were no serious scholarly and critical journals of children's literature that catered to professors' academic interests before 1945, though there were journals in the field. There were also important public debates and concern about children's education and culture before 1945, but books for children were not held in high regard or considered worthy of serious study except by teachers and librarians. Groups such as the American Library Association and the National Council for the Teaching of English made important contributions to the field and continue to do so, but it was not until the 1970s—when the Modern Language Association finally deigned to recognize it and consider it a subject— that the field at the university began to expand and gain serious recognition. Other factors also led to the rise in status of children's literature as a field at the university: the student revolution and university reforms of the late 1960s and early 1970s; the civil rights and feminist movements; the increase of capital accumulation of the universities that led to new positions and programs; the expansion of book production for young readers by publishers during the 1970s and 1980s; the formation of new organizations such as the Children's Literature Association and the Canadian Children's Literature Association; and new publications such as *Children's Literature, Children's Literature Quarterly, The Lion and the Unicorn, Children's Literature in Education, International Review of Children's Literature and Librarianship*, and others; the increase in meetings and conferences on children's literature; the establishment of special summer schools and programs such as those at Simmons and Hollins colleges; and the development of international cooperation among groups and academics concerned with children's literature. In short, the field of children's literature had always been marginalized, and it is only within the last thirty years that it has finally established itself within academics, that is, within university life. While this is a radical change in some ways, the value of children's literature as a field is still deemed to be negligible when compared to other fields of literature, and it is still somewhat tainted—there are strong remnants of attitudes that associate children's literature with kids, women, and schools of education, which are not as highly valued as the true disciplines of graduate schools of literature. In short, while the field of children's literature is no longer as marginal as before, and professors and students of children's literature have proved they can read and cite Freud, Lacan, Derrida, Bakhtin, Marx, Adorno, Benjamin, Lyotard, Baudrillard, Jameson, Eagleton, and so on as well as their peers, there is still a certain sentiment or ideological attitude that the work in the field is not as demanding and deserving of recognition as the work in other areas.

This bias, which is still changing, has in my estimation benefited the field over the past twenty years. Professors and students of children's literature—proletarians of the university—have had to confront the hierarchical structure and practices of the university. Working from marginalized positions, they have tended to take the side of the powerless, the children, to speak for them, to include them, and to fight for their rights. Being partial to children's literature means being sensitive and partial to a social critique that seeks to improve the manner in which we acculturate children. To be sure, there is also a great deal of uncritical, noncritical, and traditional scholarship in the field of children's literature that reflects accommodation and compliance with the standards of English departments and schools of education and library science or with conservative social and religious groups. In describing this development, Peter Hunt has remarked:

> Children's literature thus became a matter of, as it were, "applied culture," and found a home in departments concerned with practice and which, even now, have a lowly status in the humanities—Education

and Librarianship. Here, of course, they form only a small corner of those vast subjects; in librarianship, both the courses and the material that has emerged . . . have tended to be descriptive—an attempt to organize and classify rather than to judge; the criticism produced (and the award-giving associated with it), has been based upon a resolutely untheoretical stance, often responding directly to the views of child-readers. . . . Writers in education, similarly, have been caught between conflicting interests. . . . Literature has often been seen as an educational tool, and criticism as a tool to discriminate for practical purposes—hence the vast numbers of booklists, and "activities" based on books. As before, there is nothing in this that is intrinsically lesser than any other activity, although it has led to a great deal of anti-intellectualism and "soft" criticism.[11]

But whether these activities take place in library science or education, children's literature is still taught in many universities as a kind of appreciation course within literature departments. Survey courses in the wonders of children's books are intended to take children's literature seriously to glorify it, and future teachers are trained in pedagogically approved methods of how to improve the literacy of children through reading. Canonical survey courses predominate in the schools of education and at the university, and future teachers and professors are educated in accordance with the general requirements of the profession.

In sum, it is difficult to discuss the value of children's literature as a field and how we evaluate books produced for young readers without taking into consideration the larger institution as a whole, the habitus of a university professor as agent, and how this habitus induces subjective and objective modes of thinking and behavior that circumscribe our work. As we are all aware, to become a professor/critic/teacher of children's literature necessitates the adaptation of a particular comportment and mode of thinking that will enable one to recognize a sign system of cultural practices. If a student studies for a Ph.D. in the field of children's literature in a department of English at a university, school of education, or school of library science, he or she faces reading more books produced for young readers than any young person will ever read; fulfilling the required courses in the general field; learning the tastes and preferences of different professors; discovering what literary criticism is in fashion at the university or in the profession; choosing a topic for a dissertation that will be acceptable in the profession and enable one to obtain a job; learning how to write essays or a book for publication in the accredited and proper academic form determined by authorities in the field; recognizing how to act within the department and to accommodate oneself to routines of teaching, grading, and thinking; training oneself how to speak and think for interviews and for giving papers at academic conferences; learning to perceive how to make cultural capital out of one's work within the field of children's literature, which means exploiting one's accumulated knowledge of the literature to distinguish oneself as teacher/critic; learning how to network and how to make connections to study areas within the field of children's literature that will meet the recognition and esteem of other scholars in the field; and competing with peers for a job in a diminishing job market. It is only through disposing oneself to the positions within the field of children's literature and acquiring familiarity with the accepted practices in the field that a young person can successfully gain entrance into higher level teaching. Once arrived, the young Ph.D. will assume work as agent by relating to the codes already in place and functioning, and he or she will begin to teach, publish, and evaluate by choosing from the possibilities within the existing structure.

Even if the goal of a student who arrives at a university is not the Ph.D. but a B.A. or an M.A., and the student becomes a teacher, librarian, bookseller, literary critic, bookstore owner, publisher, editor, or parent, he or she will be exposed to the hierarchical practices in a cultural field at the university and learn to evaluate books produced for young readers in keeping with the dominant ideological and methodical trends. Though it would be misleading to speak of a chain reaction or a cycle in which professors of children's literature at the university level produce and reproduce themselves in all domains related to the field, it is important to realize how professors considered as authorities influence homologous practices in related institutions that are concerned with children's culture and also have an influence on writers of books produced for children.

While a professor of children's literature may like to think of his or her dominance or authority in the field, the habitus of this agent necessitates interacting with many more agents in schools, publishing houses, libraries, bookstores—and children themselves—which places them in a privileged marginalized position in the cultural field at large. Professors of children's literature are actually compelled—it is part of their disposition—to be more aware of the way they misrecognize the value of books and other commodities produced for children than professors occupying the more dominant positions at the university. One might be tempted to celebrate our privileged marginalized position if it were not for the fact that it is still based on how we misrecognize what children are reading and consuming and still entails evaluative processes in which we make use of our accumulated cultural capital to enhance our careers and our contested positions within the field of children's literature. It is also questionable whether professors of children's literature are willing to accept their compelling marginalized position. Temptations counsel them to compromise this position, to avoid a self-reflective social critique that would bring them into conflict with the corporative tendencies of universities, which are increasingly run like big businesses.

Having entered a new century—always dramatic if not traumatic—we might ask ourselves some important critical questions about our own habitus and the ramifications it has for children's literature. Though I have been critical of our evaluative practices, I do not think we are headed for a great predicament—unless, that is, we continue our cultural practices in the field of children's literature in bad faith and ignore the consequences of our dispositions. There is obviously no correct way into the future, but from my own critical perspective and position that I assume in the field I believe that we can exploit the value of our own powerful positions to stimulate thinking about our contradictions and the contradictions in the field. Here there are three (among many) important directions that I think we must pursue.

The first is the recognition of our misrecognition, that is, critical self-reflection about how our codes and sign systems in our cultural practices limit and prevent us from focusing on what our purported subject of study is, and why we are taking the methodological and pedagogical approach that we take in opposition to other critical positions in the field. For example, our audience at the university (the students) is in fact the real prime audience of books for the young, and it is in our interaction with them that we generate extremely important contingent values based on a sociohistorical understanding of power that enable us to grasp what historical, contemporary, and potential value a given text may possess. Though I am not necessarily a proponent of New Historicism, I think that what Mitzi Myers writes about this approach is very appropriate here:

> A New Historicism of children's literature would *integrate* text and socio-historic context, demonstrating on the one hand how extraliterary cultural formations shape literary discourse and on the other how literary practices are actions that make things happen—by shaping the psychic and moral consciousness of young readers but also performing many more diverse kinds of cultural work, from satisfying authorial fantasies to legitimating or subverting dominant class and gender ideologies, from mediating social inequalities to propagandizing for causes, from popularizing new knowledges and discoveries to addressing live issues like slavery and the condition of the working class.[12]

It is with history in mind, and not a linear, chronological predictable history, that we can become more aware of our habitus and the special way it has developed at the university and how it informs our thinking and cultural production.

To sharpen our awareness of our habitus—and this is my second point—we must subvert our positions by questioning our evaluative processes. This entails introducing material that raises questions of value formation and experimenting with pedagogical practices in the classroom that make our value systems more apparent. Two examples: I recently read Vivian Gussin Paley's book *The Girl with the Brown Crayon*, in which Paley describes a remarkable evaluative process stimulated by a little girl named Reeny, who wanted to explore all the books written and illustrated by the Italian author Leo Lionni. In the course of her individual exploration she draws Paley and the rest of the kindergarten class into personal and collective evaluations that reveal the extraordinary potential of books produced for the young. My second example: Why not do this on a college level? Why not open a class and ask students to choose for whatever reason a book or books written for the young that they esteem to find out why they esteem it? Why not continue trying to evaluate a series of books this way throughout the entire semester? Why not use such a course to reflect upon the value of evaluating books for the young?

All these "whys" lead to my final point. I would not be me and I would be dishonest if I did not end by trying to propound my own values. I do not mean to insist upon the correctness of my values but the validity for all of us to exercise social critique in our cultural practices. My own work is predicated on the immense contradiction in our attitudes and treatment of the young in American society today and how our investment strategies in the young have changed. By the beginning of the twentieth century and certainly by 1945, we were modifying our socialization practices of discipline and punishment, in which we had sought to control children through restraint. This modification completed, we now entice and cultivate children to become consumers. The investment strategy in the child has shifted, and it is no longer the family that has direct control over the child but corporations that set the tone for youth culture. Today the situation is bizarre. We deprive children by overindulging them. We dangle commodities before their eyes and shape their glances so that they envision and believe that material wealth will qualitatively improve their lives. Here the apparent shift in attitudes and depiction of children in literature and popular culture can be more clearly marked by the rise of the consumer society in the 1950s and more so-called permissive attitudes toward children. Although there are great class, ethnic, and cultural differences in the United States, and children therefore receive differentiated treatment, they have all remained the object of parents and the "proper" authorities. That is, they are targeted for experiments in child care, child raising, and education. In the first half of the twentieth century, there were many more family businesses, big and small, family farms, and intact families. Discipline and punishment of children were a family affair. Today, the family constellation has changed—there are many more divorces, single-parent families, and nontraditional constellations. Though family members still exercise some "control" over the upbringing of the children, it is generally within anonymous systems—educational, corporate, and governmental—that children are guided to realize their future and to strive for success.

The 1990s in America—and some of what I say may also pertain to other cultures—have brought about a grotesque and perverse battle over the child that can be depicted only in radical stark forms. Indulging children with the best of commodities and the best of technology and encouraging them to compete in the open market to the best of their abilities for more money to buy bigger and better toys of all kinds have led to violent forms of social relations. Children are conditioned to regard other individuals as objects and to "network" in order to profit or benefit from the relations to advance their so-called careers. They are encouraged to associate people and clothes with trademarks and to pay respect to corporate powers that have installed themselves in the family and school system. At the same time, there is a strong resistance to these pressures, and it should be stated that there has always been strong resistance. Parents have always wanted the best for their children and have sought to control them at the same time.

We are deadly serious about our children and about education. This is why there has been so much emphasis placed recently on greater discipline and structure in the schools and the return to traditional family values. This call for greater regulation and regimentation of children's lives does not come only from the Silent Majority or religious right in America, but it cuts across all social classes and political persuasions. The people who support such policies mean well. But they tend to cast the blame and responsibility for the violence and chaos in our society away from themselves onto some kind of amorphous moral decay associated vaguely with the mass media, gun laws, and the breakdown of the family. The result is that the young are caught in a vicious cycle in which they are blamed for responding demonstrably if not violently through their youth culture to a situation that they have not created. Meanwhile, the solution proposed by many adults in America is more discipline such as school uniforms, curfews, gun laws, regulations, and policing and didactic instruction and censorship. It's like hanging the Ten Commandments in the schools to solve the problems of violence. Yet most politicians and educators know full well that the present crisis of violence in American schools and in society in general is not due to miseducation of children but the pauperization of children, physically and culturally, and the greater division between rich and poor. Despite a thriving economy, the "standard" of living of the society depends on a management of psyches that renders children susceptible to the demands of market forces. Their lives have become more fragmented and at the same time more regulated and controlled than ever before in American history. The extreme pressures placed on children to compete and succeed in a socioeconomic system that pays only lip service to moral integrity have led to grotesque and barbaric situations that result in the disfigurement of our children and, too often, in self-mutilation.

It is the contradictory manner in which we invest in our children that needs to be related to the contradictory way we invest in our field of children's literature. If the field is to have a value and if our evaluating processes are to have social consequences for the manner in which we cultivate and socialize children, we must represent our position effectively as misrepresented and beleaguered and find ways we can relate to the misrepresented and beleaguered position of the young. Here is where I believe the value in evaluating the value of children's literature may lie.

NOTES

1. Barbara Herrnstein Smith, *Contingencies of Value: Alternative Perspectives for Critical Theory* (Cambridge: Harvard University Press, 1988), 43.

2. *Ibid.*, 43–44.

3. Pierre Bourdieu, *Distinction: A Social Critique of the Judgment of Taste* (Cambridge, Harvard University Press, 1984), 170.

4. *Ibid.*, 172.

5. Peter Hunt, *Literature for Children: Contemporary Criticism.* (London: Routledge, 1992), 1.

6. Rod McGillis, "The Delights of Impossibility: No Children, No Books, Only Theory," *Children's Literature Association Quarterly* 23 (Winter 1998–99): 202.

7. See also Cunningham's review essay "Histories of Childhood," *American Historical Review* (October 1998): 1195–1208.

8. Bourdieu, *Distinction*, 172.

9. *Ibid.*, 173.

10. Pierre Bourdieu, *The Field of Cultural Production* (New York: Columbia University Press, 1993), 42.

11. Hunt, *Literature for Children*, 7.

12. Mitzi Myers, "Missed Opportunities and Critical Malpractice: New Historicism and Children's Literature," *Children's Literature Association Quarterly* 13 (1988): 42.

Wanda Gág's Americanization of the Grimms' Fairy Tales

5

Wanda Gág had a life-long love affair with the Grimms' fairy tales. They were read to her in German as a child, and she read them as a child. In the introduction to her book *Tales from Grimm*, she wrote:

> The magic of *Märchen* is among my earliest recollections. The
> dictionary definitions—tale, fable, legend—are all inadequate when I
> think of my little German *Märchenbuch* and what it held for me.
> Often, usually at twilight, some grown-up would say "Sit down,
> Wanda-chen, and I'll read you a *Märchen*." Then, as I settled down in
> my rocker, ready to abandon myself with the utmost credulity to
> whatever I might hear, everything was changed, exalted. A tingling,
> anything-may-happen feeling flowed over me, and I had the sensation
> of being about to bite into a juicy big pear.[1]

She returned with a certain longing to bite once again into the
Grimms' tales during the 1930s. To be specific, from 1932 until her
death in 1946 she tried to recapture the magic of the Grimms' fairy
tales with the publication of *Tales from Grimm* (1936), *Snow White
and the Seven Dwarfs* (1938), *Three Gay Tales from Grimm* (1943),
and *More Tales from Grimm* (1947). In fact, she was literally working
on this last illustrated fairy-tale book while on her deathbed, and it
was published posthumously under the supervision of her husband,
Earle Humphreys.

What drove Gág to focus on the Grimms' tales during this period?
What was her particular contribution toward making the fairy tales
popular for an American public during the 1930s and 1940s just at a
point when anti-German sentiment was once again on the rise? Before
I try to answer these questions, I should like to outline briefly the
reception of the Grimms' fairy tales in America during the period
1919–1945 to provide a context for Gág's work and her interpretation
of the Grimms' tales as writer and illustrator.

Karen Nelson Hoyle give some of the early history of the Grimms'
tales in America in her biography of Gág:

> English-language translations of Jacob and Wilhelm Grimm's *Kinder
> und Hausmärchen* abounded before the 1930s in both England and
> the United States. Translators and illustrators in England interpreted
> Grimm for English-reading audiences. American publishers then
> reprinted the same works for several decades. This procedure was
> cheaper than paying for a new American translator and illustrator.
> Therefore, the American public read editions translated by Crane or
> Lucas and illustrated by Englishmen George Cruikshank, Walter Crane,
> Richard Doyle, Leslie Brooke, or others. These British editions then
> appeared in American libraries.[2]

In fact, fairy tales had become very popular during the first three decades of the twentieth century in the United States, and such American illustrators as Millicent Sowerby, Johnny Gruelle, and George Soper and talented immigrants such as Louis John Rhead, Eulalie, Kay Nielsen, and Fritz Kredel, along with numerous hack artists, tried their hand at illustrating collections of the Grimms' tales or individual stories. With some rare exceptions, almost all the texts were pirated from British translations of the nineteenth century, and even the exceptions were meager copies of the British books. In short, there were no complete *American* translations of the Grimms' tales, and the majority of the illustrations, except for those by Johnny Gruelle, were strongly influenced by European artists. The imitation of the florid and archaic European writing style and illustration, however, was to undergo a gradual transformation if not challenge in the 1930s. This change was due in large part to the rise of an interest in American folklore, a growing interest in American subjects on the part of American writers for children, librarians, and editors, who were all mainly women, and the rise of patriotism during World War II.

The stage was set for a serious interest in fairy tales particularly in the period during and following World War I. First of all, there was a large increase in the number of bookstores and department stores that opened sections for children's literature. At the same time, public libraries began hiring experts in children's literature and opening children's rooms with commensurate programs of storytelling. Perhaps most important were the developments in the publishing and academic world. *The Horn Book*, a journal that published reviews and essays on children's literature along with advertisements, was founded in 1924 by Bertha and Elinor Whitney, who owned one of the few bookstores in Boston that dealt exclusively with children's books. They were only part of a larger movement. As Hoyle describes the situation:

> By the end of the second date of the 1900s, enthusiasm mounted in children's book circles. Frederic Melcher, an editor of the trade journal *Publishers Weekly*, and Frank K. Mathiews, chief Boy Scout Librarian since 1912, founded *Children's Book Week* in 1919. Louise Seaman became the first full-time children's book editor, appointed in 1919 at Macmillan Publishing House. In 1922 Doubleday Page named May

Massee to a similar post; she moved to Viking in 1933. By 1926, at least eleven children's departments existed in trade publishing houses. These departments made an impact on the number and quality of children's books.[3]

The systematic organization of children's literature was dominated by editors, writers, librarians, and academics, largely on the East Coast, who set themselves up as the arbitrators of good taste and appropriate topics for childhood. As the public sphere of children's literature grew, more people, largely teachers, librarians, and academics, became involved and established regional concepts of proper reading matter for their children. But in the 1930s the tone was largely set by New York and Boston, and the issue of fairy tales, especially the Grimms' tales, and how they were to be read, taught, and told became a hot issue. Many people in America considered fairy tales frivolous, subversive, pagan, escapist, and potentially dangerous for the health and sanity of children—attitudes that mirrored puritanical sentiments in England. In this respect, the East Coast publishers, editors, librarians, and teachers who fought for the acceptance of proper fairy tales were part of a "progressive" movement seeking to "reform" the tales' reputation and to demonstrate that they were not dangerous for the psyche of the American child.

Of course, the most revolutionary breakthrough for the Grimms came in the form of a film and the reproduction of the frames from the film for picture books. I am alluding, of course, to Walt Disney's 1937 animated film, *Snow White and the Seven Dwarfs*. Disney had begun making black-and-white fairy-tale films in 1922 in Kansas City, and by the early 1930s other filmmakers, including his close friend Ub Iwerks, had made important fairy-tale films that were to influence the book publishing industry. Very few critics have remarked on the fact that the "German" fairy tales became fully "contaminated" by American artists and writers during the 1930s, especially in the Disney studios. The features of Snow White and her Prince Charming represent the all-American "healthy" ideals of beauty, prefiguring the Barbie and Ken dolls by a good twenty-five years, and the language and jokes in the film are clearly tied to American idioms and customs. Disney's success in creating his *Snow White* depended on his deep understanding of the dreams and aspirations of Middle America during the 1930s and how Americans received fairy tales. The introduction of music, sight gags, comic diversion, and Technicolor transformed the story of *Snow White* into a typical Broadway or Hollywood musical that had little to do with German folklore.[4] Other American animators followed suit in the late 1930s and early 1940s.[5] What had formally appeared in the collections of fairy tales by the Grimms, Perrault, and Andersen in book form were now mocked and turned into comic entertainment in America.

It is almost ironic that the Grimms' fairy tales flowered during the Great Depression in America in films and books. It is also ironic that this period would mark the end of the Grimms' fairy tales as particularly Germanic when the Nazis were doing their best to Aryanize the tales. Their acts of purification were matched by the American culture industry's "contamination"—a contamination that would become worldwide after 1945 in diverse ways. But there is also a logic to this flowering and contamination that I shall discuss in more detail in the next chapter. It was during the dark days of the 1930s that people were looking for some signs of hope, and of course, fairy tales, whether they be written by the Brothers Grimm, Andersen, Perrault, or Tolkien, who wrote *The Hobbit* during this period, tend to be utopian. For the most part, they end happily and reward protagonists who strive diligently and industriously to overcome obstacles to be what they perhaps only intimated. In addition, to a receptive popular audience, that is, readers and viewers looking for hope, the publishing industry and the culture industry in general had begun to realize that books, films, and artifacts that addressed children were highly profitable, and by the 1930s, as already noted, almost every major publishing house in New York was marketing an edition of the Grimms' fairy tales or single Grimms' fairy-tale books. It did not matter how pure the translations were or whether they were "Germanic" in origin. The goal was to produce "harmless" and delightful tales appropriate for children and their parents.

Enter Wanda Gág, who by this time had become a successful artist and illustrator/writer of children's books. Born 1893 in New Ulm, Minnesota, Gág grew up in a German-speaking community and was introduced to the Grimms' tales, *Struwwelpeter (Slovenly Peter)*, and many other German books and customs as a child. She also experienced many torments as the daughter of a free-thinking painter with seven children whom he could barely feed. After studying at the St. Paul and then the Minneapolis Art Institute, she went to New York in 1917, where she gradually established a reputation as commercial artist, painter, and illustrator. During the 1920s she had wanted to refresh her knowledge of German and had returned to reading the Grimms' fairy tales in German and played with the idea of translating them anew. By the end of the 1920s, thanks to the great success of her most famous children's book, *Millions of Cats* (1928), a unique fairy tale in its own right, she had a direct connection to Coward-McCann, a relatively new publishing house in New York that wanted to enter the field of fairy tales with an edition of the Grimms' tales. In 1932, after an illustration by Gág of Hansel and Gretel in front of the witch's candy house was published in the New York *Herald Tribune* and enjoyed a popular reception, she embarked on a serious plan to translate sixty tales of her choice, the least gory and most amusing, and to publish them with her own illustrations. In a 1935 letter to her friend Alma Scott, she wrote:

> I am translating the original and authentic Grimm's Fairy Tales (about 50 of them). These I plan to distribute among about 3 volumes, *Profusely Illustrated* as the old Story Books used to say. I find this very interesting and, in many cases, difficult, because what can one do with such words as *Kindlein*, *Weibchen*, *Käppchen*, etc? Little child, small wife, wee cap—are just not the same. Some words lend themselves to the *kin*, *ken*, or *let* ending, but all too few have that form. Well, I do the best I can. Mine is to be a *free* translation, true to the spirit rather than the letter, because I want to show just what *Märchen* meant to *me* as a child.[6]

This statement is highly significant because it reveals how much Gág invested herself in the tales as writer and artist and because her view is shared by many other writers and illustrators of fairy tales allegedly written for children. For instance, P. L. Travers, who published her *Mary Poppins* books about the same time Gág was producing her fairy-tale work, has stated: "You do not chop off a section of your imaginative substance and make a book for children for—if you are honest—you have, in fact, no idea where childhood ends and maturity begins. It is all endless and all one."[7] And Astrid Lindgren, who created *Pippi Longstocking* in 1945, has maintained: "I don't write books for children. . . . I write for the child I am myself. I write about things that are dear to me—trees and houses and nature—just to please myself."[8] Gág's tales were not tales for children but projections of her childhood, an endeavor to recapture her home and to recall an idyllic episode in her life. At the same time they are projections into the future, an act of sharing with children whom she never had. As we shall see, they were also part of a debate about the nature of childhood and the nature of fairy tales that continues up through the present. With the help of Anne Carroll Moore, a leading specialist in storytelling and children's literature at the New York Public Library, her sister Flavia, her friend Carl Zigrosser, and her husband Earle Humphreys, Gág worked continuously on the Grimms' project throughout the 1930s and 1940s and ended by translating and illustrating fifty-one tales before her death in 1948.

On a psychological level it is interesting to speculate why Gág spent the last twenty years or so of her life endeavoring to recapture the spirit of the Grimms' fairy tales for children. Was it an attempt to re-create an idyllic childhood that was destroyed by her father's early death when she was only fifteen? Was she seeking to create a utopian New Ulm, the real-life counterpart of which she never really wanted to return to after she left Minnesota for New York? Were the tales that Gág, who did not want to have children, conceived her way of conceiving offspring? Did the themes of the tales, in particular, the overcoming of obstacles to become successful and the reward of the persistent and diligent heroes, reflect her attitude toward life and the path that she herself had taken? After her father's death, her family could barely make ends meet. Her mother was an alcoholic, and as the oldest of seven children, Wanda became the virtual head of the family. She attended the St. Paul and Minneapolis Art Institutes on scholarships and help from friends. Money was always a problem, and Gág led very much an ascetic life and struggled against the odds to become a gifted artist.[9]

On a cultural and social level it is much clearer why she decided to embark on such a serious venture of translating and illustrating the Grimms' tales. Gág was sincerely concerned about transmitting the spirit and value system of the Grimms' tales to children in opposition to the growing tendency to commercialize, bowdlerize, and sanitize the tales during the 1930s. Her introduction to *Tales from Grimm* reveals the careful research that she had done to prepare herself for her work and especially to adapt the tales for children. As she states:

> At fourteen I was still avidly reading fairy tales and hopefully trying out incantations; but in this sophisticated age of the movies, radio, tabloids, and mystery stories, one cannot set the fairy tale age limit over eleven or twelve. I do not believe in "writing down" to children, but since the stories were originally written to include adults, it seemed advisable to simplify some sections in order that a four-to-twelve age group might be assured of getting the full value of the stories.
>
> By simplification I mean:
>
> (a) freeing hybrid stories of confusing passages
> (b) using repetition for clarity where a mature style does not include it
> (c) employing actual dialogue to sustain or revive interest in places where the narrative is too condensed for children
>
> However, I do not mean writing in words of one or two syllables. True, the *careless* use of large words is confusing for children; but long, even unfamiliar words are relished and easily absorbed by them, provided they have enough color and sound-value.
>
> The tales, coming as they do from many sources, and being composed by such widely different people as peasants and scholars, are written in a great variety of styles and tempos, which I have tried to preserve in every case.[10]

Leaving aside the questions whether one can "appropriately" write for children or actually write for children, we must ask what Gág was trying to preserve. Certainly, since Gág never set foot in Europe and since she was familiar with Germany only through these tales and other books, she could not possibly be preserving anything German or European. In fact, she was not preserving anything. On the contrary, she was creating something new, and this was her imagined conception of what it might be like to be German or European and how American children should receive something European. Her act of preservation was a reconception of what genuine European tales are supposed to be. All this she sought to do through the American language that she learned to speak in New Ulm, colored by anecdotes and information of the old country, and through her artwork. In the final analysis, she added very little to our understanding of the Grimms' tales, nor did she daringly revise or challenge some of their messages and themes. That is, her interpretations of the tales through her revisions are self-projections, as is her artwork, that do not radically alter our conceptions of the Grimms' work. In fact, her adaptations and appropriations are somewhat tame. Nevertheless, there is a quaint appealing quality to her translations that distinguishes them from other translations of this same period. Most of all, her involvement with the Grimms' tales sheds a great deal of light on her own person, her artistic development, and the debate about the contamination or Americanization of fairy tales.

Let us compare the beginning of the British translation in Fritz Kredel's illustrated *Grimms' Fairy Tales* with hers:

> Close to a large forest there lived a woodcutter with his wife and two children. The boy was called Hansel and the girl Gretel. They were always very poor and had very little to live on. And one time when there was famine in the land, he could no longer procure daily bread.
>
> One night when he lay in bed worrying over his troubles, he sighed and said to his wife, "What is to become of us? How are we to feed our poor children when we have nothing for ourselves?"[11]

Gág's:

> In a little hut near the edge of a deep, deep forest lived a poor wood chopper with his wife and his two children, Hansel and Gretel.
>
> Times were hard. Work was scarce and the price of food was high. Many people were starving, and our poor wood chopper and his little brood fared as badly as all the rest.
>
> One evening after they had gone to bed, the man said to his wife, "I don't know what will become of us. All the potatoes are gone, every head of cabbage is eaten, and there is only enough rye meal left for a few loaves of bread."[12]

Or compare the ending of *Snow White* in Johnny Gruelle's illustrated edition of 1914, translated by Margaret Hunt, with Gág's:

> But Snow White's wicked step-mother was also bidden to the feast. When she had arrayed herself in beautiful clothes she went before the Looking-glass, and said—
>
> "Looking-glass, Looking-glass, on the wall,
> Who in this land is the fairest of all?"
>
> The glass answered—

"Oh, Queen, of all here the fairest art thou,
But the young Queen is fairer by far as I trow."

Then the wicked woman uttered a curse, and was so wretched, so utterly wretched, that she knew not what to do. At first she would not go to the wedding at all, but she had no peace, and must go to see the young queen. And when she went in she knew Snow-white; and she stood still with rage and fear, and could not stir. But iron slippers had already been put upon the fire, and they were brought in with tongs, and set before her. Then she was forced to put on the red-hot shoes, and dance until she dropped down dead.[13]

Gág's:

But while this was going on in the Prince's castle, something else was happening in that other castle where lived the wicked Queen. She had been invited to a mysterious wedding, so she dressed herself in her festive best and stood in front of her mirror and said:

"Mirror, Mirror, on the wall,
Who's the fairest one of all?"

and the mirror answered:

"Thou art very fair, Oh Queen,
But the fairest ever seen
Is Snow White, alive and well,
Standing 'neath a wedding bell."

When she heard this, the Queen realized that it was Snow White's wedding to which she had been invited. She turned purple with rage, but still she couldn't stay away. It would have been better for her if she had, for when she arrived she was given a pair of red hot shoes with which she had to dance out her wicked life. But as to all the rest—the Prince and his Princess Snow White, and the seven little dwarfs—they all lived happily ever after.[14]

In comparison to most translations of the 1920s and 1930s that tended to reproduce the archaic British English language of the nineteenth century, Gág's style is succinct and idiomatically American, and her images are concrete if not primitive. Her sentences tend to be colloquial, paratactical, and melodic, and she strives for the personal tone of a storyteller sitting across from a child. Most of the tales are reduced in length, and all the redundancies are eliminated. Motivation is explained, and lurid horror is avoided. Although Gág translated freely, as she emphasized, she rarely changed the plots in a radical fashion. In this regard, she remained true to the Grimms in spirit and preserved the basic tendencies of the tales, but she did this with her free-thinking ideas and feminist sensitivity. Her personal or unique touch can be seen in her selection of tales and her splendid ear that endowed phrases and descriptions with a rural American tone and atmosphere. Gág favored tales that depicted heroes and heroines overcoming enormous obstacles with alacrity, such as "The Seven Swabians," "The Soldier and his Magic Helpers," "The Wishing Table, The Gold Donkey, and The Cudgel-in-the-Sack," and "The Hedgehog and the Rabbit." Some of the tales, like "The Six Swans," reflected her own role as caretaker of the Gág family. It is as if she wanted to minimize the difficulties in life through comforting tales in which the small protagonists triumph, but she was never cute or sentimental. On the contrary, she added a droll sense of humor to the tales, and it was humor that often stood the protagonists in good stead.

Gág's illustrations, mainly black-and-white ink line drawings, are for the most part a disappointment, even though they were nontraditional for her time. While pleasing to the eye, they do not add depth to the texts. In fact, they take away from her translations and even contradict them. In *Snow White and the Seven Dwarfs*, for example, Snow White is more like the seven- or eight-year-old Dorothy of *The Wizard of Oz*, and it is difficult to imagine her being attractive to any prince. Her stepmother is much more alluring than she is. Gág is at her best when she includes landscapes in her illustrations. Her ink drawings have a naive and almost childlike quality to them that makes them soothing but somewhat boring at the same time. There is no dramatic tension in her illustrations, or nothing that adds to our understanding of the possible psychological conflicts or social background of the stories. Gág never probed the tales; she re-created them in her own spirit. She made them into idyllic moments of pleasurable reading and seeing for her readers, children and adults alike. Her longing to recapture the Grimms' tales was actually a utopian projection of possible happiness. The joyful simple figures point toward a simplification of life, a desire for "genuine" living, which was ironically one of the reasons that her work was somewhat pivotal in the debate about fairy tales at that time.

Key here is how Gág's *Snow White and the Seven Dwarfs* was prompted and held up in opposition to Walt Disney's 1937 animated film by the same name. Hoyle writes:

> Despite a preponderance of rave reviews of the movie in the media, most children's librarians and book reviewers responded negatively to the movie and the accompanying Disney books. These editions dismayed some librarians because Disney took so many liberties with the story. He infuriated [Anne Carroll] Moore, who used all three of her powerful roles—as head of children's work at the New York Public Library, board member of the prestigious *Horn Book*, and reviewer for the *New York Herald Tribune Books*—to make scathing remarks about the Disney books. . . . She not only wrote negative reviews but actively sought a correct version of the fairy tale for children, and Wanda Gág was the logical choice. Gág's *Tales from Grimm*, published only two years earlier, was familiar to readers, but "Snow White" was not part of that volume. Moore personally pressured Coward-McCann to produce a version of the fairy tale.[15]

It is not so important to establish whether Gág's or Disney's version of "Snow White" is more or less appropriate for children or more or less valid as an adaptation and interpretation of the Grimms' tale. What is significant is the debate itself about the impossibility of the possible: Moore and others thought it was possible to make a *correct* version of a fairy tale for children, something which is inherently impossible because nobody knows what a genuine, authentic, or correct fairy tale is. The assumption was—and still is—that we know what is appropriate for children, that we know children, and that we know exactly what effects a tale will have on a child. Karín Lesnik-Oberstein has pointed out, however, that "children's fiction can be seen not only as an expression of constriction and regulation of the child for the adult's sake, but also as an expression of a paradoxical wish to resolve the self-imposed and self-defined separations: efforts to remain in touch with, and deal with, the anxieties of ignorance and knowledge, of being and becoming, of presence and absence for their own sake."[16] Both within literature and films for children, the figures of the young and childhood are constructed ideologically and aesthetically to explore the creators' own views, needs, and desires. There is no negotiation with the child because fiction and film are projections if not impositions that the young readers/viewers encounter and deal with in their own way, a way that is often already conditioned by the society and culture in which they live.

Disney and Gág cared more about their own concerns in creating their Snow Whites than the concerns of children. Disney was absorbed in his own artwork and wanted to produce a magnificent film that would make a name for himself and make the Disney name into a world trademark. He did not want to make a film just for the young but for the family, and he had no concern in producing an authentic version of a Grimm fairy tale. The fairy tale was a vehicle for him to celebrate his skills in animation and the skills of his co-creators. If there was anything radically new about his film *Snow White and the Seven Dwarfs*, it lay in his demonstrating to the world how fairy-tale reading matter could be transformed into a conventionally delightful musical about sentimental love. Gág was engaged virtually to counter the Disney version by her friends to show what poetic license Disney had taken and how he had contaminated the Grimms' true version. Though she sticks close to the Grimm text, she is unaware that there is no one authentic Grimm text, because the Grimms themselves rewrote their tale several times and "contaminated" some other texts. What Gág successfully does is to represent the figure of Snow White as a spunky, virginal, domesticated girl who looks after seven diminutive darling elves and needs looking after herself. It is tempting to ask how she imagined herself in the story, whether she imagined her own mother as dead kind mother or obsessed witch. It is tempting to ask whether she saw herself as being released from looking after the sibling dwarfs by the prince who will take her away and enable her to paint and draw to her heart's content in his castle in the country.

Of course, one could ask some of the same tempting questions about Disney's life and how he projected himself into the story and projected visions of childhood and idyllic life through cinematic images and colloquial language. In the end, however, both Disney and Gág did the exact *same* thing: they Americanized the Grimms' tale and exploited the figure of Snow White for personal and professional purposes. Snow White is nothing but a pawn in their hands, and ironically, this may account for the great appeal of Disney's film and Gág's prose narrative. Such appeal is perhaps inherent in the story itself.

I should like to suggest that Snow White appeals to both children and adults because she embodies the embattled child, abandoned by her mother, disregarded by her father, persecuted by a stepmother, used by male dwarfs, and revived from death by a prince. As a fictional figure, Snow White reflects and recalls how adults are engaged in determining the welfare and fate of children. It is a tale about hierarchical conflicts and the powerlessness of the child. Snow White must fend for herself, defend herself, but she is not in charge of her destiny. She needs a miracle, as most children continually need miracles in their daily lives to intercede on their behalf. Not that children are victims or are constantly victimized. But their lives are framed by adults who seek to play out their lives through children.

Disney and Gág do nothing much to alter our vision of children or childhood in their contaminated versions of "Snow White." As I have suggested, the tale is "Americanized" through the language and images in their works. Above all, Snow White has something of the clean-cut, rosy red, virginal features that were often associated with young girls of the 1930s in America, and it is interesting that both Disney and Gág grew up in the Midwest, for they tend to represent girls as they should be according to the ethics and morals of the Midwest. But Gág, who regarded herself as a feminist, was much more aware of the tensions that girls from her neck of the woods felt about conforming to what girls and boys should be. In contrast to Disney, she was a liberal thinker with clear socialist inclinations and contributed to left-wing publications. She lived with Earle Humphreys, who did some labor organizing, many years before she finally married him. She had great empathy for children and for the Wanda Gág of memory. Her liberal sentiments were voiced strongly in a 1939 article, "I Like Fairy Tales," published in *The Horn Book*:

> Every child goes through many phases of development, each phase with its own needs and interests. I know I should now feel bitterly cheated if, as a child, I had been deprived of all fairy lore; and it does not seem to me that we have the right to deprive any child of its rightful heritage of Fairyland. In fact, I believe it is *just* the modern children who need it, since their lives are already overbalanced on the side of steel and stone and machinery—and nowadays, one might well add, bombs, gas-masks and machine guns.[17]

One of her most successful "Americanized" Grimms' tales that reveals her social and political inclinations is "The Sorcerer's Apprentice." It not only illustrates how Gág positioned herself as child protagonist to defend the rights of the young but might also serve as a parable for the manner in which children must fend for themselves in the adult world. To my knowledge, nobody has realized what great liberties Gág took in writing this tale. In German, the title is "De Gaudeif un sien Meester," or "The Thief and his Master," and it appears in Münster dialect in the Grimms' collection. The tale begins as follows:

> Jan wanted his son to learn a trade. Therefore, he went to church and prayed to the Lord to tell him what would be best for his son. The sexton was standing behind the altar and said, "Thieving, thieving."
>
> So Jan went to his son and told him he had to learn how to be a thief because the Lord wanted it that way. He then set out with his son to look for a man who knew something about thieving. After they had traveled for a long time, they finally reached a great forest, where they found a cottage with an old woman inside.[18]

The son learns all sorts of thievery and witchcraft, but the jealous master wants to keep him in his service and prevent him from living with his father and exercising his powers. One day the master's daughter inadvertently takes the bridle off the young thief, who had been turned into a horse:

> The horse became a sparrow and flew out the door. Then the master thief also became a sparrow and flew after him. They met and held a contest in midair, but the master lost and fell into the water, where he turned himself into a fish, and they held another contest. Once again the master lost, and he turned himself into a rooster, while the boy changed himself into a fox and bit the master's head off. So the master died, and he has remained dead up to this very day.[19]

The initial setting in Gág's "The Sorcerer's Apprentice" is very different:

> A man found himself in need of a helper for his workshop, and one day as he was walking along the outskirts of a little hamlet he met a boy with a bundle slung over his shoulder. Stopping him, the man said, "Good morning, my lad. I am looking for an apprentice. Have you a master?"
>
> "No," said the boy. "I have just this morning said good-bye to my mother and am now off to find myself a trade."
>
> "Good," said the man. "You look as though you might be just the lad I need. But wait, do you know anything about reading and writing?"

"Oh yes!" said the boy.

"Too bad!" said the man. "You won't do after all. I have no use for anyone who can read and write."

"Pardon me?" said the boy. "If it was *reading* and *writing* you were talking about, I misunderstood you. I thought you asked if I knew anything about *eating* and *fighting*—those two things I am able to do well, but as to reading and writing, that is something I know nothing about."

"Well!" cried the man. "Then you are just that fellow I want. Come with me to my workshop, and I will show you what to do.[20]

In time the clever young boy learns that the man is a sorcerer, and says to himself: "Sorcery—that is a trade I would dearly love to master! . . . A mouthful of good chants and charms would never come amiss to a poor fellow like me, and with them I might even be able to do some good in the world."[21] So the boy secretly reads the sorcerer's books and practices magic while the sorcerer is away on trips. One day, however, the sorcerer discovers that the boy is his equal and is afraid that he might use the tricks of his trade to help people. So he tries to beat him to a pulp. But the boy changes himself into a bird and then a large fish, while the sorcerer transforms himself into a tiny kernel of grain and rolls into a small crack in a stone to avoid the fish. In turn, the clever boy changes himself into a rooster and eats the kernel up.

"That was the end of the wicked sorcerer, and the boy became the owner of the magic workshop. And wasn't it fine that all the powers and ingredients which had been used for evil by the sorcerer were now in the hands of a boy who could use them only for the good of man and beast?"[22]

Is this "freely translated" tale what Anne Carroll Moore and other editors, librarians, and teachers would call an appropriate or correct fairy tale for children? Gág completely contaminated the Grimms' version, and in effect, wrote a kind of autobiographical fairy tale about a young person who learns from an adult and at the same time opposes the constraints of the adult world to master art. In her struggle against the oppressive adult world, she kills off the adult, as in the case of the Grimms' tale, but in Gág's tale, there is no father left, and we do not know where the mother is. The young man is left alone to do good in the world with his art.

But Gág's tale is not just about herself; it is also about her vision of how the young must negotiate their place in the world. Written on behalf of herself, it is a tale also written in behalf of children in which the young boy becomes a fictional figure struggling to determine his own worth in equal relationship with humans and the animal world. Gág's vision here is clearly utopian, and even if she "contaminated" their so-called original messages by addressing American concerns and her own personal needs, her adaptations of the Grimms' tales still reveal what the value of fairy tales may be for young readers and viewers who continue to need creative alternatives to the complex demands and constrictions that they encounter in their daily lives.

NOTES

1. Wanda Gág, *Tales from Grimm* (New York: Coward-McCann, 1936), vii.
2. Karen Nelson Hoyle, *Wanda Gág* (New York: Twayne, 1994), 58.
3. *Ibid.*, 31.
4. For a more thorough discussion of the *Snow White* film, see the chapter "Breaking the Disney Spell" in my book *Fairy Tale as Myth/Myth as Fairy Tale* (Lexington: University Press of Kentucky, 1994), 72–95.
5. See Leonard Maltin, *Of Mice and Magic: A History of American Animated Cartoons* (New York: New American Library, 1980). There is also an important videocassette, *Cartoon Crazys Fairy Tales*, Northampton Partners, 1999. This cassette contains some of the best animated fairy tales of the 1930s, 1940s, and 1950s.
6. Alma Scott, *Wanda Gág: The Story of an Artist* (Minneapolis: University of Minnesota Press, 1949), 177.
7. Johnathan Cott, *Pipers at the Gates of Dawn: The Wisdom of Children's Literature* (New York: Viking, 1984), xxii.
8. *Ibid.*, 75.
9. For a short but insightful biography, see Michel Patrick Hearn, "Wanda Gág," *Dictionary of Literary Biography: American Writers for Children, 1900–1960*, ed. John Cech, vol. 22 (Detroit: Gale, 1983), 179–91.
10. Gág, *Tales from Grimm*, ix–x.
11. *Grimms Fairy Tales*, trans. Mrs. E. V. Lucas, Lucy Crane, and Marian Edwardes, illustr. Fritz Kredel (New York: Grosset & Dunlap, 1955), 330.
12. Gág, *Tales from Grimm*, 4–5.
13. *Grimm's Fairy Tales*, trans. Margaret Hunt, illustr. John B. Gruelle (New York: Cupples & Leon, 1914), 271.
14. Wanda Gág, *Snow White and the Seven Dwarfs* (New York: Coward-McCann, 1938), 42–43.
15. Hoyle, *Wanda Gág*, 73.

16. Karín Lesnik-Oberstein, *Children's Literature: Criticism and the Fictional Child* (Oxford: Oxford University Press, 1994), 75.

17. Wanda Gág, "I Like Fairy Tales," *The Horn Book* 15 (March-April 1939): 75–76.

18. *The Complete Fairy Tales of the Brothers Grimm*, trans. Jack Zipes (New York: Bantam, 1992), 267.

19. *Ibid.*, 269.

20. Wanda Gág, *More Tales from Grimm* (New York: Coward-McCann, 1947), 197–98.

21. *Ibid.*, 199.

22. *Ibid.*, 204–5.

The Contamination

6

of the

Fairy Tale

A curious thing happened at the end of World War II in Germany. For a brief period in 1945, the occupation forces, led by the British, sought to ban the publication of the Grimms' fairy tales. They attributed many of the atrocities and crimes committed by the Nazis to the horror and cruelty of the tales. Moreover, they asserted that the tales had given German children a false impression of the world that had made them susceptible to lies and irrationality. Even the Germans themselves began questioning the value of the Grimms' tales and whether they were appropriate for a humanist upbringing.[1] However, the attempt to ban the tales did not last long, and soon the Grimms' tales flourished in Germany in both the western and eastern sectors. Moreover, the Grimms' tales became so popular throughout the world that it is difficult today to call them German. What began in 1945 as a condemnation of the alleged nasty "Teutonic" nature of the Grimms' tales had led by the end of the twentieth century to a virtual celebration of their universal and international quality: the Grimms' tales are our proper fairy tales.

Perhaps celebration is the wrong word, because the Grimms' tales have been hotly debated, contested, and revised, particularly in Europe and North America. The revisions have been so extensive and innovative that it is difficult today to define what the nature of the contemporary fairy tale is or what constitutes a proper and authentic fairy tale. But one thing is certain: most definitions of a fairy tale begin with a fixed or imaginary notion of the Grimms' fairy tales, and there are numerous translations and picture books based on the Grimms' tales throughout the world. The Grimms, whether one admires them or not, appear to have established the model and proper fairy tale. The association of the term "classical fairy tale" with the name Grimm is not intended to deny the importance of other classical writers such as Charles Perrault and Hans Christian Andersen. They, too, have forged images in the minds of most people in contemporary society of what a fairy tale should be. But the references to the Grimms and the use of their tales far outweigh the commemorations of Perrault and Andersen.

While the Grimms' tales have served as classical models for most contemporary writers of fairy tales, they have also been the touchstone for experimentation, and in the course of the experimenting, the structure and contents of the contemporary fairy tale have been altered a great deal just as our notion of a Grimm fairy tale has kept shifting. In fact, in some ways we seem to have come full circle in our attitudes toward the Grimms' tales and fairy tales in general. Instead of condemning the Grimms, as was done in 1945, relegating the tales to the nursery or kindergarten, or analyzing them as the articulation of some mystical German spirit, we tend, like the Grimms themselves, to consider the tales as appropriate for all age groups and as representations of a profound historical development that emanates from the cultural intersection of oral and written traditions from many different countries.

In a recent essay about the fairy-tale theories of the Brothers Grimm, Heinz Rölleke makes the claim that it was not by chance that the Grimms did not use the word "German" in the title of their collection *Kinder- und Hausmärchen* (*Children's and Household Tales*, 1812–1815) at a time when numerous other writers and collectors were purposely designating their tales as German or Teutonic. According to Rölleke, the Grimms deliberately avoided titling their tales "German" because they were eminently aware of the ancient myths and tales from numerous other societies and countries that contributed to the formation of the tales they gathered for their collection. In addition, the Grimms consciously and artfully collated different versions in an effort to reproduce what they imagined was the most representative narrative of a particular tale type that had its own unique intercultural history, as they recorded in their notes. At one point Rölleke explains that, because of the depth and multicultural aspect of the tales, the Grimms were very much influenced by Goethe's advice that folk narratives should be restored and elaborated, if not contaminated to bring out their deep meanings. In fact, the Grimms were the greatest contaminators of fairy tales in the nineteenth century.

It may be at first shocking to call the Grimms contaminators, especially when the most commonly held view of them up until now has been to regard them as "purely" German. Indeed, until recently folklorists consistently sought to define their Germanic character and the German essence of their tales, a view that was held internationally by many folklorists, not just the National Socialists in the period 1920–1945. The facts are, however, that the Grimms were natives of Hessia and spent a good part of their lives in Kassel. Though they had hoped that Germans might be united one day, perhaps under Prussian rule, they were not chauvinists or conservative patriots and were always fascinated by numerous other cultures and folk traditions about which they wrote and which they respected. Their hope for German unity was predicated on the establishment of a common cultural tradition based on language and folklore, not politics, for they realized how different Germans were among themselves and how different the dialects and customs were. This is why their high German renditions of the tales they heard and borrowed from books and manuscripts were crafted with great care to appeal to all Germans, young and old. Their collection was never designed to constitute a children's book or to appeal specifically to children. Their intended audience included mainly literate adults who would potentially pass on the tales to all people in their communities and the young who would learn important moral and ethical lessons from the tales—one of the reasons why they called their work an *Erziehungsbuch* (pedagogical book). This is also why they contaminated their tales.

Contamination is a term used by folklorists to point to foreign (or alien) elements that may have been added to or have seeped into what appears to be a pure, homogenous narrative tradition. The verb "contaminate" means to render impure by contact or mixture. Synonyms are to defile, corrupt, pollute, taint, infect. A contaminated tale is one that has been somehow sullied and made impure. No longer pure, it can no longer be valid as a genuine or authentic part of a particular culture. There is something artificial about it. One could say that a contaminated tale has gone through a process of infection. But there is another, more positive way of regarding the contamination of tales. In medicine, the body is often made stronger through the injection of vaccines and other drugs that contaminate the body with the disease that might otherwise weaken it. By absorbing small amounts of the disease the body becomes immune to a particular disease and changes something that might be unhealthy for it into something more beneficial. In other words, contamination, the exposure to foreign substances, is necessary if the body is to grow stronger. Contamination can be an enrichment process; it can lead to the birth of something unique and genuine in its own right. In fact, it is practically impossible to avoid contact with foreign substances, with all kinds of bacteria, in our daily lives, and our bodies function more efficiently by learning how to incorporate the alien elements. Physically we become stronger and attain more pleasure out of life. One could argue that undergoing some contamination is necessary, and we can draw parallels with regard to inbreeding or immigration. Too much inbreeding can be destructive for a species, but without immigration we lack the possibility for developing a variety of species and variety in life. It is through the introduction of foreign elements into a family or society that the family and society become "contaminated" and thus preserve themselves and become more complex and stronger on an individual and social level.

To contaminate an oral folk tale or a literary fairy tale is thus to enrich it by artfully introducing extraordinary motifs, themes, words, expressions, proverbs, metaphors, and characters into its corporate body so that it will be transformed and form a new essence. Just as physical bodies constantly change, so do tales through retelling and reprinting. The Grimms recognized this process of narrative transformation carried on by human agents that dates back to ancient times, and they cultivated their own style and perspective to contaminate the tales that fell into their hands. In editing and re-editing their tales for close to fifty years, they (unlike the Italians Giovan Francesco Straparola and Giambattista Basile and the French Charles Perrault, Marie-Catherine d'Aulnoy, Marie-Jeanne Lhéritier, and others in the sixteenth and seventeenth centuries) effaced any trace of specific locality, nation, or character. Only through the language and proverbs and subtle references to customs could one tell that the tales were "Germanic," and even here, they were truly adaptations and transformations of narratives from many different European and Oriental regions that the Grimms artfully contaminated.

In the 1822 preface to the important *Anmerkungen (Notes)* of the *Children's and Household Tales*, the Brothers Grimm remarked: "The documentation gathered here confirms the existence of tales in various times and among various people, or it contains judgments about their value that have all the more weight because they have been articulated impartially and occasionally by men without preference and thus have retained a free and natural view."[2] In the 1856 edition of the *Notes*, Wilhelm wrote the following splendid comment:

> What all tales have in common are the remains of a faith [*Glaube*]
> that stems from the most ancient time to the present and which
> expresses itself in metaphorical views about supernatural things.
> These mythical elements are comparable to tiny pieces of a splintered
> precious stone that lie on the ground covered by grass and flowers

and can only be discovered by keen eyesight. The meaning of all this has long since been forgotten, but it is still felt and gives the tale its substance, while at the same time it satisfies the natural desire for the wonderful. The tales are never a mere kaleidoscope of the insubstantial imagination. The mythical expands the more that we go back. Indeed, it appears to have constituted the only substance of the most ancient poetry. We see how this poetry is carried by the sublimity of its subject matter without concern for bringing about harmony with reality, when it depicts the richly mysterious and terrifying natural forces and also does not reject the incredible, the horrible, and the gruesome. The poetry first becomes milder, when the observation of simple conditions is included such as the observation of the life of the shepherd, the hunter, and the farmer and when the influence of the purer morals takes effect. In astonishment we glimpse how the boundless and the monstrous appear in the North American legend directly next to the portrayal of the simple, almost idyllic life. The Tibetan legend is often filled with ugly, sometimes naked and raw things, although even here the depiction of natural relations or revelations of true feelings is not lacking. To the degree to which human and more mild customs develop and the sensual richness of poetry grows, the mythical retreats and begins to cover itself with the fragrance of distance that weakens the clarity of the outlines but elevates the grace of poetry just like painting makes the transition from sharply drawn, lean, even ugly but important shapes to the outer beauty of the forms.[3]

These remarks are extremely important for understanding how and why the Grimms shaped their tales in the manner that they did. The folk tales were for them precious gems that contained the mysteries of life and could possibly be traced back through different cultures to the most ancient of times. The tales that they collected from different German sources represented the culmination of a long-neglected and highly significant development in the civilizing process of both the East and the West, for the tales were integral parts that led to the constitution of poetry and were in and of themselves miraculous. To bring out this miraculous quality, they honed and polished them, and while they regarded their efforts as a contribution toward establishing the great legacy of the German *Volk*, they constantly insisted on stressing the Indo-Germanic roots of the tales. It is this tension that constitutes the quality of the tales, for the Grimms earnestly sought to keep alive the "mythic" meaning of the tales while appropriating them for their German readers and to establish a heritage for future readers.

To a great extent the cultural heritage that the Grimms sought to transmit exceeded their modest expectations. Not only did their collection of fairy tales become the solid foundation of most fairy tales produced in Germany in the late nineteenth and twentieth centuries, but it fixed the form and content of what a fairy tale should be for the rest of the world. Moreover—and most writers of fairy tales do not even realize this—the Grimms sowed the seeds of contamination of their own tales even as they were collecting and editing them.

Without understanding their artful insemination of foreign ingredients into their tales, it is impossible to understand the contemporary revisions and reformations of the Grimms' tales and the significance of the innovative work with their tales. In fact, contamination has made the Grimms' tales viable and crucial in addressing numerous social and political developments since 1945. There is a myriad of stimulating ways that writers and artists have contaminated the Grimms' tales throughout the world, and I should like to describe several representative works that demonstrate how the Grimms' tales have lost their specific historical legacy in German culture but have gained a worldwide legacy, ironically more in keeping with the profound multicultural motifs and themes that had been woven into their tales.

The revision and adaptation of the Grimms' fairy tales, including parodies, began in the nineteenth century and increased by the beginning of the twentieth century. For instance, in 1902 Guy Wetmore Carryl published a collection of witty verse tales that had appeared in magazines such as *The Century*, *Life*, *The Saturday Evening Post*, and *The London Tattler* under the title *Grimm Tales Made Gay*. Typical of his humor is his version of "Little Red Riding Hood," in which the promising career of a bright, ambitious young girl is cut short when she goes to visit her grandmother with a basket full of jellies, ices, chicken legs, stew, two novels, a hot-water can, a Japanese fan, and a bottle of eau de cologne. After she arrived:

> She expected to find
> Her decrepit but kind
>   Old Grandmother waiting her call,
> But the visage that met her
> Completely upset her:

It wasn't familiar at all!
With a whitening cheek
She started to speak,
    But her peril she instantly saw: —
Her grandma had fled,
And she'd tacked instead
    Four merciless Paws and a Maw!
When the neighbors came running, the wolf to subdue,
He was licking his chops, (and Red Riding Hood's, too!)

At this terrible tale
Some readers will pale
    And others with horror grow dumb,
And yet it was better,
I fear, he should get her:
    Just think what she might have become!
For an infant so keen
Might in future have been
    A woman of awful renown,
Who carried on fights
For her feminine rights
    As the Mare of an Arkansas town.
She might have continued the crime of her 'teens,
And come to write verse for the Big Magazines![4]

Carryl used his satire of the Grimm fairy tale to make fun of the suffragette movement at the beginning of the twentieth century and at the same time to question the fears of those people who were afraid of the women's movement. There is a note of frivolity in all the poems of his collection, and this frivolous use of the Grimms' tales, minimizing serious social and political issues, can be traced in such other works as Edward and Joseph Anthony's *The Fairies Up-To-Date* (1923), Joel Wells's *Grimm Fairy Tales for Adults* (1967), James Finn Garner's *Politically Correct Bedtime Stories* (1994), right up to the present in A. J. Jacobs's *Fractured Fairy Tales* (1997), based on the popular American TV show *The Adventures of Rocky and Bullwinkle and Friends*. While satire and parody have been extensively employed to rewrite the Grimms' tales for contemporary readers, and while there is always a serious side to mockery, these "contaminations" are often limited by their topical and popular references and are delightful mainly in their time. Rarely do they survive except as a footnote in the history of the genre, while other endeavors to rewrite the Grimms' tales or portray them anew seek to engage the Grimms to make a more lasting statement.

It is difficult to determine what revisions of the Grimms' tales will survive into the twenty-first century, especially since there is some doubt whether the book form itself will survive, but there have been highly significant experiments beyond simple parody that I should like to discuss, for they have made major contributions to our contemporary notion of what a fairy tale is, and their contaminations demonstrate how there can be no fixed lines drawn between children's and adult literature. The works I want to discuss are Janosch's *Janosch erzählt Grimm's Märchen* (1972, translated as *Not Quite as Grimm*), Lore Segal and Maurice Sendak's *The Juniper Tree and Other Tales from Grimm* (1973), Tanith Lee's *Red as Blood or Tales from the Sisters Grimmer* (1983), Mitsumasa Anno's *Anno's Twice-Told Tales by the Brothers Grimm & Mr. Fox* (first published in Japan in 1991), Babette Cole's *Princess Smartypants* (1986) and *Prince Cinders* (1987), Jon Scieszka's *The Frog Prince Continued* (1991), Donna Jo Napoli's *The Magic Circle* (1993), Donna Jo Napoli and Richard Tchen's *Spinners* (1999), Priscilla Galloway's *Truly Grim Tales* (1995), Vivian Vande Velde's *Tales from the Brothers Grimm and the Sisters Weird* (1995), and Emma Donoghue's "The Tale of the Spinster" in *Kissing the Witch: Old Tales in New Skins* (1997).

In dealing with these works, I shall expand upon the work of John Stephens and Robyn McCallum in *Retelling Stories, Framing Culture: Traditional Story and Metanarratives in Children's Literature*. They demonstrate that all retellings of stories must be based on a pre-text, that is, on a preexisting text, but these retellings are rarely simple replications or reproductions of their sources. Stephens and McCallum argue that:

> retellings do not, and cannot, also reproduce the discoursal mode of the source, they cannot *replicate* its significances, and always impose their own cultural presuppositions in the process of retelling, and second even the most revered cultural icon can be subjected to mocking or antagonistic retellings. The resulting version is then not so much a retelling as a *re-version*, a narrative which has taken apart

its pre-texts and reassembled them as a version which is a new textual and ideological configuration.[5]

In the process, contemporary writers who use the Grimm's tales as their pre-texts are contaminating the Grimm legacy while enriching it and forging new concepts of the fairy tale. In some cases the Grimms' tales are used as pre-texts or what I refer to as duplication.[6] Publishers, writers, and illustrators collaborate to make it appear they are copying the Grimms' tales in a proper fashion only to dupe audiences so that they can profit from the sales of the Grimms' good and proper name for profit. There are literally hundreds of publishers who produce and market cheap versions of the Grimms' tales as pretexts to conceal their profit-making motives. These duplications merely reinforce static notions of the nineteenth-century fairy tales and leave anachronistic values and tastes unquestioned. Whatever changes are made in these duplications—and changes are always made—they tend to be in the name of an ignorant conservatism that upholds arbitrary notions of propriety, for many people believe that there is such a thing as a "proper" Grimm fairy tale. In contrast, the reversions of the Grimms' pre-texts, to use the terms coined by Stephens and McCallum, adulterate the Grimms' tales by adding ingredients, taking away some elements, and reconstructing them to speak to contemporary audiences in different sociocultural contexts. As Karl Kroeber notes:

> There is nothing literary critics overlook more consistently than the fact that stories are always retold, reread, that narrative is a repeating form for discourse—in which repetition is unique. This paradox gives storytelling a strong claim to be the most important of all modes of cultural discourse. No one can dispute that narrative has been the primary means by which most societies have defined themselves. On the other hand, narrative is also the primary means by which sociocultural boundaries could be crossed, not transgressively, but unobtrusively. Stories are like plant species that move readily but unobtrusively over surprising obstacles, including vast spans of time and space, quietly adapting to foreign environments, and then changing those environments. Narrative is the discourse most amenable to translative adaptations that permit simultaneous retention and revision of its peculiarities.[7]

Therefore it is important to consider the unique aesthetic modalities that are employed to transform the ideological meanings of the pre-texts, and it is especially significant to consider how illustrations and texts are used to counter each other in unique ways. Though not all contaminated reversions of the Grimms' tales are successful artistic endeavors of retelling and may have major flaws, they are all important because they collude in transforming the Grimms' pre-texts to engender a different notion or conception of what a fairy tale should be in the twenty-first century. A few examples will demonstrate how consciously authors, artists, and writers are inspired to rewrite the Grimms for children and adults with a modern if not postmodern sensibility.

In the afterword to *Janosch erzählt Grimm's Märchen* the publisher Hans-Joachim Gelberg notes that Janosch's work owes a debt to the antiauthoritarian movement of the late 1960s and that many writers deservedly questioned the respect that canonical and traditional literature such as the Grimms' fairy tales had always received in Germany:

> This book, Janosch's fairy-tale book, distinguishes itself from all previous fairy-tale books. It lives from the lively language stamped by the oral tradition. It demands reading aloud: it is acoustic and at the same time porous enough so that the child can make something out of the telling by himself or herself. In short, the anachronistic language of the children's book that has been polished for children is missing. The form of the fairy-tale material that the Brothers Grimm had gathered loses its conservative form. In reading Janosch the reader leaves the ceremonial fairy-tale seriousness of the Brothers Grimm. This does not mean that he has less than what the brothers have too much of.[8]

Indeed, there was a very serious intention behind Janosch's publication of his retellings of the Grimms' tales. He purposely selected fifty tales from the Grimms' collection of 210 narratives to imitate the so-called *Kleine Ausgabe* (small edition), which the brothers published ten different times between 1825 and 1858. This small edition was designed to appeal to younger readers as a kind of book for the family and contained most of the well-known classical tales that are famous today. In contrast, Janosch chose numerous tales that are not widely known, and he totally rewrote them and gave them a contemporary setting. For instance, in "Hans My Hedgehog," Hans is transformed from a porcupine-looking character into a hippy rock singer who plays the harmonica. When his father gives him sunglasses and a motorcycle to get rid of him, he goes into the city and eventually becomes a movie star named Jack Eagle. In the end his father is proud of him, and everyone from his village wants to look like him. In another tale, "Doctorknowitall" a farmer and his wife realize that a doctor's life is much more comfortable than their own, and they learn to copy his trite sayings, move to the city, and set up a doctor's office. As charlatans they fit perfectly into the society and become more successful and wealthy than even they had expected they would.

Janosch, a gifted illustrator, reinforces the social critique in all his tales with hilarious black-and-white ink sketches that have a comic-book quality to them, very much in keeping with the caricatures of the petit bourgeois types that he draws in his writing. As someone who grew up during the years of the so-called economic miracle in Germany, Janosch introduces all kinds of motifs, associations, sayings, and plots that enrich the Grimms' tales. In fact, he radicalizes their tales and shows the discomfiting results of the middle-class legacy of the Grimms' tales. If many of the Grimms' tales preach industriousness, diligence, opportunism, the importance of money and power, and the domestication of women, Janosch seeks to explore the directions in which the Grimms' nineteenth-century narrative plots lead in contemporary society. His illustrations expose the shallowness of contemporary society, but they are not cynical. Janosch appears to delight in the contradictions that he depicts, and his re-versions tend to reestablish the Grimms' tales as social commentaries that speak about the foibles of the folk while, at the same time, they question where the German folk have arrived after the economic miracle years of the 1950s and 1960s.[9]

Lore Segal and Maurice Sendak took another tack in their retellings of the Grimms' tales. Their two-volume edition, *The Juniper Tree and Other Tales from Grimm* (1973), is important because of their selection and the illustrations. They chose twenty-seven tales that tend to deal with the theme of child abuse and cruel oppression. Although some of them, such as "The Frog King," "Rapunzel," and "Snow White and the Seven Dwarfs," can be found in most standard collections or selections of the Grimms' tales, most of the tales they chose are not often retranslated and reprinted, especially not for children. It is obvious that Segal and Sendak wanted to make a statement just with the title of the book, *The Juniper Tree*. This tale concerns an evil woman who has her stepson killed and serves him in a stew to his father. Eventually, the dead son wreaks revenge, thanks to a bird from the juniper tree, where his birth mother had been buried. The story is a gruesome one and has not become one of the more classical Grimms' tales for children. Clearly, Segal and Sendak revise traditional notions of the Grimms' tales just with their choice of tales and title. Since the translations are literal and do not contain any unusual changes, the selection of tales and the illustrations are the "contaminating" elements in this edition that provoke readers to rethink and perhaps revise their understanding of the Grimms and their tales. With their selection of tales focusing on the maltreatment or manipulation of children, Segal and Sendak show how the young are vulnerable to the arbitrary power of parents and adults. At the same time, they focus on the astonishing ability of children to survive even the most devastating treatment. Consequently, Sendak's black-and-white ink drawings are crucial for understanding the gist of these Grimm reversions. Two examples will demonstrate how Sendak's illustrations lend a critical contemporary meaning to the Grimms' tales, which were altered by Segal to provoke readers to reflect about the nature of oppression.

There are two volumes to the edition of *The Juniper Tree*, and each has a frontispiece. For volume 1, it is "The Goblins"; for volume 2, "Rabbit's Bride." Neither of these tales is well known, nor do they have an apparent connection to the tale "The Juniper Tree," but as we shall see, they fit perfectly into the concept developed by Segal and Sendak. As frontispieces the drawings are shocking and draw attention to two texts that are to be found unillustrated later in the volumes. The drawings are on the opposite pages of the title pages. In the first illustration, Sendak depicts six tiny men, all with grim faces and beards, dressed in medieval garb, carrying a gigantic nude baby on their shoulders. One of the men in a turban is leading the others, and he is carrying a spear with a lantern or bell dangling from the top. The baby appears to be entranced by this object, and gawks at it with his eyes and mouth wide open. The other illustration, to "Rabbit's Tale," portrays a surprised and somewhat angry rabbit who, with his long beard, resembles a billy goat while he places his arms around a straw doll holding a wooden spoon. Overlooking the rabbit are a fox with glasses and a smiling crow.

Since the readers of this edition will not know either one of the tales or the significance of the illustrations, they will have to look up the tales to grasp why Segal and Sendak placed the illustrations where they are. As a title, "The Goblins" is Segal's invention. Actually this tale appears as number 39 in the final edition of the Grimms' *Kinder- und Hausmärchen*, and there is a general title "The Elves," which incorporates three short tales. Why Segal chose the title and transformed the elves into goblins is unclear. Also, the men depicted in Sendak's illustration are far from resembling goblins or elves as they are traditionally portrayed. If anything, they look like dwarfs. The plot of the tale is simple: the elves steal a mother's child from a cradle and replace it with a changeling. The mother receives advice from a neighbor about how she might regain her rightful child. She makes the changeling laugh, and the elves appear, bringing the right child with them. Then they cart the changeling away. Sendak's illustration is striking because it leaves the viewer in doubt about the action of the little men. Are they stealing the baby or bringing the baby back to the mother? The nude child is astonished. The men appear to be angry or disturbed. We are left with an image of a vulnerable baby manipulated by men who are apparently not concerned about his welfare.

In "Rabbit's Bride," a young girl is told by her mother to shoo away a rabbit that comes to their cabbage garden. After the third time that he comes, she goes off on his tail with him to his rabbit hut, and she is told to make preparations for their wedding. The fox was to be the sexton, and the crow, the parson. But since the girl is lonely, she makes a straw doll to replace herself and gives her a wooden spoon. Then she runs back to her mother. The rabbit finds that he has been tricked and is sad. In Sendak's illustration, the rabbit has a menacing look, and his glaring image dominates the picture. The fox and the crow are onlookers or witnesses. In some respects the face of the rabbit and his eyes recall the face of the baby, even though their situations are different.

Sendak's startling illustrations to tales that cannot be immediately recalled by most readers demand that the readers inform themselves about the narratives, which deal with abduction and return home, themes very common in Sendak's other works. The demand upon the reader to become acquainted with lesser-known works by the Grimms is also a demand to explore the themes of child abuse and forced marriage and the predicament in which young people often find themselves when placed under the control of older people. In the hands of Sendak and Segal, the selected Grimms' tales become contemporary illustrated deliberations and commentaries on our treatment of the young.

Whereas it is not clear, because of its unusual composition and themes, whether *The Juniper Tree and Other Tales from Grimm* was intended for children, Tanith Lee's *Red as Blood or Tales from the Sisters Grimmer* (1983) is clearly intended solely for an adult audience. Lee, a noted British science fiction and fantasy author, was one of the first writers, along with Anne Sexton, Angela Carter, Olga Broumas, and others,[10] to critique the Grimms' tales from a feminist viewpoint and to revise the gender relations in the pre-texts. The title of her book immediately recalls "Little Red Riding Hood," death, and solemnity. It has a gothic aspect. Indeed, most of the nine tales in this collection are about revenge and murder. Not all are retellings of the Grimms' tales, but they are feminist retellings of classical fairy tales and are composed to reflect chronologically social conditions and gender relations. The first tale has a setting in Asia in the last century B.C., and in the last one takes place in the future on Earth and another planet in a story that revises "Beauty and the Beast." Though most of the tales reflect the bestial treatment of women by men that result in poisoned relations, the very manner in which Lee has structured her tales that move from antiquity to the future demonstrates a certain optimism with regard to bringing about equality between the sexes. She moves from a depiction of brutal and primitive relations between men and women to an image of mutual respect. Yet, in tales such as "The Golden Rope" (based on "Rapunzel"), "The Princess and Her Future" (based on "The Frog King"), and "Wolfland" (based on "Little Red Riding Hood"), she recalls mainly how brutally women were treated and had to sacrifice their lives for men or had to become as vile as beasts if they were to survive. "The Princess and Her Future" is a good example of her style of gothic reversion. Her beginning is ominous: "Down in the deep darkness of the green water of the cistern, where no reflection and no sunlight ever come, Hiranu waits."[11] Hiranu is the bestial creature waiting for his prey, Princess Jarasmi, sixteen years old and about to be married. At one point she receives a gift of a golden glass ball from a strange merchant, and this glass ball can tell her future. However, she accidentally loses the ball in the cistern in which

Hiranu is waiting, and she summons help from the cistern. When Hiranu returns the ball to her, it bursts, and she runs to the palace for refuge. Later Hiranu appears in her chamber, and to her surprise he is stunningly handsome. She learns that he was bound by the spell of an enemy to dwell in the mud of the well until an innocent girl would free him by some inadvertent deed. Then she agrees to marry him and drives off in a wonderful carriage. Yet the prince's behavior indicates that something dreadful is in store for the princess. Even her father, left behind, senses this. Indeed, when they are alone in the carriage, Hiranu assumes his other form, and the story ends with the narrator stating: "The sealed carriage does not reveal it. While Jarasmi's frenzied shrieks are muffled, and in any case, do not continue long."[12]

In "The Princess and Her Future," Lee carries the implications of the Grimms' pre-text of "The Frog King" to a radical, pessimistic end to jar readers into realizing that the classical text sows the seeds for such victimization. Beasts do not change. They remain vicious and dangerous, and Lee implies that the men of the eighteenth century fed off women and were not to be trusted. Many of the feminist reversions of the 1980s were similar to Lee's tales, issuing stark warnings that women had to take charge of their lives: otherwise they would be violated.

Most of the cynical, skeptical, and pessimistic tales have tended to be written by feminists or postmodern innovators like Donald Barthelme (*Snow White*, 1967) and Robert Coover (*Pricksongs and Descants*, 1970, and *Briar Rose*, 1996), who have addressed primarily adults. The writers and artists who have sought to include children in their audience have endeavored to cultivate techniques and transform motifs, plots, and characters in a more optimistic manner. A good example is the extraordinary book by Mitsumasa Anno with the title *Anno's Twice-Told Tales by the Brothers Grimm and Mr. Fox* (1993). Numerous illustrators design fairy-tale picture books based on a Grimms text, either a translation or retold tale. Some illustrators do the retelling themselves. In this case Anno has written two stories allegedly told by Mr. Fox to his son Freddy Fox that comment on the adaptations of two of the Grimms' stories, "The Fisherman and His Wife" and "The Four Clever Brothers," also known as "The Four Skillful Brothers." The concept of his book is unique: Freddy Fox finds a book in the woods and brings it to his father, Mr. Fox, who cannot read but pretends to read the tales to his son. He reads the pictures the way a nonliterate child or adult might read them, and his two stories based on the Grimms' texts appear below Anno's full-spread water-color and pencil drawings. On top of each page, the adaptations of the Grimms' tales appear as insets within the illustrations. The result is that there are numerous ways to read and view the two tales: 1) The reader can ignore Mr. Fox's stories and read only the texts by the Grimms; 2) The reader can ignore the Grimms' tales and read only Mr. Fox's stories; 3) The reader can read the Grimms' tales against the grain of Mr. Fox's stories or vice versa; 4) The reader can read the illustrations against or with the texts; 5) The reader can ignore the illustrations. The multiple possibilities do not exclude each other. Anno opens up numerous possibilities that free readers from the strictures of the proper reading of the texts and the tales. Even his images have contradictions that he probably did not envision. For instance, his version of "The Four Clever Sons," begins with: "There was once a poor farmer who had four sons." But when we look at the illustration, we see a splendid, large farm that does not seem to be in a state of disrepair. Indeed, it would seem that the farmer would need to keep his sons, as most farmers do, to maintain the buildings and cultivate the land. But he sends them away to try their luck. Mr. Fox tells his son that he imagines their father will miss them a great deal, something that the Grimms text does not reveal. Indeed, Mr. Fox proceeds to transform the Grimms' text into a tale about the circus, with comments intended to make Freddy aware about the dangers of guns, hunting, and entrapment. At one point Mr. Fox announces:

> Now the circus has begun. First the wild animal trainer comes on. Wild animals like lions and tigers are scary animals that are stronger than humans. In the old days, circuses always used lions and tigers and bears. But this circus doesn't. It has dragons and monsters, because they're even more scary. Just take their size, for instance. Look at that one. It's fifty times bigger than an elephant, and ten times bigger than a whale. "Now presenting the Dance of the Monster," says the ringmaster. That girl has lulled the monster to sleep with a song. Even a terrible monster can be calmed down with sweet music. You don't have to hit it. Modern animal trainers don't go around cracking whips. But what will happen when this monster dances? The sea will go wild and the land will shake. It will really be something to see.[13]

Mr. Fox goes on to relate how the monster becomes angry, creates a storm, and changes himself into a boat. The king who was watching the circus invites the girl to remain in his castle as a princess, and the circus moves on. This is how Mr. Fox ends his nonviolent story, which is in stark contrast to the Grimm text and the illustrations, for the four skillful brothers actually rescue the princess, who has been kidnaped by a dragon. When the dragon comes after them, they shoot him down and turn his skin into sails for the boat. They bring the princess back to her father, and since they cannot all marry her, he makes them four rich princes, and they return to live in great happiness with their father.

With tongue in cheek, Anno writes and draws reversions of the Grimms' pre-texts. He contaminates the Grimms' literary versions by adding ingredients that constantly undermine the messages of the Grimms' tales. What is important for Anno is the tender relationship between father and son, who share in a reading of a picture book. In the process, Anno transforms the traditional tale about the rescue of a princess and the killing of an animal into a carnivalesque tale in which the girl takes destiny into her own hands in a circus act that turns the world upside down. Not all illustrators are as sophisticated and subversive as Anno. Most illustrators seek to amplify or elaborate on the Grimms' texts to enrich the stories. This is the case in the work of Trina Shart Hyman, Mercer Mayer, James Marshall, Michael Foreman, Nikolaus Heidenbach, Paul O. Zelinsky, Lisbeth Zwerger,[14] and others. Though the Grimms' text may remain stable, the pictures will shed light on aspects of the stories that cannot be communicated through words. The most exciting work that is done in the illustration of the Grimms' texts in picture books involves the use of revised stories and sophisticated imagery to work against and question the pre-text. Such experimentation sets the ground for further development of the fairy tale as a genre. For instance, the British illustrator Babette Cole created the delightful parody of "The Frog King" in *Princess Smartypants* (1986), in which she also reverses the "King Thrushbeard" tale by depicting a young girl in dungarees who does not want to be married and thwarts her parents by turning her major suitor into a frog when she kisses him. In another book, *Prince Cinders* (1987), a revision of "Cinderella," the youngest of three brothers is forced to do the housework until he is rescued by a zany fairy and a princess. In all her books Cole displays an uncanny sense for explosive situations that she captures in bright, often dazzling illustrations made with dyes. Although she has been dubbed an anarchic writer and illustrator, there is always a clear provocative purpose in her fairy-tale reversals that compel the reader immediately to rethink their notions of what a fairy tale is. *Prince Cinders* begins by presenting a prince who is small and scrawny, and on the opposite page we are presented with his three big hairy and macho brothers glaring at him. They tease him about his looks, but by the end of the tale they are turned into three house fairies who flit about Prince Cinders's palace to do the housework forever and ever.

Such comic turns are evident in Jon Scieszka's *The Frog Prince Continued* (1991), with paintings by Steve Johnson. In this wry version of the Grimms' tale, Scieszka debunks the notion of a happy ending by creating a prince who could not get rid of his nasty frog habits; the princess becomes so disturbed that the prince feels he must run into the woods to look for a witch who will transform him back into a frog. After many adventures with spooky witches and a clumsy fairy godmother, the prince manages to return home, thankful and content to have such a wonderful wife in the princess. He gives her a kiss, and immediately they turn into frogs and hop happily into the forest. Scieszka's satire on fairy tales and happy endings is cleverly illustrated by Johnson's stark oil paintings that portray the prince in modern dress. Clothed in green, the prince's eyes bulge and his tongue catches insects. He and his wife resemble wooden puppets pulling at the strings of the dictates of the traditional fairy tale. There is a surrealistic quality to Johnson's illustrations that transforms the cheery fairy tale into an eery one, despite the alleged happy ending.

Whereas Cole's and Scieszka's retellings of the Grimms' tales have been published as picture books that appeal to a young audience as well as adult readers, Donna Jo Napoli's reversions of the Grimms' tales are clearly more sophisticated and demand greater linguistic skills and familiarity with the pre-texts of the Grimms. Most of her works are novellas or short novels which focus on the psyches of the characters and could be considered psychological case studies. *The Prince of the Pond: Otherwise Known as De Fawg Pin* (1992) is a revision of "The Frog King" told from the viewpoint of Jade, a female frog, who recalls how she helped a bewildered prince, who was transformed into a frog by a wicked hag, to survive in the wilderness and regain his human form. In a sequel, *Jimmy, the Pickpocket of the Palace* (1995), a frog who was sired by the prince when he was a frog is turned into a human when he tries to save the pond from the hag, and discovers that he does not like human life in the palace. In *The Magic Circle* (1993), a powerful retelling of "Hansel and Gretel," Napoli investigates the prehistory of the witch with great sympathy, and she reveals that the witch was at one time a good healer but became transformed into an ogress by evil spirits. The brother and sister do not overcome evil in Napoli's tale. They witness the self-destructive capacity of a good human being and thus expose the potential for cruelty that exists in "good" people when circumstances turn against them. Napoli also examines the dark side of fairy tales in *Zel* (1996), a revision of "Rapunzel," in which she explores the psychology of the three main characters: the girl locked in the tower, the prince who wants to save her, and the witch/mother who wants to keep her, by allowing each one to tell the story and by shifting perspectives. In all her retellings Napoli explores the motives of the characters and adds ingredients that make the rereading of the Grimms' tales more disturbing than pleasant. While she does not move the setting of the tales to the present, her contamination of the pre-texts introduces elements that enable readers to have more empathy for characters troubled by twisted emotions. Ultimately her retellings reveal that happiness comes at the end of long, painful inner journeys. One of her more recent books, *Spinners* (1999), written with Richard Tchen, is a disturbing psychological exploration of the Grimms' "Rumpelstiltskin." They begin the book by describing an illicit affair between a farmer's daughter and a tailor who wants to marry her. However, her father wants her to wed the rich miller. Frustrated, the tailor promises to spin a dress of gold for the daughter, and the farmer gives him a month to do this. Otherwise his daughter will belong to the miller. Out of desperation the tailor steals a magic spinning wheel from an old woman, and this deed will mark him for the rest of his life. The spinning wheel enables him to spin a dress of gold, but as he does this he turns ugly and gnarled. The farmer's daughter is so horrified by his transformation that she marries the miller even though she is pregnant and bearing the tailor's baby. When she gives birth she dies, and her daughter, Saskia, is raised in brutal fashion by her drunken father, the miller. It is the miller who boasts to a sinister king that she can spin straw into gold, and it is the disfigured tailor as Rumpelstiltskin who comes to her aid. Later, after Saskia gives birth, the tailor wants to claim his grandchild out of vindictiveness and revenge. But Saskia gets to know his name and unknowingly brings about his death. She is left with her child, but lives in a sadomasochistic marriage with the king.

Napoli and Tchen add numerous levels to the personalities of all the characters, providing them with psychological motivation. The prehistory to the traditional Rumpelstiltskin plot explains the mystery of this character, but not in any rational way to make sense out of it. Napoli and Tchen are more interested in the irrational side of life, in how we cannot "spin" our stories and how we become enmeshed in webs that destroy the joyful impulses and creative potential that we have.

Priscilla Galloway, a Canadian writer, also explores the psychological ramifications of the Grimms' tales. In her collection of eight stories, *Truly Grim Tales* (1995), which are not entirely based on the Grimms' pre-texts, she writes:

> whoever plays with the grand old stories owes a huge debt to centuries of storytellers who have gone before, those who have told and retold, and those who have written down and collected. They have given me such delight, and so much to ponder. Nonetheless, I've always known they left out a lot and were unaware of even more. It has not been easy to discover the truth, but I have persisted. Gradually the stories behind the stories have come clear.[15]

There is something presumptuous about this statement, as if Galloway knows the truth or could even find the truth about old fairy tales. It would be more fitting, of course, to claim that she has found her own truths through the exploring and rewriting fairy tales, and what she fills in through contamination may be somebody else's untruth. In effect, it is the playing with truth that accounts for the quality of Galloway's stories. In her intriguing revision of "Rumpelstiltskin," which she gives the title of "The Name," she transforms the tale into a first-person narrative told by a misshapen nobleman who had been stricken with disease as a boy. He informs us that he later had a relationship with a country maiden, who became pregnant with his child, but his father would not permit him to marry beneath him.

So she was married off to the miller. Dejected, the narrator tells us that he left his father and went to live in a hut in the countryside. Years later, when his father dies, the narrator returns to take over his rich estates, and he learns that the country maiden had given birth to a daughter and then had been abused and beaten to death by the miller. It is this same greedy miller who boasts to the king that his daughter can spin straw into gold, and the king seeks her out and threatens her with death unless she does so. Consequently, the rich narrator intervenes in his daughter's life by bribing the king's guards and by bringing gold to his daughter, providing that she give him her firstborn. When she becomes queen and gives birth to a daughter, the narrator arrives to claim the baby, but his daughter, the queen, resists. He challenges her to guess his name within three days. If she succeeds, he will relent. On the first two days, she fails. The only way she can succeed is if he helps her, and he debates at the end of the narrative whether he will leave his daughter ignorant and raise the child himself or send her a messenger to let her know the elfish name of which his father had been so proud. There is no closure to the tale. We never learn the narrator's name. Nor is there any indication as to what choice he is inclined to make. If we learn anything, we learn the truth about Rumpelstiltskin's true identity. But even this truth is questionable because narrators are not always reliable truth-tellers, and we do not even know whether Rumpelstiltskin is narrating this tale. Galloway is a master of ambivalence, and in the course of her retelling, we are inspired to have more compassion for the maligned Rumpelstiltskin, to doubt the Grimms' pre-text, and to explore human motives more fully before we make rash judgments.

Her version can be compared to Vivian Vande Velde's "Straw into Gold" in her book *Tales from the Brothers Grimm and the Sisters Weird* (1995), a collection of thirteen fractured fairy tales which, unlike Galloway's story, make no claim on truth. The tone and style of her "Rumpelstiltzkin" is farcical as the beginning indicates:

> Once upon a time, in the days before Social Security or insurance companies, there lived a miller and his daughter, Della, who were fairly well-off and reasonably happy until the day their mill burned down. Suddenly they had nothing except the clothes they were wearing: No money, nor any way to make money, nor any possibility of ever getting money again unless they came up with a plan.[16]

Together they manage to concoct a plan to trick people into believing that Della can spin straw into gold. However, the plan backfires when a vain and greedy king locks Della in his castle and threatens her with death unless she performs magic. Fortunately, Della is helped by an elf who not only immediately reveals his name as Rumpelstiltzkin, but also befriends her and provides her with gold. The callous king marries Della, but he never has time for her or cares for her. Even when she gives birth to a baby daughter and when she and Rumpelstiltzkin invent a plan to arouse his concern in the daughter, the king remains aloof and narcissistic. So, in the end, Della asks Rumpelstiltzkin to take her and her daughter to his kingdom, where they live happily ever after.

Though retold in a light vein, this reversion has its serious side. Again the bad reputation of the mysterious little creature is restored. Rumpelstiltzkin is the caring, compassionate person, who does not want to profit from Della's predicament. The king as oppressor and egotist is depicted as the villain, not dissimilar to many a contemporary father who has no time for his family and is not pleased to have a baby daughter. Vande Velde's feminist version of "Rumpelstiltskin" brings out the authoritarian nature of the pre-text while projecting a male model of gentleness in the figure of her Rumpelstiltzkin.

Indeed, the feminist movement that has been so important for revising the Grimms' tales has produced a number of significant retellings of "Rumpelstiltskin" that reveal how gender relations have changed greatly during the last thirty years. One of the best of the more recent versions is "The Tale of the Spinster" in the Irish writer Emma Donoghue's collection *Kissing the Witch: Old Tales in New Skins* (1997), which is a series of linked retellings of twelve classical fairy tales. One character in each tale becomes the narrator of the next. Like all of Donoghue's retellings, the spinster's tale is a terse poetic meditation on dilemmas faced by contemporary women. In this narrative we learn that the spinster's mother had been very poor and mean and yet boasted about her daughter's gift for spinning. Indeed, she even madly maintained at the end of her life that her daughter could spin shit into gold. By the time of the mother's death, the spinster had been driven to set up a spinning cottage industry that consumes her. She becomes so caught up in the drive for success and money that she will stop at nothing to expand her business. One day she hires an exceptional young woman who does not speak very much. The spinster calls her Little Sister, and she comes to depend upon her for spinning the flax and making her wealthy. Little Sister accepts no pay except room and board, and when she wants to return to her home, the spinster tries to bribe her, but Little Sister agrees to stay only if she can have the spinster's firstborn. Since the spinster becomes even richer and mingles with wealthy merchants, she enjoys herself without worrying about the consequences. One consequence is an illegitimate daughter. The spinster is ashamed of her, but Little Sister takes care of the baby and saves her from her abusive mother by taking her away.

There is a telling passage in this story that sums up its meaning. It comes at a time when Little Sister agrees to stay and help the spinster for a long time. "Nothing could have made me happier," the spinster declares:

> With Little Sister at home, spinning up her magic, I could go out again, feel the sun pinking my face. I dressed even richer than I was and paid calls on fine ladies, dined with weavers, drank with money-men. Not that I was idling; everything I did was for the sake of business; each courtesy to a merchant, an arrow aimed true. And, finding my vocation, I learned that my mother was right after all. Work was a rope on a ship in rough water, a candle on a creaking staircase, a potato in a beggar's embers. It kept me sane and bright-eyed; it kept me from dwelling on the past; it even kept me from remembering that I was a woman.[17]

Donoghue transforms the Rumpelstiltskin story to contemplate legacies, and in this respect her tale is highly significant in regard to the legacy of storytelling and fairy tales that the Grimms have passed on to the world at large. Of course, Donoghue's intention was not to make a grandiose statement about the value of fairy tales for the world. Her aim is more modest, for she analyzes specifically how mothers can destroy the humanitarian instincts of their daughters through abusive behavior and treatment. Unconsciously, the spinster, a symbolic figure for the spinner of tales, inherits the worst aspects of her mother's personality and allows them to possess her. It is against this type of inheritance that Donoghue writes. To be a woman is to be a compassionate human being like Little Sister, sensitive and aware of the feelings of other, different human beings.

Whether the spinster will ultimately succumb to the destructive forces that hinder her humane feelings from emerging is left up in the air. We know she has abducted a young boy in an effort to regain a child—a touch of humanity—and that she tells a tale that reveals she knows what she has lacked. It is also a tale of retelling that serves to challenge and go beyond the legacy of the Brothers Grimm.

In her important study, *Postmodern Fairy Tales: Gender and Narrative Strategies* (1997), Cristina Bacchilega maintains that:

> postmodern fairy tales reactivate the wonder tale's "magic" or mythopoeic qualities by providing new readings of it, thereby generating unexploited or forgotten possibilities from its repetition. As "borderline enquiries," postmodern re-visions of traditional narratives do more than alter our reading of those narratives. Like meta-folklore, they constitute an ideological test for previous interpretations, and in doing so, postmodern fairy tales exhibit an awareness of how the folktale, which modern humans relegate to the nursery, almost vindictively patterns our unconscious and "secretly lives in the story."[18]

Not all "contaminated" retellings of the Grimms' tales are, strictly speaking, postmodern tales. However, the retellings do perform transformations in much the same manner as postmodern narratives. As they explore neglected issues and dimensions of the Grimms' tales, they define themselves in relation to these traditional pre-texts and thus provide a new understanding of the Grimms' works while determining and predetermining the fairy tale in contemporary society.

Curiously, as Bacchilega points out, the postmodern and even conservative retellings of the Grimms' tales depend on patterns of past folklore and continually reuse techniques and themes that the Grimms employed to contaminate their tales. While the Grimms' tales are crucial as the pre-texts for contemporary postmodern experimentation, their most important contribution to their own legacy is their method of contamination that refurbishes the conventional form and frame of folklore to question both past and present social conditions and gender relations. Thus it is not by chance in the postmodern film *Ever After* (1998) that it is framed with the Brothers Grimm visiting a distinguished French noblewoman, played by the majestic French actress Jeanne Moreau, who proceeds to tell them a fascinating tale about Cinderella, a feisty rebel, played by the very American actress

Drew Barrymore. According to the Frenchwoman, Cinderella, raised by an enlightened father who dies at the beginning of the film, is inspired by Thomas More's *Utopia* and enchants the prince of France by her intelligence and human compassion. This "contemporary" Cinderella turns the prince and France upside down, and in the end she marries him and is seen urging him to bring about social reforms in the final frames. At the end of the story within the framework of the film, the Grimms are stunned and can hardly believe their ears, but the French noblewoman shows them as evidence the silver glass slipper that her great-grandmother, Cinderella, had worn to her wedding. Fiction becomes fact in this fictitious film. The frame is like a magic mirror held up to us so that we can recall the Grimms' tale and see how they were astonished to find that they had missed a real source for their tale. At the same time the film plays with our conventional notion of who the Grimms were and the concerns of their tales and what might be lacking in their tales for present audiences. The Grimms' tales will never be the same in the twenty-first century, but we shall remember them well by continuing to transform and contaminate their works with an eye to the future. What else is "once upon a time" but a look into the future?

NOTES

1. See Gerhard Boettger, "Das Gute und Böse im Märchen," *Lehrerrundbrief* 3 (1948): 290–91; Walter Gong and Karl Privat, "Vorschule der Grausamkeit? Eine Diskussion um die Märchen der Brüder Grimm," *Der Tagesspiegel*, February 7, 1947, np; Johannes Langfeldt, "Märchen und Pädagogik," *Pädagogische Rundschau* 2 (1948): 521–25; Werner Lenartz, "Von der erzieherischen Kraft des Märchens," *Pädagogische Rundschau* 2 (1948): 330–36. Wolfgang Petzet, "Verteidigung des Märchens gegen seine Verleumder," *Prisma* 1 (1947): 3, 11.

2. Jacob and Wilhelm Grimm, *Kinder- und Hausmärchen*, ed. Heinz Rölleke, 3 vols. (Stuttgart: Reclam, 1980), 10.

3. *Ibid.*, 421–22.

4. Guy Wetmore Carryl, *Grimm Tales Made Gay*, illustr. Albert Levering (Boston: Houghton Mifflin, 1902), 26–27.

5. John Stephens and Robyn McCallum, *Retelling Stories, Framing Culture: Traditional Story and Metanarratives in Children's Literature* (New York: Garland, 1998), 4.

6. See my discussion of duplication in *Fairy Tale as Myth/Myth as Fairy*

Tale (Lexington: University Press of Kentucky, 1994), 8–9, and in the chapter "The Contemporary American Fairy Tale," 139–61.

7. Karl Kroeber, *Retelling / Rereading: The Fate of Storytelling in Modern Times* (New Brunswick, NJ: Rutgers University Press, 1990), 3.

8. Janosch, *Janosch erzählt Grimm's Märchen* (Weinheim: Beltz & Gelberg, 1972), 254.

9. About the same time in Germany Iring Fetscher produced a similar radical reversion of the Grimms' tales, *Wer hat Dornröschen wachgeküßt? Das Märchen Verwirrbuch* (Hamburg: Claassen, 1972). His satirical tales were accompanied with montages, and they mocked not only the tales themselves but also the scholarly approaches and interpretations of the tales.

10. For more details about the rise of the feminist fairy tale, see my book *Don't Bet on the Prince: Contemporary Feminist Fairy Tales in North America and England* (New York: Methuen, 1986).

11. Tanith Lee, *Red as Blood or Tales from the Grimmer Sisters* (New York: Daw, 1983), 82.

12. *Ibid.*, 90.

13. Mitsumasa Anno, *Anno's Twice-Told Tales by the Brothers Grimm and Mr. Fox* (New York: Philomel, 1993), c. 44–45. (pages unmarked).

14. All of these artists have created important illustrations of the Grimms' tales in picture books and editions of the Grimms' fairy tales. For information about their work, see the entries in Jack Zipes, ed., *The Oxford Companion to Fairy Tales: The Western Fairy Tale Tradition from Medieval to Modern* (Oxford: Oxford University Press, 2000).

15. Priscilla Galloway, *Truly Grim Tales* (New York: Bantam, 1995), ix.

16. Vivian Vande Velde, *Tales from the Brothers Grimm and the Sisters Weird* (New York: Harcourt Brace, 1995), 1.

17. Emma Donoghue, *Kissing the Witch: Old Tales in New Skins* (New York: HarperCollins, 1997), 124–25.

18. Cristina Bacchilega, *Postmodern Fairy Tales: Gender and Narrative Strategies* (Philadelphia: University of Pennsylvania Press, 1997), 22.

The Wisdom and Folly of Storytelling

7

In his 1987 novel *The Story-teller*, the Peruvian writer Mario Vargas Llosa explores one of the vexing contradictions of contemporary life, namely that the more we advance to civilize the world, the more it seems we breed intolerance and barbarism. In particular he raises the question whether genuine storytelling and *communitas* are possible in advanced civilized societies. Vargas Llosa sends his narrator, who has a writing block and is suffering from ennui, on a trip to Florence, where he visits a gallery that is exhibiting a collection of photographs of the Machiguenga Indians in the Amazon Jungle. As the narrator gazes at a photo of an *hablador*, or spiritual teacher, telling a story to a circle of Indians, he realizes that the man looks a lot like Saul Zuratas, a friend from college who had disappeared from his life some twenty years earlier. An outcast because of a blemish on his face and because of his mixed Jewish and Indian ancestry, Saul had become intimate with the Machiguengas while doing anthropological work in the Amazon and, impressed by their spiritual dignity, had decided to live with them and help them resist colonization.

What Vargas Llosa's narrator finds baffling is how someone raised in contemporary Western culture could become an *hablador*—a task that would involve, among other things, mastering the Machiguengas's demanding art of storytelling. "Talking the way a storyteller talks," the narrator says,

> means being able to feel and live in the very heart of that culture, means having penetrated its essence, reached the marrow of its history and mythology, given body to its taboos, images, ancestral desires, and terrors. It means being, in the most profound way possible, a rooted Machiguenga, one of that ancient lineage who . . . roamed the forests of my country, bringing and bearing away those tales, lies, fictions, gossip, and jokes that make a community of that people of scattered beings, keeping alive among them the feeling of oneness, of constituting something fraternal and solid.[1]

In contemporary Western society we are not exactly suffering from a shortage of storytellers and stories. Every day we are inundated by one tale after another on TV and radio, in newspapers and magazines, at work and at the family dinner table, over the World Wide Web. But despite this deluge, something important is missing. As Vargas Llosa reveals, we have lost the gift of genuine storytelling, which every Machiguenga understands implicitly and which was an integral part of Western culture until the early part of the twentieth century. It's the gift of using the power of story to share wisdom and build a meaningful sense of community.

Yet for us, stories are marketable commodities and are to be used to market the interests of big corporations or to promote ourselves. It is a somewhat pathetic if not deplorable situation. On June 25, 1999, a headline caught my attention, "Biotech Industry Bets Its Future on Storytelling," and I read that Jeremy Rifkin, the ecology activist, had unexpectedly been invited to attend an industry meeting at the headquarters of Monsanto Company:

> It was not Monsanto's idea to seek his input as the company was quick to tell anyone who asked. The 54-year-old Rifkin was called in by Ulrich Goluke, a consultant hired by Monsanto and 13 members of the World Business Council for Sustainable Development, to help them paint a portrait of the biotechnology landscape of the year 2030 and how it evolved. The exercise, known as story building or more formally as scenario creation, is a specialized form of crystal-ball gazing that big corporations in the United States and abroad are increasingly turning to as an early warning system for how their strategies could go astray.
> "Every child knows you get the really big issues across with stories," Mr. Goluke said.[2]

Ad agencies use cleverly written stories to "move product." News commentators discuss the creative aspect of advertising. Newspapers and magazines print sensational stories to titillate their readers. TV talk-show hosts coax people into divulging their most intimate stories on the air and doing preposterous things, all to score big ratings. People who commit atrocious crimes sell their stories to book publishers for unspeakable amounts of money. Politicians are trained to tell stories to entertain audiences in the fashion of comedians. Comedians imitate politicians trying to act like comedians. Even the new breed of professional or platform storytellers in North America and Europe are caught up in the game. They charge high fees for their services in schools, libraries, and community centers and perform in a manner that has more in common with Hollywood than the talking circles of the Amazon rain forest. Though many of them are gifted, their primary mission is not to share wisdom, but to amuse, distract, entertain, and to celebrate their art.

idealizing the past, let's recognize the significant qualita-
nce in the manner in which tales were told and used up to
th century. The work and customs of small tribes, vil-

lages, towns, reading circles, court societies, and small communities shaped storytelling, but today market forces, mass media conglomerates, and the Internet determine how stories will be spread. There is an intricate "web of dictation," an arbitrary set of rules based on profit and power, that limits how far and how deep storytellers can go. In his 1936 essay "The Storyteller," written when fascism was enveloping Europe, the renowned German literary critic Walter Benjamin outlined how the capitalist market system had created enormous barriers to the free exchange of experience. Therefore one of the key roles of storytellers, according to Benjamin, is to be subversive, to pierce through the myths of the ruling elite in order to free people to recognize who they really are. At other times in history, the myths that came to be challenged were those of Greco-Roman religion, feudalism, Christianity, and communism. But now a new—and some would argue, more insidious—myth looms: the myth of freedom.

We think we speak freely in free societies. We think there's a free exchange of ideas. Yet our ideas are often pre-scripted, our words often petrified before we speak them. Roland Barthes demonstrated how words are frozen in myths that endorse the ruling ideologies of a given society. He argues that myth:

> is constituted by the loss of the historical quality of things: in it, things lose the memory that they once were made. The world enters language as a dialectical relation between activities, between human actions; it comes out of myth as a harmonious display of essences. A conjuring trick has taken place; it has turned reality inside out, it has emptied it of history and filled it with nature, it has removed from things their human meaning so as to make them signify a human insignificance. The function of myth is to empty reality: it is, literally, a ceaseless flowing out, a hemorrhage, or perhaps an evaporation, in short a perceptible absence.[3]

Linguistic standards, word choices, expressions, and gestures are molded into a semiotic system manipulated by politicians, religious leaders, and corporate heads to create myths that serve to consolidate the power structure. This system fosters the thoughtless consumption of products, faiths, and laws that inhibit the free expression of ideas. But, as Benjamin pointed out, the web of dictation is not seamless. By challenging and exploding the putative truths of the myth of freedom, we can make room for truthful and imaginative expression. Here is where genuine storytelling comes in.

Benjamin maintains that the ability to exchange experience, what he calls *Erfahrung*, which means the moment in which one learns something about oneself and the world, is at the heart of genuine storytelling—and that ability, which at one time seemed inalienable, has all but disappeared because shared experiences are not the basis of story anymore. According to Benjamin, traditional forms of storytelling have been eclipsed, and shared experiences mediated by a wise storyteller have given way to individualized experiences that reflect the growing alienation in society.

In this respect, Benjamin and Vargas Llosa are very close in describing the predicament of storytelling and the genuine storyteller in contemporary Western society, and this deep concern in the fate of storytelling has been echoed even more recently in Karl Kroeber's thoughtful study *Retelling/Rereading*:

> The world is becoming with accelerating swiftness a single culture, and narrative has always been rooted in localisms—the personal, the family, the tribe, even the nation. In a unitary worldwide civilization perhaps narrative discourse has little or no significant function. Walter Benjamin thought that story was obsolete in societies in which mechanical reproduction is popular as well as feasible. But even he did not foresee the extent and rapidity with which reproductive technologies would spread. In a world capable of instant electronic transmissions and rapid and inexpensive reproduction of images, for example, the patience required of a narrative audience, its willingness to let a story unfold at its own pace, may not be a valuable attribute.[4]

The threats to genuine storytelling are many: homogenization, depersonalization, fragmentization, and obsolescence, but I should like to step back a moment from the critique of the transformation of storytelling by Benjamin, Llosa, and Kroeber to reexamine their premises and to discuss the potential impact of storytelling on children. There tends to be a nostalgia in their works for a type of storytelling that is practically impossible in today's advanced technologi~~~ ties that foster globalized networks. Storytelling has tself in accordance with socioeconomic changes, perhaps ter, but there is still the possibility for "genuine" story- the general tendency to make every story the same,

ONES

that is, devoid of its subversive and antiauthoritarian qualities, which, for Kroeber, is the essence of storytelling. My focus will be on the situation of storytelling largely in the United States, but I shall also discuss some of my own experiences in Europe to question the notion of genuine storytelling and what it means for children more broadly.

There is no doubt that the art of storytelling and the types of storytelling that have existed in Western societies—and in the East as well—have undergone immense changes since the 1930s. Yet I believe that it was a gross exaggeration on Benjamin's and Vargas Llosa's part (while Kroeber is much more perceptive)[5] to suggest that "genuine" storytelling has declined with the decline of close communities, what the Germans call *Gemeinschaft*, which suggests communality. As I have argued, there is a nostalgic tinge to their writing that leads them to espouse a myth about past storytelling or storytelling in small communities. I am reminded here of a small tale by Hermann Hesse, himself a storyteller, who venerated the past and the Orient, in which he portrayed the suffocating conditions and the darkness of people in a tribe living deep in a forest at the dawn of civilization. "Der Waldmensch" ("The Forest Dweller") depicts the degrading conditions under which the people of the forest tribe live because their priest, Mata Dalam, hates the sun and spreads lies about light so that they all fear him and the sun. In particular, they are scared to leave the darkness of the forest and are held under the spell of the stories of Mata Dalam, who becomes more and more tyrannical in establishing ritual and law. When Kubu, an intelligent and curious youngster, who represents the dissatisfied young people, tries to expose the lies of the swindling Mata Dalam, he finds himself expelled. Hesse then describes his situation this way:

> So he [Kubu] walked around the forest and pondered his situation. He reflected about everything that had ever aroused his doubts and seemed questionable, especially the priest's drum and his rituals. And the more he thought and the longer he was alone, the clearer he could see. Yes, it was all deceit. And since he had already come so far in his thinking, he began drawing conclusions. Quick to distrust, he examined everything that was considered true and holy. For instance, he questioned whether there was a divine spirit in the forest or a holy forest song. Oh, all that too was nothing. It too was a swindle. And

as he managed to overcome his awful horror, he sang the forest song in a scornful voice and distorted all the words. And he called out the name of the divine spirit of the forest, whom nobody had been allowed to name on the pain of death—and everything remained quiet. No storm exploded. No lightning struck him down![6]

In fact, as Hesse goes on to narrate, Kubu leaves the forest and discovers the truth and beauty of the sun. He becomes enlightened because he breaks the spell of the alleged wise priest/storyteller and tears through his web of fabrications.

I cite this tale because much of what we call traditional storytelling was also swindle, lies and untruths. Many of the traditional tales were told as religious and political propaganda to uphold and correspond to rituals that either celebrated a particular kind of totemic worship or reinforced the power relations of the dominant people in a tribe or community. And many tales were also told in reaction to the status quo. In my own research on the interaction of the oral storytelling tradition and the rise of literary genres such as the fairy tale, fable, and legend, I have found that we know very little about the lives of "genuine" storytellers or genuine stories and how they functioned in the oral tradition. Most of the research on storytellers in the oral tradition is speculative since so little was written about them until the nineteenth century. Moreover, few scholars have dared question the dangerous tyrannical aspect of priests, priestesses, shamans, holy men, administrators, court officials, scribes, and so on. We know next to nothing about simple people who spread and listened to stories. If we just examine storytelling since the rise of Christianity in Europe, we know that all types of tales were told from the medieval period to the present, and there were many different kinds of storytellers, some paid by aristocratic patrons, while others were members of a family or community who freely told their tales. The tellers came from all sectors of society—slaves, priests and priestesses, peasants, fishermen, sailors, soldiers, spinners, herb gatherers, troubadours, wandering scholars, housewives, merchants, innkeepers, hunters, actors, heretics, criminals, bandits, administrators, scribes. People told stories in all walks of life, and they fitted their stories to the situation. Oral storytelling was always functional and purposeful and remains so today. There were no doubt "genuine" storytellers who grasped the essence of their cultures, and there were probably many among them who used the power of story to fabricate and to maintain power.

If we turn our glance to this history, we can see that there were all types of settings in which tales were told in spontaneous and organized moments: marriage, birth, and death ceremonies called for different kinds of tales. Numerous religions and ethnic groups developed particular creation stories to explain how the earth was formed and how the gods came into being. Festivals and holidays were all associated with particular stories. Soldiers recounted great heroic feats that became legends. Farming and the conditions of life in the country formed the backdrop of tales told at harvest time or around the hearth. Rumors and stories were spread about bandits, duplicitous priests, and miraculous events by merchants and travelers. Each trade, such as blacksmith, tailor, and spinner, and each profession, such as priest, peddler, sailor, had stories associated with it. Aristocrats organized court spectacles and pageants that included storytelling. Rulers sought entertainment through storytellers, and salons were formed by aristocrats and bourgeois women in which artful conversation and storytelling played important roles. Factories, churches, synagogues, temples, bathhouses, brothels, shops, prisons, schools, hospitals, saloons, and many other settings were the places that generated generic kinds of tales linked to the experiences that people had in these places. Hundreds, thousands, and millions of tales were told there and continue to be told in similar settings today. They were told to instruct, warn, satirize, amuse, parody, preach, question, illustrate, explain, and enjoy. It all depended on the teller and auditors in a given social situation.

So what is genuine storytelling? Kroeber argues:

> Genuine storytelling is inherently antiauthoritarian. Even a true believer in an official dogma cannot help articulating a received truth in his own fashion—for stories are told by individuals, not groups. Inherent to all such individuation is the potentiality for subversion, especially because a story is "received" by individuals, no matter how large and homogeneous the audience of a telling, each of whom simply by interpreting for himself or herself may introduce "unauthorized" understanding—all the more dangerous if unintended.[7]

But are we to believe, then, that we are all potentially subversive? How do our truth claims test the ethical standards of a society through our narratives? Is there an ideal social context in which tales are to be told that is much more preferable to others? Can the quality or value of a tale be separated from its function?

These questions demand sincere and frank answers, and I want to try to answer these questions briefly before I turn my focus to the changing function of storytelling and the storyteller in the last thirty years, and how these changes may affect children.

The notion that there is such a thing as "genuine" storytelling has always been appealing to me, and in previous essays on storytelling I have tried to define what the possibilities for "genuine storytelling" are. But upon further reflection I fear that I, too, fell under the sway of Benjamin's "storytelling," and perhaps that of Vargas Llosa, for it is practically impossible to distinguish between genuine and artificial storytelling, except in the most obvious cases. In fact, a tale that resonates as genuine may often depend on the artifice or art of a storyteller to engender an aura of genuineness. A sincere and honest story can be boring and does not necessarily reveal the essence of a culture or the essential purpose of the narrator.

But the impossibility of defining the "genuine" storytellers or "genuine" stories does not mean that they do not exist or that we should abandon the project of seeking to know what distinguishes genuine from artificial. We could begin with a working definition such as: Genuine storytelling is the frank presentation and articulation of experience and knowledge through different narrative modalities in order to provide a listener with strategies for survival and pleasure and to heighten one's awareness of the sensual pleasures and dangers of life. Kroeber insists on the importance of retelling and the ethical nature of genuine storytelling: "All significant narratives are retold and are meant to be retold—even though every retelling is a making anew. Story can thus preserve ideas, beliefs, and convictions without permitting them to harden into abstract dogma. Narrative allows us to test our ethical principles in our imaginations where we can engage them in the uncertainties and confusion of contingent circumstance."[8] But then, such genuine storytelling has probably always taken place and is still all around us. Again, this is not to say that there is no such thing as genuine storytelling, but the definition will most often depend on the critic's ideological perspective.

For me, genuine storytelling is not only subversive but magical in that it transforms the ordinary into the extraordinary and makes us appreciate and take notice of the little things in life that we would normally overlook. Genuine storytelling is more often spontaneous and unrehearsed than it is planned and studied. I don't mean that it is not necessary to remember and recall tales we have told in the past, or that we should not create a repertoire of tales that we like to repeat in an artful manner. I mean more that a genuine tale or storytelling arises out of a particular occasion and suits that occasion for both teller and auditor. It is the coming together of the teller and audience that creates a genuine aspect to a moment that, unless recorded or taped, remains fleeting. This is why one cannot categorically define the genuine tale or genuine storyteller, for it is the sociohistorical context that gives rise to the event. And this is also why one cannot determine what wisdom or ethical principles the teller will pass on to the listener and what the teller will learn from her audience. Surely, *all* tales teach. Even in the most banal joke or anecdote there is something to be learned. But the wisdom of a tale depends on the teller's clear realization that what she is telling may be folly. To speak, to take center stage, to appropriate the role of storyteller, to be the focus of attention, is to assume power and command the minds and imaginations of listeners. The storyteller persuades listeners by any means possible (incantation, music, rhythm, gesture, tone, instruments, costumes, etc.) to enter a realm for a moment and to abandon themselves to the conceptual power (or lack of power) of the teller. In any event, the teller seeks to convince listeners that there is some iota of truth, something that the listeners can carry away with them that might make them more insightful. Paradoxically, the storyteller—and here I am trying to define the genuine storyteller—must be convinced that the tale may be folly, that she may be creating a hoax. The genuine storyteller is a skeptic, a doubter, whose wisdom is conveyed by the realization that there may be no wisdom or ethic to be passed on. It is by challenging the truth value of the very words that the storyteller speaks that she becomes genuine and that wisdom may be conveyed.

There is obviously no ideal social context in which a tale can be or should be told. The telling can occur across a kitchen table or as a goodnight story. It can occur on television or on a stage; it can be a confession or a declaration. With children it can be in a classroom, on a school playground, in the halls of a school, in a car, at home, on the streets, at a ball game—all kinds of occasions may call for a story, and no occasion is preferable over another, although I would argue that some social contexts are intrusive and manipulative and are purposely intended to prevent critical and imaginative thinking on the part of the listeners. In such instances, the quality or value of the tale is diminished. If the storyteller wants to be absolutely convincing and to gain power over the minds of the people in the audience, the tale itself will suffer, no matter how artful the teller is. It is in the absolutism—the absolute art of the teller—that deceit enters. Obviously, if a tale is told spontaneously to suit an occasion, there is no time for immediate self-reflection on the part of the storyteller, but there is time for reflection, and it is in the critical reflection afterward about a tale told or twice told that value is revealed. The same tale can be told over and over again by different tellers, and it will never be the same. Its value will depend on the occasion and how the teller responds to the occasion, and it will also depend on whether the teller seriously questions the efficacy and message of the narrative and the occasion.

The value of telling tales to children has been a subject of debate for centuries. There is a well-known expression in English which seems to serve as a marker to determine whether a tale should or should not be told to children. We generally say that something is not fit for children's ears when we hear foul language or when the story contains a disturbing and horrid event. Ever since the twentieth century—and this has not always been the case—we have sought to protect our children from hearing and seeing what we deem to be inappropriate and harmful. Exactly what is appropriate and harmful has always been a matter of taste and a matter of social class, just as the mastery of language, spoken and written, has been subjected to taste and class. Storytelling for children in America became at the end of the nineteenth century the domain of librarians, schoolteachers, church educators, and recreation workers, mainly women, up through the middle of the twentieth century.[9] It was also regarded as the mother's duty to tell goodnight stories to soothe the souls of children before they went to sleep, although fathers sometimes also participated in the goodnight ritual. In some cases, gifted regional storytellers practiced their craft outside institutional settings, but there was no deep-rooted tradition of folktale telling in America with two exceptions: the great storytelling tradition of Native American tribes (largely eradicated or silenced in the American public sphere), and African-American storytelling roots and customs (also torn apart and confined in America). These traditions were not destroyed, but they underwent transformations and became important means (often subversive) to maintain community connections. The Europeans who settled America told stories, of course, but the notion of creating a special status for the storyteller or conventionalizing storytelling customs never took deep root. This may have something to do with the lack of fixed rituals, changing communities, and socioeconomic mobility in America. In many countries throughout the world, the vocation or profession of storyteller has been and still is highly regarded. In the case of the United States, there have always been storytellers but no such thing really as a professional storyteller, and more than often, in the early part of the twentieth century, the storytellers read aloud from books in libraries and schools at appointed story hours, or they more or less memorized literary fairy tales and stories written for children.

All this changed somewhat radically in the 1970s. In his important book on the revival of storytelling in America, Joseph Daniel Sobol focuses on the period from 1970 until approximately 1995. He writes:

> The resurgent mythological imagining of the storyteller as artist and cultural healer provided the impetus for storytellers to move out of those institutional settings and out of their family and community backgrounds to form a network of free-lance professional performers. These new professionals are supported largely by those earlier institutions—libraries, schools, and recreation centers—but also by a national network of storytelling festivals, modeled on the National Storytelling Festival in Jonesborough [Tennessee]. In the process they have developed a web of connections among support personnel in established "art worlds"—publishers, media producers, arts councils, arts journalists, and public sector folklorists. All of these interlocking networks of storytellers and support people have come to constitute an "art world" of its own.[10]

Ironically, for the first time in American history, professional storytellers began trying to establish ritual and myth in a "demythologizing time."[11] As Sobol incisively remarks, the storytelling movement emanated from the civil rights and antiwar movement of the late 1960s and the diverse cultural radicalism of the 1970s, when many different ethnic groups in America began seeking their roots and when the disenchantment with American politics and the inability to change the society led many people to seek spiritual and ecological solutions to social problems. By the beginning of the 1980s, the fracturing of the myth of the American Dream and the questioning of the moral values of American society, caused by the strife of the 1960s and 1970s, also led to what Christopher Lasch called the age of narcissism and produced massive cult movements, a strong conservative religious revival based on traditional family values, the rise of right-wing militia groups, identity politics, and New Age cults. Many people were willing to try anything to bring about both inner and outer peace or to stake their claims as to what it meant to be American. In addition, many ethnic groups sought to recuperate anything they could from their past to discover what it meant to be Native American or African American.

One of the things people began to explore was storytelling, or, to be more precise, storytelling as a mode of bringing about a new sense of community and new sense of self. Therefore the organization of the storytelling, its professionalization and institutionalization, which owed a great debt to the foundation in the early 1970s of the National Association for the Preservation and Perpetuation of Storytelling (NAPPS) in Jonesborough, Tennessee—now called the National Story Association (NSA)—was most instrumental in creating formal and informal networks of storytellers and a new myth about storytelling in America. Of course, as Kay Stone, in her fine study *Burning Brightly: New Light on Old Tales Told Today* (1998), points out:

> The dramatic rise of organized storytelling is not only a North American phenomenon. . . . Organized storytelling, both as a child-centered activity and as a performance art for adults, has continued to flourish in countries of continental Europe and the British Isles, and in other parts of the world, most notably in Asia (especially Japan) and Australia. . . . The folk revival on this continent is yet another expression of the hunger for an imagined era of the lost simplicity.[12]

Sobol and Stone agree that many amateur storytellers who turned professional were drawn to storytelling by intense personal experiences—almost epiphanies—that had ignited their desire to tell tales: they longed to bring about harmony and community against the growing technologization of society, and they yearned to heal wounded souls. Call the period from 1980 to the present postmodern, postin-

dustrialist, post-whatever—there has been a growing sense throughout the world that the imagination has taken a back seat to
rationalization, that alienation and fragmentation are determining
factors in the psychic and social behavior of most people, and that
most public talk is shallow, hypocritical, and deceitful.

Therefore an underlying motive of the new professional storytellers
in America (and probably elsewhere in the world) was to recapture
talk, to purify talk, and to make talk serve the people and spiritual
ends rather than to induce people to buy products or buy and sell
other human beings. In the eyes of many of the revivalist storytellers,
the purpose of the storyteller became something mystical, even divine.
Sobol claims that the revival of storytelling was:

> an idealistic movement and remains so at its deepest wellsprings. It
> consistently invokes a revival dialectic—basing itself on artistic and
> communal ideals located in an imagined past to heal a present bro-
> kenness and awaken an ideal future. The storyteller is the mediating
> image of restored wholeness, a prism of heightened presence through
> which these idylls of past and future can shine, clarifying the social
> matrix for at least the duration of the performance event.[13]

This is undoubtedly the positive side of the professionalization of
storytelling in America, and storytellers began entering hospitals,
retirement homes, prisons, businesses, asylums, parks, reservations,
churches, synagogues, and even shopping malls to demonstrate how
stories could transform people's lives and engender a new sense of
communal spirit. They performed for large and small crowds and
organized their own festivals, shared stories and experiences, and
expanded their outreach to work in some instances with Jungian therapists and in other instances with teachers, clergy, and social workers,
often offering workshops to train new "disciples" of the revivalist
movement.

In every movement, however, cliques and ruling groups form, and
then the movement grows beyond the expectations of its founders.
And so it happens that many storytellers who become well known or
famous develop a distorted sense of their power and seek to become
cultural icons or gurus. Moreover, the necessity to accommodate the
needs of the institutions the storytellers depend on for income has
led many storytellers to become commercial and neglect the original
spiritual impulse of the revival. The competition among storytellers

has contaminated the sense of artistic community. The commodification of the profession has led to its division into two large camps: those commercial storytellers who perform largely for the sake of performance and who have forgone any sense of cultural mission, and those professional storytellers who continue to reflect on their role as storyteller and question the value of storytelling. Of course, generalizations about storytellers in a country as large as the United States—or in any country, for that matter—are bound to have numerous exceptions. But my main point here is that as soon as the storytellers began a vital movement, organized themselves, and became professional, they also began to undermine their movement because they had to subject themselves to market conditions that transformed them into entertainers and performers compelled to please audiences and their customers, certainly not to provoke or challenge them.

Given this situation, storytellers are faced with a nonchoice: complying with the market system and seeking popular success, or complying with it and resisting it at the same time. For instance, some regard children and schools as clients, and for the right price they will come to a school, do a performance or two before large audiences, answer some questions, talk about multiculturalism or some distinct ethnic culture, and then leave the youngsters (and teachers) in awe. The learning experience for the youngsters and teachers is minimal. They remain passive. And why not? What has happened in their presence? The storyteller could be any kind of good performer. But many superb storytellers are doing more than artful performances. They are striving to question both themselves and their stories, and to use their skills and repertoire to enable the young to become their own storytellers. For instance, Lynn Rubright, a professor and storyteller in St. Louis, received a three-year federal grant in 1971 for her Project TELL—Teaching English through Living Language, the purpose of which was to demonstrate how storytelling and other arts can serve as pivotal approaches to teach reading and writing. In her invaluable book *Beyond the Beanstalk: Interdisciplinary Learning through Storytelling*, she shows how the project resulted in training and transforming both students and teachers. She lists some of the basic agreements among teachers who have used storytelling in their classes. Here are just a few:

The more teachers and their students open themselves to playful experimentation with stories, the more possibilities there are for varieties of renderings to unfold.

Through storytelling workshops, teachers recognize and experience their own potential as skilled storytellers, and by modeling storytelling in their classrooms, they enable their students to become more effective storytellers too.

Storytelling, combined with dramatic play, allows children to try on many roles, helping them develop their ability to empathize, increasing understanding of those different from themselves.

Teachers are often surprised at the insights children reveal as they ponder the complex meanings of fables, folktales, and other literature they have heard or read.

When children tell stories they often reveal gifts and talents that have gone undiscovered with traditional approaches to learning.

Storytelling offers many children an opportunity to develop skills and excel in oral expression, gaining respect that they had not experienced before from peers.[14]

What is crucial in Rubright's ongoing work as a storyteller is her awareness that storytelling is a means to bring students and teachers together and to develop their skills and talents, not to highlight the prowess of the storyteller as priest, shaman, guru, or healer. The storyteller's role is more that of an animator who uses story to empower his auditors and to establish a realm in which the students can explore themselves and the world in imaginative and critical ways. There are many, indeed numerous, methods and approaches to storytelling and helpful guides to becoming a storyteller such as Doug Lipman's *The Storytelling Coach: How to Listen, Praise, and Bring Out People's Best*. But the point in working with students is not to train them to become future storytellers but to provide them with skills and confidence. Through storytelling they can learn not only that what they have to say is significant, but also that they will have to struggle to have their viewpoints represented or interwoven into the stories fabricated around them.

There are a plethora of ways to empower young people through story, especially in schools. In England, Michael Wilson, professor and storyteller, and others have sought to animate adolescents to form their own storytelling clubs and circles and guide them so that they would acquire the skills to collect and tell their own stories. The cooperative work with adults, especially with teachers, is crucial, especially when the children are between the ages of five and twelve. Throughout her work, writer and teacher, Vivian Paley has demonstrated how she has managed to draw children to stories, to draw out stories from children, and to be inspired by them to reflect on their interactions, problems, and needs. One of her most recent books, *The Girl with the Brown Crayon*, is a fascinating account of how Reeny, a five-year-old girl, is attracted to the books of the Italian author Leo Lionni, and because of her great interest, the entire class begins listening to and reading all of Lionni's books. In addition, discussions of the stories lead to discussions of race, gender, and identity. The classroom is transformed into a laboratory of life through the conversations and stories that the children and teachers tell.

Transforming the classroom into a laboratory, theater, or playroom is important because it breaks down borders and boundaries. Children can trespass and, in doing so, they can become acquainted with unknown dimensions of their personalities and the material conditions surrounding them. In Pistoia, Italy, a municipal laboratory called "Di Bocca in Bocca" ("From Mouth to Mouth") explores the local Italian oral tradition in six-week programs. Since Italian schools often end at 1 P.M., children are often left to themselves or looked after by parents in the afternoons. Several years ago, the city of Pistoia organized free municipal programs that focused on storytelling, mask making, design, and other activities to enable children to learn more about the oral tradition in their region and to bring about a stronger sense of community. During 1998 and 1999 I made several trips to Pistoia to witness a fairy-tale project in which the storyteller Marisa Schiano used her story to animate the children to form their own characters using masks and outfits. Then the students created their own stories using what they had made. The long-term work with the students included writing and acting out stories, which were collected in little pamphlets or hung on the walls.

The choice of a venue for storytelling with children depends on the customs and regulations of a particular country or community. In Pistoia, the venue was municipal. In the United States, storytelling for children now takes place in public libraries, bookstores, recreation centers, churches, synagogues, parks, and other domains outside the school. Yet school may be the best venue because it enables the storyteller to establish a relationship with the teacher, students, school community, and parents. In returning again and again to a particular class, the storyteller goes through a learning process. That storyteller can then help train teachers to use the techniques and methods of storytelling to develop the critical and creative talents of the students. In Minneapolis, I am involved in a project called "Neighborhood Bridges" in collaboration with the Children's Theatre of Minneapolis and two urban schools, Whittier and Lucy Laney. For three years I have worked with seven actors, whom I coached as storytellers in a special program to introduce children to different genres of storytelling, acting, and writing, and several teachers and two classes of fifth-graders. The overall goal of the program is to transform their classrooms for two hours each week so they can try out and test their skills in storytelling, improvisational skits, writing, and drawing. In the process they have produced some printed stories and created their own plays which they have performed for their schoolmates, parents, and teachers, and they have traveled to the other school at the end of the year to build community bridges.

The effects, as Lynn Rubright has already noticed in her work, were multiple and probably not always recognizable with regard to the future development of these students. By this I mean it is difficult to measure quantitatively the improvement in the lives of the students and teachers, but anyone involved in a storytelling program or experiment of this kind will see immediately that in the long run this storytelling will be a significant impetus for individual growth. Through storytelling programs centered on critical literacy, young people acquire the confidence to stand before others and articulate their views, to invent stories, to write and illustrate their own narratives, to appreciate and question the tales they hear from others, to move and use gestures that dramatically aid their articulated views, and to think for themselves.

Yet the focus of school authorities and politicians tends to be on testing, more testing, and rote learning. The value of storytelling as a means of strengthening learning and cultivating skills has generally been neglected by schools, though teachers are generally receptive to innovative storytelling when exposed to it. For most school officials, parents, and politicians, storytelling is performance or platform storytelling, good and healthy amusement for the children, but not related to the learning processes that they hope will make the children successful—successful in their careers, as citizens, and as consumers. But performance/platform storytelling has very little to do with genuine pedagogical storytelling.

It is not my intention to examine the manifold ways in which market conditions and relations of work have penetrated families and schools except to say that the corporate model of doing business generates models in the public and private spheres that influence our behavior. Communities become seen as markets, individuals as "types" or, worse, as objects. We treat other people as objects and are treated as objects ourselves. In the United States, this has led to an intensification of reification and alienation in all areas of life. At the same time, the discontent that many people feel—as Freud might say, *das Unbehagen*, in his book *Civilization and Its Discontents*—has produced a deep longing for tranquility, harmony, spirituality, and community. As various critics have noted, this longing, related to a lack or gap in our lives, has been part of the driving force behind the revival of storytelling in North America and in the world. In reaction to the work and living conditions that undermine the possibilities for creating communities and fixed traditions, storytellers have tried to foster a mythical and mystical sense of community in and through their stories. This intention is certainly understandable, even laudable. But to my mind, genuine storytelling today cannot pretend that ideal communities and cults are within our reach. If it is to capture the essence of our contemporary societies, then genuine storytelling must reflect conditions that produce alienation and invent stories and strategies to combat the conditions. It need not do this with pessimism but with the hope that suffering can lead to joy and candor to wisdom. Mythological storytelling in unmythological times only masks the predicament of fragmentation in which we find ourselves today.

A few years ago, while visiting Germany, I saw a disturbing TV documentary on storytelling and sects. Part of the show focused on a group of people in Hamburg that gather to tell stories about their actual experiences watching and listening to fairies. Another segment featured a group of men who congregate regularly in a forest to run about naked, commune with nature, and tell stories to strengthen their bonds of brotherhood. In the final segment, male and female witches gathered in the woods to celebrate medieval rituals that endow them with spiritual powers as storytellers. In all the interviews with the storytellers and their followers, the people appeared to be sincere. They believed devoutly in the stories they concocted. Their folly in my eyes was wisdom in theirs. And the truth of the matter is that both the folly I perceive and the wisdom they feel result from the same widespread malaise. The folly and wisdom are of our own making, and we often confuse the two.

When people form secret societies, they are striving to fill gaps in their lives left by a technological society that discounts human feelings. The problem is that they are often unaware of the extent to which their behavior conforms to market expectations and unknowingly helps sustain a myth of freedom because, on the surface, they appear to be acting freely. However, in my opinion, most of these groups' rituals are little more than conditioned responses to intolerable circumstances—responses that are tolerated by society because they do not endanger the status quo. On the contrary, these groups reinforce it by serving as so many zany sideshows for the rest of us— just another form of entertainment—while confirming that our norms are normal and good.

In a world in which entertainment has also been largely commodified by large corporations, genuine storytelling, and especially storytelling with and for children, has a special mission—to expose the wisdom and folly of all storytelling. If our young are to have a chance to ground their lives in any kind of tradition, then they must learn hopeful skepticism, how to play creatively with the forces dictating how they are to shape their lives, and how to use storytelling to reshape those conditions that foster sham and hypocrisy.

NOTES

1. Mario Vargas Llosa, *The Storyteller*, trans. Helen Lane (New York: Farrar Straus Giroux, 1989), 244.

2. Barnaby J. Feder, "Biotech Industry Bets Its Future on Storytelling," *International Herald Tribune* (June 25, 1999): 13.

3. Roland Barthes, *Mythologies* (London: Granada, 1973), 142–43.

4. Karl Kroeber, *Retelling/Rereading: The Fate of Storytelling in Modern Times* (New Brunswick, NJ: Rutgers University Press, 1990), 187.

5. "If we understand that storytelling did not simply disappear with the advent of the twentieth century, we open the way to different kinds of critical understanding that might enable us to break free from constrictive theoretical conceptions." Kroeber, *Retelling/Rereading*, 188.

6. Hermann Hesse, *The Fairy Tales of Hermann Hesse*, trans. Jack Zipes (New York: Bantam, 1995), 190.

7. Kroeber, *Retelling/Reading*, 4.

8. *Ibid.*, 9.

9. This is fully documented in Richard Alvey's study, "The Historical Development of Organized Storytelling for Children in the United States," Ph.D. diss., University of Pennsylvania, 1974.

10. Joseph Daniel Sobol, *The Storytellers' Journey: An American Revival* (Urbana: University of Illinois Press, 1999), 14.

11. *Ibid.*, 15.

12. Kay Stone, *Burning Brightly: New Light on Old Tales Told Today* (Peterborough, Ontario: Broadview, 1998), 8–9.

13. Sobol, *The Storytellers' Journey*, 29.

14. Lynn Rubright, *Beyond the Beanstalk: Interdisciplinary Learning through Storytelling* (Portsmouth, NH: Heinemann, 1996).

The Perverse Delight of *Shockheaded Peter*

8

It seems there must always be something Germanic about perversity, gloom, and torture in the arts. Therefore, if you had not known it right away, you might have guessed the origins of the haunting and tantalizing production of *Shockheaded Peter: A Junk Opera* by the Tiger Lillies, a three-piece band with a large cult following in London: their outrageous play has been inspired by some gruesome tales from the most famous German children's book in the world—*Der Struwwelpeter* (1845), known in English as *Slovenly Peter*. Hilariously grotesque though they may seem, the verse stories and illustrations in this book, created by one Dr. Heinrich Hoffmann, give rise to many disturbing questions: How could they have been intended for children in the nineteenth century? Did some sadist write and illustrate these verse tales? Did the Germans believe in maiming their children to keep them under control? What could have moved the Tiger Lillies, Michael Morris of Culture Industry, and Phelim McDermott and Julian Crouch of Improbable Theatre, to adapt this macabre book for the stage? Why have audiences on the junk opera's world tour been so receptive to their ludicrously grim performance? Is this cultural phenomenon, marked by revelry in perversity, another sign of the sickness of our age? Or does the appeal reflect our desperate, well-intentioned endeavors to manage children in a world unfit for children?

Indeed, the delight in perversity has something paradoxical about it because it actually reflects a deep concern for the welfare of children, and in this regard Hoffmann's book and the efforts by the Tiger Lillies and company are all connected to provocative historical performative acts on behalf of children by artists who seek to draw attention to the crazed manner in which adults want to save the young from themselves by destroying their curiosity and adventurous spirits. What may appear to be "German" cruelty in *Shockheaded Peter* is actually a widespread Western benevolent attitude toward children that assumes highly ambivalent forms of rewards and punishments. What makes the McDermott and Crouch production of *Shockheaded Peter* different and disturbing is that it heightens Hoffmann's "enlightened" cruelty toward children in such a graphic and sadistic manner that it becomes difficult to laugh at the relentlessly repeated punishments the child puppets are compelled to endure on stage. Yet laugh we must.

I believe Dr. Hoffmann himself might have been upset by this production because it carries his well-intentioned dictums to an extreme. Born on June 13, 1809, in Frankfurt am Main, one of the few powerful free cities in the Holy Roman Empire during the Napoleonic Wars,

Hoffmann was to become a prime representative of the progressive forces that constituted the educated bourgeois elite of Germany. His father, Philipp Jacob Hoffmann, was an architect and urban engineer who helped build the first modern sewage system in Frankfurt. Hoffmann's mother died one year after his birth, and though his father remarried, he took charge of his only son's education. Typical in a well-to-do middle-class family were rules and regulations, and every minute of every day was planned. The young Hoffmann, though not a rebel, had difficulty complying with his father's directives, and he was not an especially good student. He was more the dreamer and artist than an achiever, and one day he found the following letter from his father on his desk:

> Since Heinrich continues to be undisciplined, frivolous, and forgetful and is no longer whatsoever capable of controlling his active nature according to his own free will in an intelligent and useful way, and as a consequence of this disorderliness, is a disgrace to his parents and has become the greatest disadvantage to himself, I hereby want once again to remind him of his duty and to ask him to return to: order, discipline, industriousness, reasonable division of his time so that he can become a useful member of bourgeois society and so that his parents are at least justified in expecting that he does not drown in the flood of daily common life.[1]

It was thanks to such a stern and caring father that Hoffmann mended his ways, and by 1829, when he was ready to attend the university in Heidelberg, he had become a diligent student and a prudent aspiring member of bourgeois society. Hoffmann did not entirely lose that "spark of dreaminess" or his artistic bent that led to his writing children's stories and poems, as we shall see. More important, however, was Hoffmann's great desire to please his father at all costs. Therefore he completed his medical studies at the universities of Heidelberg and Halle by 1833 and then spent one year in Paris as an intern at a hospital. In 1835, he returned to Frankfurt and helped establish one of the first clinics for the poor.

Hoffmann had a strong social conscience. Influenced by the revolutionary movements of the 1830s, he was committed to democratic change but he never participated in radical movements. Instead, Hoffmann preferred the more traditional bourgeois clubs and associations of a liberal persuasion, such as the Freemasons and community choirs. He loved to write songs, ditties, and poems that he performed to commemorate or celebrate particular events. He joined a club called "Tutti Frutti," which organized lectures and readings, and he supported such causes as free speech for the press.

In 1840 Hoffmann married Therese Donner, daughter of a respectable Frankfurt businessman, and the following year his wife gave birth to their first son, Carl. They were to have two more children, Antonie Caroline in 1844 and Eduard in 1848. During the early 1840s Hoffmann established himself as a competent doctor, but just as significant was his participation in the cultural life of Frankfurt. He was known and respected by his friends and the public as an occasional poet who could write songs and poems for all kinds of gatherings and events. He had wit and finesse, and often there was a barb of social criticism in his poetry. In fact, Hoffmann's poems became so popular that he published a collection in 1842. However, they did not contribute anything to his fame as his unusual children's book would three years later.

Actually, the concrete origins of *Struwwelpeter* can be traced to sometime before Christmas of 1844. Hoffmann went looking for a suitable children's book as a present for Carl, then three years old, but the more he looked in the Frankfurt bookshops, the more discouraged he became. The books were too sentimental, didactic, or boring. So he bought a notebook, composed five stories in verse, and sketched pictures in color. When he came to the end of the book, there was an empty page, on which he drew the famous Struwwelpeter and composed his delightful rhyme about the ghastly boy who does not cut his nails or hair and thus is repulsive to all who happen to see him.

> See Slovenly Peter!
> Here he stands,
> With his dirty hair and hands.
> See! His nails are never cut;
> They are grim'd as black as soot;
> No water for many weeks,
> Has been near his cheeks;
> And the sloven, I declare,
> Not once this year has combed his hair!

Anything to me is sweeter
Than to see shock-headed Peter.[2]

Actually, not many people were intended to see the icon of Slovenly
Peter at first, since the book was a Christmas present for Carl, but
Hoffmann's friends who happened to read it encouraged him to have
it published before his son—as children are wont to do—ripped it to
shreds. The original title of the book was *Der Struwwelpeter oder
lustige Geschichten und drollige Bilder für Kinder von 3–6 Jahren
(Slovenly Peter or Amusing Tales and Droll Pictures for Children from
3 to 6)* by "Reimerich Kinderlieb." It contained five tales in rhymed
verse: "The Story about Naughty Frederick," "The Story about the
Black Boys," "The Story about the Wild Hunter," "The Story about the
Thumbsucker," and "The Story about Soupy Caspar." The first edition
of fifteen hundred copies was sold out within four weeks. When the
second edition was published in 1846, Hoffmann added two more
tales: "The Very Sad Story about the Matches" and "The Story about
Fidgety Phillip." He also changed his pseudonym to Heinrich Kinderlieb. By the fifth edition in 1850, "The Story about Hans Who Never
Looked Where He Was Going" and "The Story about Flying Robert"
were added; Struwwelpeter's image and ditty were moved to the front
of the book and have remained there since, and Hoffmann allowed his
real name to appear on the cover of the book. The original pseudonym, "Reimerich Kinderlieb," loosely translatable as "the colorful
rhymster who loves children," is fascinatingly ambivalent, for the
entire debate that ensued about *Struwwelpeter* concerns whether the
author of the book really did love children, or whether he had a sadomasochistic urge that he concealed in his putative love for children.
What indeed did he intend to pass on to children through his comical
and frightening pictures? Why have there been more than seven hundred different German editions and one hundred translations, not to
mention hundreds of imitations and parodies throughout the world?
Why have we kept this book alive, and what does the Tiger Lillies'
production mean?

We might find some answers in the emphatic delight that Hoff-
mann took in exploring the theme of discipline and punishment in
Struwwelpeter's comic verses and how *Shockheaded Peter* critiques
Hoffmann by showing the drastic results of adult abuse of power in

the present. Clearly, Hoffmann strongly believed that without self-discipline and self-control there can be no self-realization. Life can be enjoyed and made pleasurable only if one denies one's "unruly" desires, curiosity, and erotic inclinations. The imagination and sensuality are to be curbed in the name of learning and productivity and for the benefit of the community. The soothing, playful voice that speaks Hoffmann's rhymes seeks to persuade and seduce the child reader into heeding the advice illustrated by the pictures. It is a voice that wants panoptically to oversee the children's reading and make sure that they learn from the horrific lessons represented by the illustrations.

Struwwelpeter is a funny manual of good sense. It is not nonsensical, as some critics have claimed. Rather, it is eminently reasonable and straightforward. Without pretension it tells children, especially middle-class children, in graphic detail exactly what will happen to them if they do not do as they are told. With the exception of the story about Pauline and the matches and another about the wild hunter, the verses all concern naughty boys who are severely punished for disregarding bourgeois rules of decency. Thus Frederick must lie in bed in pain while the dog that he mistreated gets to eat his sumptuous dinner. Wilhelm, Ludwig, and Caspar are dipped in black ink for making fun of a young black boy. Conrad's thumbs are snipped off by the tailor with a gigantic scissor because he cannot stop sucking his thumb. Caspar wastes away and dies because he refuses to eat his soup as he is supposed to do. Fidgety Philip brings the wrath of his parents upon him when he leans back in his chair and tears down the tablecloth with the family meal on it. Hans falls into a pond, loses his school briefcase, and almost dies because he does not look where he is going. Robert is carried off by the wind and disappears forever because he does not stay at home during a storm. Implicit in the book is that boys are much more unruly than girls. Typically, Pauline's frightful tale is a domestic tragedy. The girl burns herself to ashes inside the house.

According to Hoffmann, none of these lessons in verse would have much effect on children without the illustrations. In his autobiography he wrote:

> The child learns simply only through the eye, and it only understands
> that which it sees. It does not know anything whatsoever to do with

moral prescripts. The warnings—Don't get dirty! Be careful with matches and leave them alone! Behave yourself!—are empty words for the child. But the portrayal of the dirty slob, the burning dress, the inattentive child who has an accident—these scenes explain themselves just through the looking that also brings about the teaching.[3]

In other words, it is through the process of gazing at a picture telling a story or illustrating a lesson that the child learns what to do in specific situations. This may be true for children between the ages of three to six, the intended audience of the book. But this book was never really conceived and created for children. Like all "good" children's literature and performances for children, *Struwwelpeter* had to appeal to the tastes and values of adults. Therefore it is also important to ask what adults did and do learn from *Struwwelpeter*, a question at the heart of the *Shockheaded Peter* production, which implies that we have learned nothing in the last 150 years and continue to maim our children in good conscience.

Hoffmann, whose own values and behavior were determined by his father's sadomasochistic treatment of him, sought to rationalize the overbearing punishment and abuse he had endured as a child. His light verse and naive comical sketches undermine the cruelty that many of the characters suffer. Through humor, Hoffmann tried to minimize the power that his father had held over him while also pursuing a new strategy to gain control over his own son. The exaggerated features in the drawings and the preposterous situations commented on by a voice that speaks in doggerel are not bound to scare readers. More likely they will and did evoke smiles. Nevertheless, Hoffmann's book is nothing to smile about either, because it reveals a deadly process of dampening instinctual drives in the name of bourgeois civilization.

In *Struwwelpeter*, the voice that speaks and the hand that draws are authoritative and directive and reflect general Western attitudes toward children. Hoffmann does not write and draw because he is "kinderlieb"; he is more concerned with maintaining the strictures of bourgeois training than with caring for children. He wants them to respond to the directives that *he* responded to from *his* father—directives that he internalized, modified, and sought to pass on through stories and pictures. The formation of the verse and pictures is to lead to conformity and inhibition. But the clear intention of the author, questioned at the same time by his own humor, reveals a certain ambivalent attitude toward such socialization and his own experience growing up with a father who virtually ordered and ordained his superego. It is the ambivalent tension between the funny rhymes and the caricatures that made *Struwwelpeter* such a curious book, a curio, and propelled its popularity, for it rationalized the torture and abuse that parents practiced with clear consciences in raising their children. It is highly likely that the book struck a chord in middle-class readers of all ages, allowing them to gain a certain distance from the pressure of regimentation and to laugh at themselves—but to laugh without changing the way children were being and would continue to be manhandled.

The production of *Shockheaded Peter* responds to both the book's popularity and the perpetuation of child abuse in Western society. This junk opera breaks with affirmative children's literature and fairy-tale theater, perverting the norm to question normalcy. We must remember that *Struwwelpeter* was a typical book (despite Hoffmann's desire to create something new) and did not approach the question of cruelty, sadism, and punishment very differently from other children's books and fairy tales during the first half of the nineteenth century. The fairy tales by the Brothers Grimm included many in which young people are battered, abused, abandoned, and murdered. Eyes are pecked out. Hands are cut off. Heads are chopped off. In Hans Christian Andersen's "Little Red Shoes," a poor girl is punished by having her feet sliced off. "If you spare the rod, you spoil the child" was the mantra of parents during the nineteenth and early twentieth centuries. Throughout Europe and North America, children were faced with stories and images of the inferno and the devil, who was waiting for them to make a mistake so he could drag them to hell. Corporal punishment was commonplace. Children were expected to obey their elders no matter how deceitful and brutal the adults were. Few laws governed the exploitation of child labor or protected them from abusive parents. Family and new school systems gradually institutionalized childhood in order to produce hardworking, productive, and manipulable individuals who would understand how to rationalize their lives for the benefit of the market and sociopolitical order. The danger, of course, was that as more people learned to read and write and were exposed to different forms of discourse, they could easily develop a consciousness that could not be controlled. This is why children's literature became so important during the nineteenth century, and why a book like *Struwwelpeter* had such a significant reception and resonates with us today. It formed part of a normative discourse through which parents contended for power through the bodies of their children.

Children's literature was in its infancy in the first half of the nineteenth century, and as it instituted itself, the texts, used in many different ways, became the arena in which battles were fought over the bodies and souls of children. (And it is not much different today, although we now rely more on the visual images in film and on the TV screen to create impressions of young people's bodies and minds.) The debate about proper reading habits and reading matter for children, how to delight and instruct at the same time, originated in the eighteenth century as the middle classes were assuming power. In the nineteenth century a general consensus had been reached, and the publication of books, texts, pictures, and other artifacts for children reflected a deep, enlightened belief that human beings could be molded, improved, and civilized. Even Jews could be acculturated. Blacks and Indians were another matter. But the missionary zeal of the white Christian middle classes was great, and first among their concerns were their own children, who formed the majority of the readers/gazers because the majority of children in Europe and North America were not literate. Therefore the design of most children's books tended to rationalize the vested interests of bourgeois institutions in the making, and the logical narrative structure of the stories and the reading process itself were often geared to bring about obedience to the codes and strictures of civil society.

In Germany, *Struwwelpeter* was especially valuable for the middle-class socialization process because it was among the first books with pictures to be created for the three-to-six-year-old age group. The explicit drastic punishments that the children experience in the stories were to be held before the eyes of children (and adults) as warnings of what awaited them if they were to make the same mistake. Though there were many other kinds of literature being produced for children during the middle of the nineteenth century, no other book of its kind unleashed a series of imitations that celebrated corporal punishment in the way it did. In numerous picture books that followed and imitated *Struwwelpeter*, children are brutally beaten, thrown into dark cellars and dungeons, tortured by doctors, kidnapped, eaten by animals, placed on exhibition in a cage, starved to death, fed until they burst, and transformed into ghastly beasts. Some critics have claimed that *Struwwelpeter* was a very Teutonic book and revealed a great deal about the sadomasochistic nature of the German national character. Yet the imitations of *Struwwelpeter* were not limited to Germany. In one of the early adaptations of the book, *Slovenly Peter's Story Book, Containing the Dirty Little Child, The Little Glutton, Tom the Thief, Little Jacob, Sammy Tickletooth, Untidy Tom, Little Suck-a Thumb, Johnny Sliderlegs, Carri and the Candle, Rocking Philip* (1860), we find the following story:

Little Jacob, and How He Became Fat

The Little Jacob was so small,
He could not smaller be;
When he took off his little coat,
Just like a stick look'd he.
His parents, therefore, anxious were
About their little Jake,
And said, "Oh, dear! What can we do
Our Jacob fat to make?
All sorts of nice things we must get
For our dear boy to eat;
Meats boil'd and roasted, baked and fried,
And pies and puddings sweet.
And then, besides, we'll let him drink
Plenty of wine and beer;
And if this does not make him fat,
Why nothing will, we fear."
This diet, then, they put him on,
And soon, to their great joy,
They found that fat and fatter grew
Their darling little boy.
When six months pass'd, and he had grown
Fat, as you see him here,
His parents said, "You need not now
Eat quite so much, my dear;

For, oh! If you become too fat,
We then may try in vain,
Unless we give you bitter pills,
To make you thin again.
But Jacob would not then obey,
He only ate the more,
Until, at length, he grew as fat
As he was thin before.
One day a hearty meal he made,
But still was not content;
Cake, wine, and beer he slily took
And to the fields he went.
There, for a while, like any pig,
He ate and drank alone;
But suddenly his mother heard
Her Jacob moan.
Out of the house, off to the fields
Swift as a flash she flew;
Alas! Alas! what saw she there?
Her Jacob burst in two.
I'll say this much to boys and girls,
If they be thick or thin;
That, be this story true or false,
Sure, gluttony's a sin.[4]

This *American* story, written in "*Struwwelpeter* fashion," is highly significant not simply because of its clear imitation of Hoffmann's narrative technique and pedagogy, but because it was one of hundreds that were disseminated throughout Europe and North America for middle-class readers, and because it indicated, like its predecessor, a shift in attitude toward children and what children were to become not only in Germany but throughout the Western world.

The irony of *Struwwelpeter* is that the figure of the slovenly boy and the platform on which he stands were built on the enlightened notion of human perfection. That is, the psyches that produced *Struwwelpeter* and all the imitations, and the psyches of the young and old readers who responded to it were not caught up in sadomasochistic fantasies. Rather, they were convinced that there was a true opposite to the figure of Struwwelpeter, and this good and obedient and wonderful child was the goal of the bourgeois civilization process that embraced Western Europe and North America. The child became the object of intense love and care, a projection of the parents' desire for perfection and immortality. Throughout the nineteenth century the child became regarded more and more as an investment for the future and the measuring stick of the moral and ethical qualities of a particular family and society. Therefore the failure of a child reflected upon the stature of the parents. This is why children's literature was formed to forge perfect children and contained warnings galore like fat Jacob and slovenly Peter.

Of course, much has changed in the socialization of children in the twentieth century, and there is no longer great faith in the power of children's literature to strengthen the moral character of our children. (Today many other cultural institutions and products, such as comic books, films, games, gadgets, clothes, and toys, have a more powerful influence on children's thinking and behavior.) In fact, given our society's emphasis on consumerism and violent competition, the stories in *Struwwelpeter* are more like harmless jokes than anything else, and the evident sadism is more funny than shocking. In my opinion, this social normalization of cruelty prompted the Tiger Lillies to stage *Struwwelpeter* for adults as an act of confrontation. In their hands, a book that was intended to mollify adults' bad consciences and produce guilt in children is transformed into a bitter, if not cynical, attack on complacent adults who believe that we have grown more civilized in our attitudes toward children.

The history of how the production came to be realized reveals important links to the origins of *Struwwelpeter* in the nineteenth century and how the production's creators sought to critique attitudes toward the book and toward children. In a 1999 interview with the journalist Lyn Gardner, Michael Morris, founder of Cultural Industry (the production company behind *Shockheaded Peter*), remarked: "I can't remember any other books we had in the house when I was a child during the sixties, but I do remember *Struwwelpeter*. It was a book you wanted hidden but at the same time always wanted to know where it was. It was just a question of trying to bring out what was already there. I just upped the death rate."[5] Of course, Martyn Jacques, the lead castrato crooner of Tiger Lillies, did much more. He wrote all the songs and music, a blend of French cabaret, Kurt Weil, and Central European folk melodies, investing them with deeply sarcastic and gruesome overtones. But the sublimely nasty music and songs needed a structure and plot, and after Morris and Jacques discarded the idea of a variety show, they decided to ask Phelim McDermott and Julian Crouch, the directors and designers of Improbable Theatre, to create a show through improvisation and the use of puppets. After coming up with the idea of a self-contained Victorian toy theater for the set, they had difficulty finding a narrative thread with a focus on children. But then, as McDermott explains, "one day Julian suddenly said we shouldn't be thinking about the children but about the parents. That was the breakthrough. We sat down on the computer and wrote a story beginning Once upon a time. We took turns to write just one word each and we came up with a story about a couple having a child and there's nothing wrong with the child but because it was not exactly this couple's idea of perfection they tried to get rid of it."[6] Crouch adds, "We wrote three pages. It was very weird and rich, kind of shamanic or writing by ouija board. It created a structure—that if you buried something under the floorboards in the first scene it would have to come up later. I thought of it as my own feelings about being a parent coming up through the floorboards."[7]

And so the return of the repressed was transformed into the frame for the play. A young couple wish very much to have a child (the beginning of many a fairy tale), yet when the stork puppet brings the repulsive Shockheaded Peter with motley hair and clawlike fingers, they stuff him under the floorboards of a Victorian toy theater and try to forget about him. But Peter keeps returning, and in between his repeated nightmare visitations we learn of other children's atrocious punishments when they do not live up to the expectations of their parents. All of these scenes are presided over by a sinister master of ceremonies in top hat and are enacted by lavishly dressed actors and puppets that move to the tune of bizarre music. The characters are almost automatons, almost characters from the imagination of another Hoffmann, the formidable E. T. A. Hoffmann, whose horrifying story *The Sandman* depicts a hero falling in love with a mechanical toy and dying from his hallucinations. In *Shockheaded Peter*, everything is hallucination, except that we are eminently aware of the illusion being created for us. The horror of sadism is so deliberately exaggerated that we are compelled to laugh, while the accordion-playing Jacques's high falsetto—vacillating between snarlingly aggressive and lovely tones, and accompanied by two loony percussionists—creates such an eerie atmosphere that we can take pleasure in returning to the repressed while reflecting on how different we are today.

Take "The Story of the Man That Went Out Shooting." It begins with the following verses (adapted by Jacques):

> This is the man that shoots the hare;
> This is the coat he wears:
> With game bag, powder-horn and gun
> He's going to have some fun.
>
> The hare sits in the leaves and grass
> And laughs to see the green man pass.
>
> As the sun gets very hot,
> And he a heavy gun has got,
> He lays down to sleep under a tree,
> He goes to sleep, as you can see.
>
> The hare sneaks up hip hop
> And takes the gun and then hops off.
>
> The green man wakes and sees the hare's face,
> the gun is shoved in his face,
> He screams and runs away;
> The hare chases him all day,
> The hare is trying all that she can,
> To shoot the sleepy green-coat man.
> Help! Help! Fire the Hare!
>
> At last he stumbles at the well,
> Arse over tit and in he fell.
> The hare takes aim, and hark!
> Bang! Goes the gun, and hits the mark![8]

But the hare is not finished after she kills the hunter. She shoots the green man's wife, then turns the gun on her own child, and finally commits suicide. A strange tale about the victimized's violent acts that ends in the victimized victimizing herself. Is there a moral here? Are we being told that children who play with guns will turn them on themselves, just as Harriet, who plays with matches, scorches herself and dies? Or is this some sort of parable about how we the hunters have created the conditions that drive the oppressed to violence and

THE STORY OF THE WILD HUNTSMAN

The green man wakes, and sees her place
The spectacles upon her face.
She pointed the gun at the hunter's heart,
Who jumped up at once with a start.
He cries, and screams, and runs away,
"Help me, good people, help! I pray."

At last he stumbled at the well,
Head over ears, and in he fell.
The hare stopp'd short, took aim, and hark!
Bang went the gun!—she miss'd her mark!
The poor man's wife was drinking up
Her coffee in her coffee-cup;
The gun shot cup and saucer through;
"O dear!" cried she, "what shall I do?"
Hiding close by the cottage there,
Was the hare's own child, the little hare;
When he heard the shot, he quickly arose,
And while he stood upon his toes,
The coffee fell and burn'd his nose;
"O dear," he cried, "what burns me so?"
And held up the spoon with his little toe.

self-destruction? All of these "messages" appear likely or possible today, and it is irrelevant whether they are true or defensible interpretations of the ghastly comic scenes from *Struwwelpeter*. What is significant is the perverse political implication of the songs and acts. This perversity becomes even clearer when the English text is compared to Hoffmann's original, for Hoffmann did not have the hare kill her offspring or commit suicide. In fact, the hare misses her mark and is unable to kill the hunter:

The hare stopp'd short, took aim, and hark!
Bang went the gun!—she miss'd her mark!
The poor man's wife was drinking up
Her coffee in her coffee-cup;
The gun shot cup and saucer through;
"O dear!" cried she, "what shall I do?'
Hiding close by the cottage there,
Was the hare's own child, the little hare;
When he heard the shot, he quickly arose,
And while he stood upon his toes,
The coffee fell and burn'd his nose;
"O dear," he cried, "what burns me so?"
And held up the spoon with his little toe.[9]

Whereas Hoffmann sought to minimize brutality and perhaps even apologize for it, the skits and songs of *Shockheaded Peter* seek to unnerve us: there is no reconciliation possible for the return of the repressed, and there is no justice for the maligned and maimed in Western society's contemporary farcical reforms of nineteenth century bourgeois maltreatment of children. Therefore we can only delight in sarcastic acts of revenge, perverse resistance to correct behavior.

In one of the production's most horrifying skits, "The Story of the Bully Boys," we are purposely pushed to the limits of laughter because of the murderous act of the authoritative figure of Agrippa. The changes to Hoffmann's text reveal a contemporary social critique, not simply of Hoffmann's book but of our vicious treatment of those we consider misfits or rowdy. Here is Hoffmann's text, which has racist overtones and yet seeks a creative way to curb racist attitudes:

The Story of the Inky Boys

As he had often done before.
The woolly-headed black-a-moor
One nice fine summer's day went out
To see the shops and walk about;
And as he found it hot, poor fellow,
He took with him his green umbrella.
Then Edward, little noisy wag,
Ran out and laugh'd, and waved his flag,
And William came in jacket trim,

THE STORY OF THE INKY BOYS

Then Saint Nicholas fóams with rage:
Look at him on this very page!
He seizes Caspar, seizes Ned,
Takes William by his little head;
And they may scream, and kick, and call,
But into the ink he dips them all;
Into the inkstand, one, two, three,
Till they are black, as black can be;
Turn over now and you shall see.

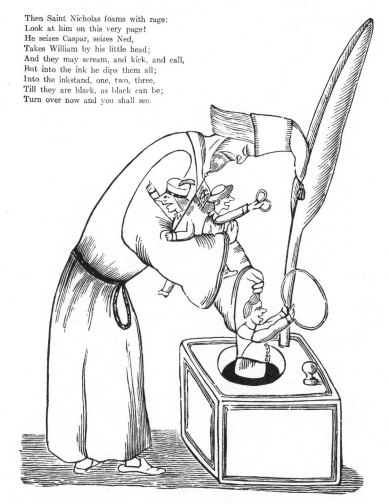

And brought his wooden hoop with him;
And Caspar, too, snatch'd up his toys
And joined the other naughty boys;
So one and all set up a roar,
And laughed and hooted more and more,
and kept on singing,—only think!—
"Oh! Blacky, you're as black as ink."

Now Saint Nicholas lived close by,—
So tall he almost touched the sky;
He had a mighty inkstand too,
In which a great goose-feather grew;
He call'd out in an angry tone,
"Boys, leave the black-a-moor alone!
For if he tries with all his might,
He cannot change from black to white."
But ah! they did not mind a bit
What Saint Nicholas said of it;
But went on laughing, as before,
And hooting at the black-a-moor.
Then Saint Nicholas foams with rage;
Look at him on this very page!
He seizes Caspar, seizes Ned,
Takes William by his little head;
And they may scream, and kick, and call,
But into the inkstand, one, two, three,
Till they are black, as black as can be;
Turn over now and you shall see.

See, there they are, and there they run!
The black-a-moor enjoys the fun.
They have been made as black as crows,
Quite black all over, eyes and nose,
And legs, and arms, and heads, and toes,
And trowsers, pinafores, and toys,—
The silly little inky boys!
Because they set up such a roar,
And teas'd the harmless black-a-moor.[10]

Compare this with Jacques' text:

The Story of the Bully-Boys

As he'd often done before,
My neighbour from next door
One fine summer's day went out
To the shops to walk about;
And as he found it hot, poor fella,
He took with him his green umbrella.

When Edward, noisy little wag,
He came out and waved his flag;
And William came in jacket trim
And brought his wooden hoop with him;
and Arthur brought his toys,
And joined the other bully boys.
Well, tall Agrippa lives close by,
So tall he almost touches the sky!
He calls out in an angry tone,
To leave my neighbour alone.
But they didn't mind a bit,
What Agrippa said of it.

Well, tall Agrippa foams with rage,
Just look at him on this very page!
He seizes Arthur, seizes Ned,
He smashes all their tiny heads!

Then they don't scream, and they don't call,
They are corpses one and all!
Three little corpses, one, two, three,
They are all dead as can be!

Silly little Bully boys
They've lost more than their toys.
Because Agrippa they annoyed,
Silly little Bully boys.[11]

There is no room for mistakes in contemporary Western society, even though we pride ourselves on freedom of movement. Whereas Hoffmann jokingly spared the three naughty boys by transforming them into blacks so that they could learn what it feels like to be mocked and maltreated, the play in *Shockheaded Peter* turns mean. There is no way to transform or reform the boys because they will not toe the line. So they must be killed. They have defied authority in the form not of St. Nicholas, Santa Claus's predecessor, but of Agrippa,[12] the ruthless deputy of the Roman emperor Augustus and defeater of Antony and Cleopatra, who reflects a corporate killer mentality. Such defiance is dealt with harshly; children cannot win. Their rebellious spirits must be crushed. Jacques and his coproducers do not want us to laugh with the children in their defiance. Rather, our laughter is to be snide if not desperate. Contemporary Western films and plays that portray young people triumphing over their stupid or naive parents create an illusion of benign and caring governance of the young. What Bakhtin described as the radical carnivalesque humor in his book on Rabelais is impossible today because we cannot turn society on its head. The revolutionary has become impossible. We are left with truncated forms of mad gestures that belittle authoritarianism but offer little hope for alternative forms of communication. *Shockheaded Peter* is a helplessly hopeless opera that is disturbing because the songs and acts leave us with comforting despair. When Jacques squeals his lines rhythmically in fateful sentences, he pointedly mocks the voice of authority and punishment and relishes doing so. Therefore when Conrad indulges in sucking his thumbs and has them cut off, we are left with his mother condoning his death (though in Hoffmann's original he did not die):

> Well, Mama comes home, and here Conrad stands,
> And he looks quite sad, as he shows his hands—
> Ha! Ha! Said Mama, I knew he'd come
> For naughty little Suck-a-Thumb.
>
> Snip, snip, the scissors go,
> And Conrad cries out: Oh!
> Snip, snip, they go so fast,
> And Conrad bleeds to death at last.[13]

The mother and the great tall tailor who cuts off Conrad's thumbs are ridiculous figures of authority, but they are left ruling the hearth. They may be caricatures of our worst nightmares and be mimicked in songs and music, yet they remain standing there, and we can only snip at them through laughter and by siding with wrongheaded children (largely puppets), who are destroyed or destroy themselves before our eyes. Only through perverse delight in opposing what is right and reasonable can we grasp the insanity of our laws and customs today and understand the ambivalence that adults feel when they become parents.

McDermott and Crouch's idea to frame the *Struwwelpeter* tales within a Victorian toy theater and to focus on parents is inspired.

Though many adults desperately want children, children bring problems when they arrive and complicate their parents' lives in ways that the parents might never have anticipated. But the real problem, as *Shockheaded Peter* reveals, concerns the parents who abuse, neglect, and abandon children or who set arbitrary rules that pose as civilized means to guide children through life. Internalized, these parents are housed within us, and perverse laughter is one of our strongest means to get rid of them. However, like Slovenly Peter they keep returning through the floorboards of our lives, and this is what makes McDermott and Crouch's production so chilling and unsettling, even as we laugh.

The frame of the Victorian toy theater cannot contain these grotesque figures running amok through doors and trapdoors. The action threatens to spill out into the audience, but the actors and puppets remind us blatantly that their antics are pure theater. No pretension is made to speak soothingly down to children, no idyllic images of what children should be like are offered. In contrast to most plays for children, there is no resolution. This is not a play for children but a play to prick the conscience of adults. The "junk opera" sings ruthlessly and candidly about perverse behavior and severe punishment that mold the psychic bonds between parents and children. *Shockheaded Peter* is thus a radical psychodrama that transforms the nineteenth-century *Struwwelpeter* into a dramatic twenty-first-century conflict between adults and children. This dramatic adaptation is no longer for children because the images, music, and messages might tell them frightening truths that "normal" children's theater and cinema conceal.

Shockheaded Peter's appeal is not just a sign of the times but a critical reflection about the desperate manner in which we seek to script and control the painful irrationality and traumas of our childhood. The well-known psychiatrist Alice Miller has written numerous books about this topic—*The Drama of the Gifted Child* (1981) and *For Your Own Good: Hidden Cruelty in Child-Rearing and the Roots of Violence* (1983)—and there have been great controversies during the past twenty years about uncovering childhood abuse and victimization through recovered memory. Whether we can really learn about how mistreated we were by recalling childhood trauma through the help of therapy is an open question. Moreover, it is not clear what we should do with all the disturbing memories. *Shockheaded Peter* adds fuel to the fire not by telling us anything new or how to overcome the return of the repressed but by insisting that we cannot keep repressing the victimization of children, as can be seen from the final victimized image of the large puppet representing Slovenly Peter at the end of the play. By baldly confronting us with the horrors of trauma that cannot be grasped except through laughter, the play compels us to wonder why or if we should laugh. Laughter does not resolve or dissipate the horrors, but the play's delight in mimicking perversity allows us a more conscious awareness of our ambivalent and contradictory attitudes toward children and our past. No wonder that the German *Struwwelpeter* was a bestseller for well over 150 years and that it has come back to haunt us in the form of *Shockheaded Peter.*

NOTES

1. Heinrich Hoffmann, *Lebenserinnerungen* (Frankfurt am Main: Insel, 1985), 26.

2. Heinrich Hoffmann, *Slovenly Peter, or Cheerful Stories and Funny Pictures*. From the twenty-third edition of the celebrated work of Dr. Henry Hoffmann (Philadelphia: Henry T. Coates & Co., c. 1900), title page.

3. Hoffmann, *Lebenserinnerungen*, 106.

4. Heinrich Hoffmann, *Slovenly Peter's Story Book* (New York: McLoughlin Brothers, 1860), unpaginated.

5. Lyn Gardner, "Theatre of Blood," *The Guardian*, January 23, 1999, 4.

6. *Ibid.*

7. *Ibid.*

8. *Der ultimative Struwwelpeter oder Horrorgeschichten und grässliche Bilder: The Ultimate Shockheaded Peter or Horrible Stories and Noisy Pictures. A Junk Opera*, Original Text by Dr. Heinrich Hoffmann adapted by Martyn Jacques of the Tiger Lillies. Pictures adapted by Ralf Alex Fichtner (Berlin: Autorenhaus-Verlag, 1999), 17–18.

9. Heinrich Hoffmann, *Slovenly Peter, or Cheerful Stories and Funny Pictures for Good Little Folks* (Philadelphia: Winson, 1915), 13.

10. *Ibid.*, 8–11.

11. *Der ultimative Struwwelpeter*, 13–15.

12. Marcus Vipsanius Agrippa (63–12 B.C.) was a military commander and deputy of Augustus, the Roman emperor. He led the victory over Mark Antony at the Battle of Actium in 31 B.C. and was later responsible for suppressing rebellions in the Roman Empire. It is interesting that the Tiger Lillies use him as the figure of authority and not St. Nicholas, as Hoffmann did. Agrippa

has much more of a vicious mentality and feeds into the perverse delight in the changes made by the Tiger Lillies.

13. *Der ultimative Struwwelpeter*, 23. Here, too, the translated text of the original German is very different. Conrad does not die:

> Mama comes home; there Conrad stands,
> And looks quite sad, and shows his hands; —
> "Ah!" said Mamma, "I knew he'd come
> To naughty little Suck-a-Thumb." (*Slovenly Peter*, 15)

The Phenomenon
of Harry Potter, or
Why All the Talk?

9

Although there are now

four published books in the Harry Potter series,

it is difficult to assess them as literature *per se*.[1]

We must talk about a phenomenon, and it is a

mind-blowing phenomenon because it reveals

just how difficult it is to evaluate and analyze children's literature or works that purport to be literature for the young.[2]

Anyone working in the field of children's literature cannot avoid Harry Potter. This past April, I made a passing remark in an interview for an article published in the "Variety Section" of the Minneapolis *Star Tribune* about my work with fairy tales that swept me into this phenomenon.[3] Mary Jane Smetanka, the journalist who was writing about my work with fairy tales, asked me at one point what I thought about the Harry Potter books, and I replied that I felt they were formulaic and sexist. The article was long and dealt with many different aspects of fairy tales and storytelling. However, this one remark caught the eye of numerous readers, and before I knew it, I had received several phone calls from members of the mass media who wanted either to interview me or to quote me in some feature about the Harry Potter books. At one point I agreed to appear on a public radio talk show at KNOW in St. Paul, and I was aggressively attacked by ninety percent of the callers (all adults) for demeaning J. K. Rowling's works, which they felt had done wonders for their children and children's literature.

This interview caused another chain reaction—more requests from the press and radio programs for my opinion about the Harry Potter books. It was as if I had suddenly become the only critic to have "negative" things to say about a worldwide phenomenon in the realm of children's literature that millions of readers cherished. But I knew this was not the case because I had talked to numerous colleagues, specialists in children's literature, and authors of children's literature and young adult books, and they shared a good many of my critical views.

I am not certain whether one can talk about a split between a minority of professional critics, who have misgivings about the quality of the Harry Potter books, and the great majority of readers, old and young, who are mesmerized by the young magician's adventures. But I am certain that the phenomenal aspect of the reception of the Harry Potter books has blurred the focus for anyone who wants to take literature for young people seriously and who may be concerned about standards and taste that adults create for youth culture in the West. How is it possible to evaluate a work of literature like a Harry Potter novel when it is so dependent on the market conditions of the culture industry? Given the changes in the production and reception of children's and youth literature in the last ten years, what criteria can one use to grasp the value of a best-seller, especially when the buyers and readers are to a large degree adults? What constitutes a good fairy-tale novel? How do the Harry Potter books compare to other fantasy works? Is it fair to question the value and quality of J. K. Rowling's books, which have allegedly helped readers of all ages to read again with joy, just because they are so successful?

I believe that it is exactly because the success of the Harry Potter novels is so great and reflects certain troubling sociocultural trends that we must try to evaluate the phenomenon. In fact, I would claim that the only way to do Rowling and her Harry Potter books justice is to try to pierce the phenomenon and to examine her works as critically as possible, not with the intention of degrading them or her efforts, but with the intention of exploring why such a conventional work of fantasy has been fetishized, so that all sorts of magic powers are attributed to the very act of reading these works. The phenomenon is indeed beyond her control. She herself did not even conceive of its possibility. Yet "everyone" appears to be spellbound and drawn to read the Harry Potter books. Might the stories about quaint Harry transform one's own life?

What has actually happened, as I have tried to show throughout this book, is that the conditions under which literature for the young is produced and received have been transformed through institutional changes of education, shifts in family relations, the rise of corporate conglomerates controlling the mass media, and market demands. Phenomena such as the Harry Potter books are driven by commodity consumption that at the same time sets the parameters of reading and aesthetic taste. Today the experience of reading for the young is mediated through the mass media and marketing so that the pleasure and meaning of a book will often be prescripted or dictated by convention. What readers passionately devour and enjoy may be, like many a Disney film or Barbie doll, a phenomenal experience and have personal significance, but it is also an *induced* experience calculated to conform to a cultural convention of amusement and distraction. It is this highly important connection between the conventional and the phenomenal that I want to explore in my essay on the Harry Potter books in an effort to take children's literature seriously within the political context of current globalizing trends predicated on fostering sameness throughout the world.

There are two common meanings for the word phenomenon. It generally refers to some kind of *occurrence*, change, or fact that is directly perceived; quite often the event is striking. Or the term is used to describe an extraordinary *person*, someone with exceptional talent, a *phenom*, whiz kid, or super star. Whether an occurrence or person, there is something incredible about the phenomenon that draws our attention. We hesitate to believe in the event or person we perceive, for a transformation has unexpectedly taken place. One of the reasons we cannot believe our senses is because the phenomenon defies rational explanation. There seems to be no logical cause or clear explanation for the sudden appearance or the transformation. Yet it is there, visible and palpable. The ordinary becomes extraordinary, and we are so taken by the phenomenon that we admire, worship, and idolize it without grasping fully why we regard it with so much reverence and awe except to say that so many others regard it as a phenomenon and, therefore, it must be a phenomenon.

Reason no longer applies after a phenomenon has appeared, especially when there is a series of phenomena that contribute to the "Harry Potter phenomenon" such as:

- The rise of the myth of J. K. Rowling, single mother on welfare, sitting in a café and writing the books while raising a daughter by herself. This myth is the old rags-to-riches story and in our day and age has been spread through the mass media. It is the fairy tale about the diligent, hardworking girl who is recognized as a princess and lives happily ever after.

- The rejection of the first novel, *Harry Potter and the Sorcerer's Stone*, by several publishers before being accepted by Bloomsbury Publishing in London. Neither the editors at Bloomsbury nor those at Scholastic, Inc. in New York would have predicted that the Harry Potter books would attract so much popular attention and sell in the millions. The long shot finishes a phenomenal first.

- The astonishing appeal of Harry Potter, the hero of all the books, a slight, modest, but confident boy who wears broken glasses. Despite his potentially nerdlike qualities, he has supernatural gifts that enable him to perform heroic deeds and defeat cynical forces of evil much like the knights of Arthurian legend. But Harry is much more successful—a postmodern whiz kid.

- The strange controversy surrounding the Harry Potter books caused by conservatives, even though the works are clearly didactic and moralistic and preach against the evil use of magic. But they have drawn the ire of the American religious right, which seeks to ban these books from schools, libraries, and bookstores because Harry is a wizard. Perhaps if Harry were seen as a Christian knight (which he actually is), he might be pardoned for his magical sins. But his stories, considered sinful, have stirred a phenomenal debate in the States.

All these incidental phenomena can be understood as tendencies that form the "dialectics of the phenomenal" operative in the case of the Harry Potter phenomenon. What appears as something phenomenal turns or is turned into its opposite through a process of homogenization: the phenomenal thing or occurrence must become a conventional commodity that can be grasped or consumed to fit our cultural expectations. Otherwise it is not a phenomenon. There are other contributing factors operating here.

J. K. Rowling has overcome hardships and appears to have remarkable endurance and an extraordinary imagination. A divorced mother, she has written four compelling novels and has turned her ordinary life into the extraordinary. Therefore her personal story, or the little we know of it through newspapers, magazine articles, and various Websites, captures our attention and our hearts because of the astonishing turnabout that has occurred in her life, which follows our conventional wish fulfillment of rags to riches.

Her books are phenomenal because, they, too, are ordinary and yet have become extraordinary. There is nothing exceptional about Rowling's writing in comparison with that of many other gifted writers of children's and young adult literature. I am thinking here of such fantasy writers as Lloyd Alexander, Natalie Babbitt, Diana Wynne Jones, Francesca Lia Block, Philip Pullman, Jane Yolen, Donna Jo Napoli and many others who are constantly experimenting in innovative ways—and not always successfully. What distinguishes the plots of Rowling's novels, however, are their conventionality, predictability, and happy ends despite the clever turns of phrases and surprising twists in the intricate plots. They are easy and delightful to read, carefully manicured and packaged, and they sell extraordinarily well precisely because they are so cute and ordinary.

Harry Potter as a fictitious character is ordinary on first appearance because he more closely resembles a bookworm than a hero. Yet, like Clark Kent, he has more to him than his appearance would indicate. He is one of the mythical chosen heroes, called upon by powers greater than himself to rescue his friends and the world from diabolical evil. He is David, Tom Thumb, Jack the Giant Killer, Aladdin, and Horatio Alger all in one, the little guy who proves he's bigger than life. But because he does not fight in the name of Judeo-Christianity, he is suspect and causes controversy.[4]

There is something wonderfully paradoxical about the phenomena surrounding the phenomenon of the Harry Potter books. For anything to become a phenomenon in Western society, it must become *conventional*; it must be recognized and categorized as unusual, extraordinary, remarkable, and outstanding. In other words, it must be popularly accepted, praised, or condemned, worthy of everyone's attention; it must conform to the standards of exception set by the mass media and promoted by the culture industry in general. To be phenomenal means that a person or commodity must conform to the tastes of hegemonic groups that determine what makes up a phenomenon. It is impossible to be phenomenal without conforming to conventionality. Whether you are a super athlete, actor, writer or commodity—and there is tremendous overlap in these categories—you must be displayed and display yourself according to socially accepted rules and expectations of "phenomenality." In American and British culture, the quality of what rises to the top is always appropriated, and if the phenomenon does somehow contain some qualities that are truly different, they are bound to be corroded and degraded, turning the phenomenon against itself and into a homogenized commodity that will reap huge profits until the next phenomenon appears on the horizon. Difference and otherness are obliterated in the process. What appears unique conceals the planned production of commonality and undermines the autonomy of judgment. A phenomenon can sway us from ourselves. We become dizzy and delirious.

In the case of the Harry Potter books, their phenomenality detracts from their conventionality, and yet their absolute conformance to popular audience expectations is what makes for their phenomenality. So far there are four novels: *Harry Potter and the Sorcerer's Stone* (1998), *Harry Potter and the Chamber of Secrets* (1999), *Harry Potter and the Prisoner of Azkaban* (1999), and *Harry Potter and the Goblet of Fire* (2000). Each one is well over 300 pages. Indeed, the last novel, a tour-de-force, that demands patience and perseverance on the part of valiant readers, amounts to 734 pages. These works have been followed by Harry Potter commodities, with a film in the planning stages. Rowling has intended from the beginning to write seven novels altogether, a magic number, but if you've read one, you've read them all: the plots are the same, and in my opinion, the story lines become tedious and grating after you have read the first. Here is the formula for each novel:

Part I. Prison   Harry the imaginative hero, the chosen one, lives in the home of Vernon and Petunia Dursley because he is an orphan. They have a fat slob of a son named Dudley, who becomes more disgusting and unlikable with each novel. All three are referred to as Muggles because they are not wizards. In other words, they lack imagination and are materialist philistines. Their home is more like a prison than anything else, or to be more precise, it is the domain of banal reality. The Dursleys and their kind are devoid of imagination. Indeed, they are afraid of magic and the world of fantasy.

Part II. The Noble Calling   Since Harry is special a member of the elect, he receives a summons, calling, invitation, command, or reminder to attend Hogwarts, the school for wizards, at the end of each summer after he has reached the age of ten. To accomplish this task, Harry must break out of the Dursleys' home.

Part III. The Heroic Adventures   Harry travels in some magical fashion to Hogwarts, where he will be tested in various ways, but he is always pitted against his archenemy Voldemort, a sinister wizard, who killed Harry's parents and tried to kill the boy as well. Thanks to his mother's sacrifice, Harry survived Voldemort's first attempt to murder him, but the evil wizard is on a mad quest to finish the job. Hogwarts and the environment (including a Forbidden Forest and a town called Hogsmeade) constitute the mystical realm in which Harry with his noble sidekick, Ron Weasley, fight against the sadistic Draco Malfoy and his cruel pals Crabbe and Goyle. Their fights, which often take place on the playing field of quidditch (a bizarre spatial game that resembles computerized baseball, basketball, and hockey played on broomsticks) are only the backdrop for deadly battles with the forces of Voldemort. Cheering Harry on are two girls, Hermione Granger and Ginny Weasley, Ron's younger sister. Whatever happens—and the plots always involve a great deal of manly competition and some kind of mystery—you can be sure that Harry wins.

Part IV. The Reluctant Return Home   Exhausted, drained, but enlightened, Harry is always victorious by the time summer recess is about to begin. Unfortunately, Harry must always return to the banal surroundings of the Dursley home.

The plots of the first four novels thus far resemble the structure of a conventional fairy tale: a modest little protagonist, typically male, who does not at first realize how talented he is and who departs from his home on a mission or is banished until he fulfills three tasks. He generally enters a mysterious forest or unknown realm on his quest. Along his way he meets animals or friends who, in return, give him gifts that will help him. Sometimes he meets an old sage or wise woman, who will provide him with support and aid. At one point he encounters a tyrant, ogre, or competitor, whom he must overcome to succeed in his mission. Invariably, he defeats his opponent and either returns home or settles in a new domain with money, wife, and happy prospects.

Rowling's novels are, of course, much more complicated and complex than your classical fairy tale. They have clearly been influenced by mystery novels, adventure films, TV sitcoms, and fiction series, and they bear all the typical trademarks that these popular genres exhibit. Indeed, the last novel, *The Goblet of Fire*, even had scenes modeled on the European soccer championship matches replete with cheerleaders and hooligans. Perhaps it is because the novels are a hodgepodge of these popular entertainments that her novels are so appealing.

In keeping with the tendency in Western popular culture, one story is never enough, especially if it sells well and sits well with audiences.

Repeat it, tweak it, and milk it until the ratings diminish. The problem for the author of a series is how to inform new readers or remind readers of what has happened in the previous books, and after the first novel Rowling has had to resort to hackneyed tricks of the trade to fill in gaps. In the second novel, *Harry Potter and the Chamber of Secrets*, she had to spend the entire first chapter more or less summarizing the first novel, just as she had to do in the third novel, *Harry Potter and the Prisoner of Azkaban*:

> The Dursley family of number four, Privet Drive, was the reason that Harry never enjoyed his summer holidays. Uncle Vernon, Aunt Petunia, and their son, Dudley, were Harry's only living relatives. They were Muggles, and they had a very medieval attitude toward magic. Harry's dead parents, who had been a witch and wizard themselves, were never mentioned under the Dursleys' roof. For years, Aunt Petunia and Uncle Vernon had hoped that if they kept Harry as downtrodden as possible, they would be able to squash the magic out of him. To their fury, they had been unsuccessful. These days they lived in terror of anyone finding out that Harry had spent most of the last two years at Hogwarts School of Witchcraft and Wizardry. The most they could do, however, was to lock away Harry's spellbooks, wand, cauldron, and broomstick at the start of the summer break and forbid him to talk to the neighbors.[5]

And in the fourth novel, *Harry Potter and the Goblet of Fire*, we learn:

> Uncle Vernon, Aunt Petunia, and Dudley were Harry's only living relatives. They were Muggles who hated and despised magic in any form, which meant that Harry was as welcome in their house as dry rot.[6]

Though Rowling misinterprets history when she criticizes the Dursleys' attitude toward magic as "medieval," a period that evidenced a strong belief in magic and an acceptance of miraculous happenings, we get the picture: the Dursleys are coarse, pragmatic materialists, frightened by people as different as Harry.

But is Harry really different? He is white, Anglo-Saxon, bright, athletic, and honest. The only mark of difference he bears is a slight lightning-shaped scar on his forehead. Otherwise, he is the classic Boy Scout, a little mischievous like Tom Sawyer or one of the Hardy boys. He does not curse; he speaks standard English grammatically, as do all his friends; he is respectful to his elders; and he has perfect manners. He would definitely help a grandmother cross the street, perhaps even fly her across on his broomstick. He is a straight arrow, for he has a noble soul and will defend the righteous against the powers of evil. This means that Harry the scout must play the role of a modern-day TV sleuth in each novel. In novel one, he is given the task of discovering what the sorcerer's stone is, who invented it, and how to prevent Voldemort from obtaining it. In novel two, he must discover who is turning his friends into stone, in particular Ginny, whose soul and body are controlled by a sinister force. In novel three, he helps capture the notorious escaped prisoner of Azkaban, Sirius Black, only to learn that Sirius did not aid Voldemort in killing his parents, nor does he want to kill Harry. Surprisingly he turns out to be Harry's godfather, who will look after him in the future. In novel four, he completes three difficult tasks in the Triwizard Tournament and then thwarts Voldemort's attempt to kill him once again. His great discovery here is that Voldemort has regained human form and is assembling Death Eaters and Dementors ostensibly to take over the world through black magic. The plots in each one of these novels take numerous arbitrary and inventive twists and turns, and in the third and fourth books, the mysteries become so involved and intricate that it is almost impossible to follow the clues. Nevertheless, Harry can and does. He is the ultimate detective, and Ron, as in all buddy/cop films, is always at his side. Typically, the girls are always left to gawk and gaze at Harry's stunning prowess. The cultural critic Christine Schoefer perceptively remarks:

> Harry's fictional realm of magic and wizardry perfectly mirrors the conventional assumption that men do and should run the world. From the beginning of the first Potter book, it is boys and men, wizards and sorcerers, who catch our attention by dominating the scenes and determining the action. Harry, of course, plays the lead. In his epic struggle with the forces of darkness—the evil wizard Voldemort and his male supporters—Harry is supported by the dignified wizard Dumbledore and a colorful cast of male characters. Girls, when they are not downright silly or unlikable, are helpers, enablers and instruments. No girl is brilliantly heroic the way Harry is, no woman experienced and wise like Professor Dumbledore. In fact, the range of female personalities is so limited that neither women nor girls play on the side of evil.[7]

But what are we to expect when women are generally accessories in most TV police shows, detective novels, and mysteries? In the Harry Potter books they fulfill stereotypical roles, but so do most of the characters. As Schoefer has demonstrated, Professor Dumbledore is Harry's spiritual father, the ultimate saintly wizard, who operates behind the scenes to guide and help Harry. Then we have the bumbling but good-hearted giant Hagrid, who provides comic relief; the strict assistant principal Minerva McGonagall; the rich snob Draco Malfoy, Harry's nemesis at the school; Professor Snape, the snide teacher who holds a grudge against Harry, but will undoubtedly unveil a positive side; Argus Filch, the nosy caretaker; Ron Weasley, the dependable, faithful friend; Ginny Weasley, who has a love interest in Harry; Sirius the protective godfather; and last but not least, Hermione Granger, the bookish and bright girl, who always comes up with the right answers and can be a pain in the neck because of the strange causes that she supports. There are others, but these one-dimensional characters are planted in each one of the novels to circle around Harry with his phallic wand and to function in a way that will highlight his extraordinary role as Boy Scout/detective. There is indeed nothing wrong in being a Boy Scout, and I suspect that this is why many adults, especially parents, like Harry: he is a perfect model for boys because he excels in almost everything he undertakes. But this is also his difficulty as a literary character: he is too flawless and almost a caricature of various protagonists from pop culture. Like young heroes today, Harry appeals to young readers (and adults) because Rowling has endowed him with supernatural powers of the sort we can see in *The Power Rangers*, *X-Men*, *Star Wars*, *Buffy the Vampire Slayer*, and numerous other TV shows and films. Harry "acts out" his role with wand, invisible cape, and broomstick to determine his destiny, and though adults may help him, he is literally the one who has the power to use for the benefit of goodness.

From the Manichean concept of the world in the novels it might seem clear what good and evil are, but these concepts prove amorphous. There appear to be two major types of evil in the books: the vicious sadism of Voldemort and the cruel vindictiveness of the Dursleys. They have evil written over their faces, even though the nature of their evil is different. Therefore it is easy to empathize with Harry. Voldemort is a killer who stalks Harry, and Rowling is expert at creating an atmosphere of frenzy and fear in which Harry must hunt the evil one as he is being stalked. Almost everyone except Harry refers to Voldemort as "You-Know-Who," rather than naming him, for it is believed that naming him will mean calling him. Rowling likes to play with names using foreign associations and phonetics to induce associations. Volde evokes some German and Scandinavian names. *Wold*, which stems from old high German and has Scandinavian cognates, means woods or open field and is pronounced *vold*. Then there is the old Norse *vole* which means field mouse or rat. We use the word *vole* today to describe a common rodent. *Mort* is clearly French for death. So we have evil as a death field mouse or a death rat. But the meaning is irrelevant. It is the association of Voldemort with uncontrollable evil that is important. He keeps shifting shapes and is hard to define, so that Harry is called upon to protect himself and others at every turn he takes and, it would seem, every second he is at Hogwarts. (It is interesting that Voldemort pursues Harry mainly when he is at the place where he should feel most protected.)

Is this why young readers (and perhaps adults as well) are drawn to Harry and his numerous encounters with and fights against evil? Are we living in such a paranoid world, in which children and adults feel violence might occur at any moment, that we must live our lives constantly on guard? Are pedophiles, kidnappers, serial killers, and mass murderers all around us? Do the mass media create an atmosphere of hysteria so that white England and white America paint dark forces surrounding them, seeking to invade their homes and steal their children? Just as it is difficult to place our finger on evil in the real world, evil is elusive in the Harry Potter novels, and yet it lurks around every corner and on almost every page.

Even in Muggleland, or suburban England, evil exists in the shape of the Dursley family. Vernon and Petunia abuse Harry by depriving him of food, locking him in a closet, and preventing him from having contact with friends, while their son picks on Harry at every chance he gets. All three are sadists, and Harry is psychologically starved for love and affection—although he always appears chipper and perseveres. Rowling is heavy-handed in her depiction of the Dursley family that bears some resemblance to cartoon characters of the TV Simpson family. They are so plainly uncouth and comical that they pose no great threat to Harry, who always finds a way (through cleverness or help from friends) to avoid them. Still, they are evil not only because they treat him like scum but because they lack imagination and compassion.

If evil in the Harry Potter books is defined by the actions of Voldemort, the Dursleys, and like-minded individuals such as Malfoy, Malfoy's father, Barty Crouch, and Wormtail, then goodness is, of course, embodied by Harry and his friends. And unlike most children entering puberty, they have pure souls; in fact, they do not drink, smoke, or take drugs. They do not curse or fail to show their elders respect. They study hard and attend all classes. They rarely break the rules of Hogwarts, and when they do, they have a good reason or guilty consciences. They do not talk about sex, although their hormones seem to have risen in the last novel. They are fearless when it comes to facing the murderous forces that threaten their clean-cut existence. Left alone, they would probably grow up and become dutiful and pleasant wizards and witches like the gentle and conscientious ones who teach in their school. Goodness is doing unto others what you would like done to you, and Harry and his friends are gentle Christian souls. So much for fearing wizards and witches!

One of the difficulties in reading fairy tales and fairy-tale novels is that you know from the beginning that evil will be overcome. A fairy tale is not a fairy tale that does not have a happy end. Of course, this is not entirely true. In fact, the optimism of the classical fairy tales (Perrault, Grimm, Andersen, MacDonald, Baum, Tolkien) has been challenged by numerous postmodern and magic-realist writers who have turned fairy tales upside down and inside out to voice a certain skepticism about the original messages of conventional fairy tales and the meaning of traditional happiness. Not so Rowling. She remains within the predictable happy-end school of fairy-tale writers. You know from beginning to end that Harry will triumph over evil, and this again may be one of the reasons that her novels have achieved so much popularity.

In a world in which we are uncertain of our roles and uncertain about our capacity to defeat evil, the Harry Potter novels arrive and inform us (as do many films and TV series) that if we all pull together and trust one another and follow the lead of the chosen one, evil will be overcome. The scheme of things is very similar to the Disney corporation's *The Lion King*, which celebrates male dominance and blood rule. In fact, there are people "chosen" for the task of leadership because they have the right magical skills and good genes. It doesn't matter that they happen to be all white, all British, all from good homes, and that the men and boys call the shots. What matters is a feeling of security that we gain after reading one or more of Rowling's novels. They are carefully crafted to make us delight in the good clean way that her protagonists set the world aright without questioning the real conflicts that the majority of children in the United Kingdom and North America face.

In the last novel, *The Goblet of Fire*, Rowling seemed to be touching on some serious problems such as violence, soccer hooliganism, and union organizing. However, she never explores these topics in depth. For example, Hermione's support of the house-elves is generally mocked by the boys, and Rowling also depicts the elves (common laborers) resisting Hermione's attempts to organize them because they enjoy their work and slavery. Is Rowling trying to show that workers have such a low political consciousness that they will not listen to an enlightened leader like Hermione? Certainly, Rowling's own ideological position of enlightenment is contradictory: on the one hand, she condemns the viciousness of Voldemort and his followers who abuse magic and the imagination. On the other hand, she celebrates competition in a male world at every turn of the page. Though *The Goblet of Fire* is her most intriguing novel, wands appear to be flying out like drawn pistols on every page in her phallocentric world, and the test of a male's virtue is whether he will win contest after contest with his wand. Though Harry does not want to win at any cost, he thrives on competition as do all the characters in her novels, and Rowling thrives on contriving all sorts of tests and inventions to keep her readers guessing and in suspense. But there is very little excitement when we know the narrator will always help her winner.

In one of the more incisive short analyses of the Harry Potter books, the critic Richard Bernstein commented in the *New York Times*:

> When I began to read them, having heard how great they were from my several addicted nephews, it was hard for me to understand what all the sensation was about. Conservative Christians have criticized the Harry Potter books, saying they lead their young readers in the direction of paganism. For me the problem was that Ms. Rowling's world of sorcerers, gravity-defying broomsticks, spells, potions, unicorns and

centaurs, goblins, trolls, three-headed dogs and other monstrous and magical creations seemed to be so divorced from any reality as to kill off the narrative excitement. But whereas adults see in Harry Potter a fairly conventional supernatural adventure story—one not nearly as brilliant or literary as, say, *The Hobbit* or the *Alice in Wonderland* books—something more fundamental evidently reverberates in the minds of children, something as powerful as the witch of "Hansel and Gretel." And read from this point of view, the Harry Potter books do indeed contain many of the elements that Bettelheim identified in the Grimm tales. Ms. Rowling's success in this sense may show the continued power of the form and the archetypes that those long-ago Germans perfected."[8]

Bernstein points out that Harry represents the vulnerability and powerlessness that children feel, and the Potter books, like fairy tales, may indeed enable children as readers to deal therapeutically with issues of abandonment, loneliness, and alienation. Yet we have no proof whatsoever that fairy tales operate this way. One could make the opposite case and argue that many of the classical fairy tales have helped disseminate stereotypical notions of gender and race and have indoctrinated children through stereotypes—not through archetypes —to believing in set patterns of behavior in accord with patriarchal codes. Even "Hansel and Gretel" can be read as a rationalization of the abusive treatment of defenseless children who forgive their father (not their mother) for his abandonment of them. Ever since Jacqueline Rose's important book *The Case of Peter Pan*, critics in the field of children's literature have studied the fictional child and how writers manipulate readers through personal projections of children to deal with and perhaps rationalize their own desires and needs.

Rowling, too, has her own psychological need to project children and a realm of childhood in which she consciously and subconsciously manipulates her figures to please herself. As she has stated, "I just write what I wanted to write. I write what amuses me. It's totally for myself. I never in my wildest dreams expected this popularity."[9] But she also wants to generate an emotional effect in readers commensurate with the pleasure that she hopes to attain. The mechanisms that she uses are part and parcel of popular culture and the conventional repertoire of the fairy tale. Harry Potter is her fictional child; she is all-powerful and controls arbitrarily all the characters and events in the Harry Potter books. They are nothing without her—without her ideological perspective, desires, cravings, and craft.

Whether the books will have the effect on readers that she desires is another question. Bernstein, for instance, reads the books, dismisses them, and then reevaluates them from Bettelheim's questionable perspective—certainly not from his nephews' personal perspectives, because he did not explore the effects that the books had on them. My guess is that even if he had done this, he would have gotten different results: children do not all read the same way, nor do all children read best-sellers, especially when they are over 700 pages long.

This past February I did a storytelling session at the Marcy School in Minneapolis with fifth- and sixth-graders. At the end of the session I discussed the Harry Potter books with them and why they liked or disliked the books. There were about twenty-two youngsters in an integrated group, half girls, half boys. The teacher had bought all three hardcover novels, which were prominently placed in the classroom. (The fourth book had not yet appeared.) She bought them because she felt that they would stimulate the boys to read more. However, when I asked how many of them had actually read the first novel, only half the students raised their hands, and they were mostly girls. The students knew the novel mainly because the teacher was reading it to them. She had not gotten beyond the first novel. Only one of the girls and one of the boys had read all three; a few others had read two. Some of the students called the books boring. For the most part, they liked what was being read to them, but they liked other books equally well. When I criticized the books for being sexist, several girls rose to the defense of Rowling and argued that Hermione was a key figure in the books, and without her Harry would not be able to solve the mysteries. Yet after I explained my viewpoint, some agreed that Hermione was more an accessory than the major active protagonist. Many hesitated to discuss the novels because they had not read them all. One of the girls revealed that when she had been asked by her parents whether she had wanted to use her allowance money to buy a Harry Potter novel or to wait until Christmas, when she would receive it as a gift, she chose to wait until Christmas. Indeed, while children are not adverse to reading the Harry Potter adventures and other books, they are adverse to spending money on them. They certainly do not buy them. Adults have clearly been buying the majority of the Harry Potter books.

In the June 9, 2000, issue of *USA Today*, there is a graph showing that 43 percent of the Harry Potter books were bought *for* people over age fourteen, while 57 percent were bought *for* people under age fourteen.[10] However, this graph and the article (entitled "Harry Potter's Simplicity Lures Kids of All Ages") contain little meaning because they do not reveal whether the books were actually read, who did all the buying, and what social classes, ethnic groups, and genders are reading the books. Indeed, there are no reliable and thorough demographic studies concerning the purchase of the Harry Potter books and their reception among adults and children. Nevertheless, we can make educated assumptions about the dissemination and reading of the books. For example, in the United States, the first four novels have appeared mainly in hardback editions costing around twenty dollars. Only recently has a softback edition of *Harry Potter and the Sorcerer's Stone* appeared. Given the purchasing tendencies of Americans, we can assume that adults are buying the books for children *and* themselves, and that most of the purchasers are well-to-do. Since the books are very long, the attention span of most youngsters is short, and since children watch on the average of three hours of television a day, we may also assume that a very small minority of children (and adults) is actually reading the books and reflecting on them. It may be that this minority is large and vocal and not to be discounted for courageously reading all four books. But I want to emphasize that this reading public is probably limited to affluent white children and their parents, and that all these readers react in highly diverse ways to the Harry Potter books. I cannot speculate about the positive psychological effects that these novels are having on children and adults. On the other hand, Rowling's books *conventionally* repeat much of the same sexist and white patriarchal biases of classical fairy tales.

In a recent article in *The Horn Book*, Brian Alderson, one of the most astute contemporary critics of children's literature in England, recalls a disturbingly common experience he had at the seventy-fifth birthday party of Joan Aiken, one of the most inventive writers of fairy tales and fantasy novels in the world today. Attending the party was a young lady, a children's books editor for one of England's national newspapers, whom he describes as "one of those bright eager souls who seem to be ubiquitous here on the lower slopes of journalism and in publishers' publicity departments."[11] At one point she asked him who his favorite writer for children was, and he responded with great hesitation, wary about the question and the questioner:

"Well—I'm an unrepentant admirer of William Mayne." "Ooh," says she, "who's he? What age does he write for?"

Will it surprise you if I confess that I was not altogether unsurprised by that ingenuous remark? I've met its equivalent quite a lot just lately and I'm sage enough to realize that greybeards like me can't expect instant apprehension of knowledge that we've taken decades to acquire.[12]

He continues in his brief article to discuss the problems that arise when young people who know very little about the history of children's literature assume positions of arbiters of taste and judgment and pontificate about children's books, and at the same time he ponders whether "old professionals" like himself, who know too much about the quality of "past splendors," may have difficulty in appreciating contemporary children's books that are given undue praise without comparison to numerous other outstanding works in the field. For Alderson, the situation is indeed absurd as he contemplates how the overwhelming phenomenon of Harry Potter detracts from the profound accomplishments of Joan Aiken and other writers such as Mayne, Rosemary Sutcliff, Ursula LeGuin, and Janni Howker.

Roger Sutton, the editor of *The Horn Book*, writes that he received a letter accompanying a reader's copy of *Harry Potter and the Prisoner of Azkaban* from Scholastic, Rowling's publisher in New York, in which Scholastic said of the Harry Potter books: "all of this attention focused on a children's book can only be good for the visibility of children's literature in general—everyone wins."[13] Of course, Scholastic wins most of all and is rolling in money, but it is not fair to blame the publisher for the success of the Harry Potter books. Still, the statement is self-serving and deceptive. Children's literature was big business and a huge success long before the Harry Potter books appeared on the scene. The field of children's literature did not need nor does it now need these books to become more visible. Do these books prove the quality of children's literature? Certainly not. Books of quality—including those for young adults—are unfortunately not being read as widely as the "phenomenal" books. Is everyone winning? Does Scholastic mean that more children are being motivated to read? Is this true? And if it is, should we rejoice? This reminds me of the old argument that it does not matter what children read as long as they read. (We want them functionally literate. That is all that matters.) Well then, the Harry Potter books, I say, as an unabashed adult reader, will certainly help children become functionally literate, for they are part of the eternal return to the same and, at the same time, part of the success and process by which we homogenize our children. Making children all alike is, sadly, a phenomenon of our times.

NOTES

1. In her article, "At Last, The Wizard Gets Back to School," Janet Maslin comments: "The frenzy that has greeted the fourth book in the series, *Harry Potter and the Goblet of Fire*, would seem to go beyond any reasonable response to fiction, no matter how genuinely delightful that fiction happens to be. Instead, the current wave of Harrymania brings the Potter series to a fever pitch better associated with movie hype, major sports events and hot new Christmas toys," the *New York Times* (July 10, 2000): B1.

2. In a short editorial, Roger Sutton, editor of *The Horn Book*, alludes to the phenomenon and the difficulty it causes in evaluating children's literature: "I don't have any opinions about *Harry*; at least I *didn't* have any opinions until J. K. Rowling's series became a 'publishing phenomenon' (ghastly but apt phrase) and . . . children's books became All About Harry. So I'm not feeling suckered—neither by the book nor by the publisher, but by the cosmic forces that have ordained that this likable but critically insignificant series become widely popular and therefore news, and therefore something I'm supposed to have an opinion about." "Potter's Field," *The Horn Book* 75 (September/October 1999): 1.

3. Mary Jane Smetanka, "Once Upon a Time," *Star Tribune* (April 2, 2000): Section E, 1, 4.

4. This controversy is actually very old. Religious groups beginning with the Catholic Church in the fifteenth century and individual tyrannical kings and governments up through the Nazi and communist regimes have tried to ban, censor, and burn books. One of the first major assaults in America was on L. Frank Baum's *The Wizard of Oz*, and there will be many more to come. It is not unusual for narrow-minded religious groups and authoritarian governments to want to destroy something or people in the name of morality. For a sober discussion of the religious viewpoint, see Kimbra Wilder Gish, "Hunting Down Harry Potter: An Exploration of Religious Concerns about Children's Literature," *The Horn Book* 76 (May/June 2000): 262–71. While pleading for

tolerance on both the right and the left, Gish does not deal with the contradictions in the Bible, which is filled with a great deal of magic and folklore.

5. J. K. Rowling, *Harry Potter and the Prisoner of Azkaban* (New York: Scholastic, 1999), 2–3.

6. J. K. Rowling, *Harry Potter and the Goblet of Fire* (New York: Scholastic, 2000): 19.

7. Christine Schoefer, "Harry Potter's Girl Trouble," *Salon.com* (January 23, 2000), 1.

8. Richard Bernstein, "Examining the Reality of the Fantasy in the Harry Potter Stories," *New York Times* (December 2, 1999): B1.

9. Alan Cowell, "All Aboard the Potter Express," *New York Times* (July 10, 2000): B6.

10. Deirdre Donahue, "Harry Potter's Simplicity Lures Kids of All Ages," *USA Today* (June 9, 2000): 10B.

11. Brian Alderson, "A View from the Island: Harry Potter, Dido Twite, and Mr. Beowulf," *The Horn Book* 76 (May/June 2000): 349.

12. *Ibid.*, 349.

13. Sutton, "Potter's Field," 501.

Bibliography

Abernethy, Rose L. "A Study of Existing Practices and Principles of Story-telling for Children in the United States." Ph.D. diss., Northwestern University, 1964.

Adorno, Theodor. *The Culture Industry: Selected Essays on Mass Culture*. Ed. J. M. Bernstein. London: Routledge, 1991.

Alberghene, Janice M., and Beverly Lyon Clark, eds. *Little Women and the Feminist Imagination: Criticism, Controversy, Personal Essays*. New York: Garland, 1998.

Alderson, Brian. "A View from the Island: Harry Potter, Dido Twite, and Mr. Beowulf." *The Horn Book* 76 (May/June 2000): 349–52.

Allison, Alida, ed. *Russell Hoban / Forty Years: Essays on his Writing for Children*. New York: Garland, 2000.

Alvey, Richard G. "The Historical Development of Organized Storytelling for Children in the United States." Ph.D. diss., University of Pennsylvania, 1974.

Anno, Mitsumasa. *Anno's Twice-Told Tales: The Fisherman and His Wife & Four Clever Brothers by the Brothers Grimm & Mr. Fox*. New York: Philomel, 1993.

Anthony, Edward, and Joseph Anthony. *The Fairies Up-to-Date*. London: Thornton Butterworth, 1923.

Arbuthnot, May Hill. *Children's Books Too Good to Miss*. Cleveland: Press of Case Western University, 1948.

_____. *Children and Books*. Chicago: Scott, Foresman, 1957.

Ariès, Philippe. *Centuries of Childhood*. Harmondsworth: Penguin, 1973.

Associated Press. "Survey Finds Low Levels of Literacy." *Star Tribune* (December 11, 1997): A6.

Avery, Gillian. *Behold the Child: American Children and Their Books 1621–1922*. London: Bodley Head, 1994.

Babbitt, Natalie. "Read This, It's Good for You." *New York Times Book Review* (May 18, 1997): 23–24.

Bacchilega, Cristina. *Postmodern Fairy Tales: Gender and Narrative Strategies*. Philadelphia: University of Pennsylvania Press, 1997.

Barthelme, Donald. *Snow White*. New York: Atheneum, 1967.

Barthes, Roland. *Mythologies*. London: Granada, 1973.

Bazalgette, Cary, and David Buckingham, eds. *In Front of the Children: Screen Entertainment and Young Audiences*. London: British Film Institute, 1995.

Bazalgette, Cary, and Terry Staples, "Unshrinking the Kids: Children's Cinema and the Family Film." In *In Front of the Children: Screen Entertainment and Young Audiences*, eds. Cary Bazalgette and David Buckingham, 92–108. London: British Film Institute, 1995.

Beckett, Sandra L. *Reflections of Change: Children's Literature since 1945*. Westport, CT: Greenwood Press, 1997.

_____, ed. *Transcending Boundaries: Writing for a Dual Audience of Children and Adults*. New York: Garland, 1999.

Benjamin, Walter. "The Storyteller." In *Illuminations*, trans. Harry Zohn, 83–109. New York: Harcourt, Brace & World, 1968.

Bernstein, Richard. "Examining the Reality of the Fantasy in the Harry Potter Stories." *New York Times* (December 2, 1999): B1–2.

Bettelheim, Bruno. *The Uses of Enchantment: The Meaning and Importance of Fairy Tales*. New York: Alfred A. Knopf, 1976.

Bigelow, Bill. "Masks of Global Exploitation: Teaching about Advertising and the Real World." *Rethinking Schools* 14 (Winter 1999/2000): 14, 16.

Bingham, Jane, ed. *Writers for Children: Critical Studies of Major Authors since the Seventeenth Century*. New York: Scribner's, 1987.

Boettger, Gerhard. "Das Gute und Böse im Märchen." *Lehrerrundbrief* 3 (1948): 290–91.

Bottigheimer, Ruth. "The Publishing History of Grimms' Tales: Reception at the Cash Register." In *The Reception of Grimms' Fairy Tales: Responses, Reactions, Revisions*, ed. Donald Haase, 78–101. Detroit: Wayne State University Press, 1993.

Bourdieu, Pierre. *Distinction: A Social Critique of the Judgment of Taste*. Cambridge: Harvard University Press, 1984.

————. *The Field of Cultural Production*, ed. Randal Johnson. New York: Columbia University Press, 1993.

Boynton, Robert. "The Hollywood Way." *The New Yorker* (March 30, 1998): 48–54.

Bruner, Jerome. *The Culture of Education*. Cambridge: Harvard University Press, 1996.

Butts, Dennis, ed. *Stories and Society: Children's Literature in Its Social Context*. London: Macmillan, 1992.

Carryl, Guy Wetmore. *Grimm Tales Made Gay*. Illustr. Albert Levering. Boston: Houghton Mifflin, 1902.

Cashorali, Peter. *Fairy Tales: Traditional Stories Retold for Gay Men*. San Francisco: Harper, 1995.

Cassell, Justine, and Henry Jenkins, eds. *From Barbie to Mortal Kombat: Gender and Computer Games*. Cambridge: MIT Press, 1999.

Chambers, Adrian. *The Reading Environment: How Adults Help Children Enjoy Books*. South Woodchester: Thimble Press, 1991.

Chavanu, Bakari. "Seventeen, Self-Image, and Stereotypes." *Rethinking Schools* 14 (Winter 1999/2000): 14, 18.

Clark, Beverly Lyon. *Regendering the School Story: Sassy Sissies and Tattling Tomboys*. New York: Garland, 1997.

Clark, Beverly Lyon, and Margaret Higonnet, eds. *Girls, Boys, Books, Toys: Gender in Children's Literature and Culture*. Baltimore: Johns Hopkins University Press, 1999.

Cole, Babette. *Princess Smartypants*. London: Hamish Hamilton, 1986.

————. *Prince Cinders*. London: Hamish Hamilton, 1987.

Coover, Robert. *Pricksongs and Descants*. New York: Dutton, 1970.

————. *Briar Rose*. New York: Grove Press, 1996.

Cott, Jonathan. *Piper at the Gates of Dawn: The Wisdom of Children's Literature*. New York: Viking, 1984.

Cowell, Alan. "All Aboard the Potter Express." *The New York Times* (July 10, 2000): B1, 6.

Cross, Gary. *Kids' Stuff: Toys and the Changing World of American Childhood.* Cambridge, MA: Harvard University Press, 1997.

Cunningham, Hugh. *Children and Childhood in Western Society since 1500.* London: Longman, 1995.

_____. "Histories of Childhood." *American Historical Review* (October 1998): 1195–1208.

Danesi, Marcel. *Cool: The Signs and Meanings of Adolescence.* Toronto: University of Toronto Press, 1994.

Denby, David. "Buried Alive: Our Children and the Avalanche of Crud." *The New Yorker* (July 15, 1996): 48–58.

Donahue, Deirdre. "Harry Potter's Simplicity Lures Kids of All Ages." *USA Today* (June 9, 2000): 10B.

Donoghue, Emma. *Kissing the Witch: Old Tales in New Skins.* New York: HarperCollins, 1997.

Engelhardt, Tom. "Reading May Be Harmful to Your Kids: In the Nadirland of Today's Children's Books." *Harper's Magazine* (June 1991): 55–62.

_____. "Gutenberg Unbound." *The Nation* (March 17, 1997): 18–29.

Feder, Barnaby J. "Biotech Industry Bets Its Future on Storytelling." *International Herald Tribune* (June 25, 1999): 13–14.

Ferguson, Andrew. "Inside the Crazy Culture of Kids Sports." *Time* (July 12, 1999): 52–60.

Fetscher, Iring. *Wer hat Dornröschen wachgeküßt? Das Märchen Verwirrbuch.* Hamburg: Claassen, 1972.

Finnegan, William. "The Unwanted." *The New Yorker* (December 1, 1997): 61–78.

Flynn, Richard. "The Intersection of Children's Literature and Childhood Studies." *Children's Literature Association Quarterly* 22 (Fall 1997): 3.

Freire, Paulo. *Pedagogy of the Oppressed.* Trans. Myra Bergman Ramos. New York: Herder and Herder, 1971.

_____. *Pedagogy of Hope.* Trans. Robert R. Barr. New York: Continuum, 1997.

Freud, Sigmund. *Civilization and Its Discontents.* Trans. James Strachey. New York: Norton, 1961.

Gág, Wanda. *Millions of Cats.* New York: Coward-MacCann, 1928.

_____. *Tales from Grimm.* New York: Coward-McCann, 1936.

_____. *Snow White and the Seven Dwarfs.* New York: Coward-McCann, 1938.

_____. "I Like Fairy Tales." *The Horn Book* 15 (March-April 1939): 75–80.

_____. *Three Gay Tales from Grimm.* New York: Coward-McCann, 1943.

_____. *More Tales from Grimm.* New York: Coward-McCann, 1947.

_____. *The Sorcerer's Apprentice*. Illustr. Margot Tomes. New York: Coward, McCann & Geoghegan, 1979.

Galloway, Priscilla. *Truly Grim Tales*. New York: Bantam Doubleday Dell, 1995.

Gannon, Susan R. "Children's Literature Studies in a New Century." *Signal* 91 (January 2000): 25–40.

Gardner, Lyn. "Theatre of Blood." *The Guardian* (January 23, 1999): 4.

Garner, James Finn. *Politically Correct Bedtime Stories*. New York: Macmillan, 1994.

_____. *Once Upon a More Enlightened Time: More Politically Correct Fairy Tales*. New York: Macmillan, 1995.

Giroux, Henry A. *Popular Culture: Schooling and Everyday Life*. New York: Begin & Garvey, 1989.

Gish, Kimbra Wilder. "Hunting Down Harry Potter: An Explorations of Religious Concerns about Children's Literature." *The Horn Book* 76 (May/June 2000): 262–271.

Gong, Walter, and Karl Privat. "Vorschule der Grausamkeit? Eine Diskussion um die Märchen der Brüder Grimm." *Der Tagesspiegel* (February 7, 1947): np.

Gordon, Karen. *The Red Shoes and Other Tattered Tales*. Normal, Ill: Dalkey Archive Press, 1996.

Gray, Paul. "Wild about Harry." *Time* (September 20, 1999): 66–72.

Grimm, Jacob, and Wilhelm Grimm. *Grimm's Fairy Tales*. Trans. Margaret Hunt. Illustr. John B. Gruelle. New York: Cupples & Leon, 1914.

_____. *Grimms' Fairy Tales*. Trans. Mrs. E. V. Lucas, Lucy Crane, and Marian Edwardes. Illustr. Fritz Kredel. New York: Grosset & Dunlap, 1945.

_____. *Grimms' Fairy Tales*. Trans. Margaret Hunt and Rev. James Stern. Illustr. Josef Scharl. New York: Pantheon, 1944.

_____. *Kinder- und Hausmärchen*. Ed. Heinz Rölleke. 3 vols. Stuttgart: Reclam, 1980.

_____. *The Complete Fairy Tales of the Brothers Grimm*. Trans. Jack Zipes. New York: Bantam, 1992.

Griswold, Jerome. *Audacious Kids: Coming of Age in America's Classic Children's Books*. New York: Oxford University Press, 1992.

Gross, Martin. *The Conspiracy of Ignorance: The Failure of American Public Schools*. New York: HarperCollins, 1999.

Haase, Donald, ed. *The Reception of Grimms' Fairy Tales: Responses, Reactions, Revisions*. Detroit: Wayne State University Press, 1993.

Harris, Irving B. *Children in Jeopardy: Can We Break the Cycle of Poverty?* New Haven: Yale University Press, 1997.

Hazard, Paul. *Les livres, les enfants et les hommes*. Paris: Flammarion, 1932. (*Books, Children and Men*. Boston: The Horn Book, 1944.)

Hearn, Michael Patrick. "Wanda Gág." In *Dictionary of Literary Biography: American Writers for Children, 1900–1960*, ed. John Cech. Vol. 22, 179–91. Detroit: Gale, 1983.

Hearne, Betsy. "Margaret K. McElderry and the Professional Matriarchy of Children's Books." *Library Trends* 44 (Spring 1996): 755–75.

————. "Midwife, Witch, and Woman-Child: Metaphor for a Matriarchal Profession." *Story: From Fireplace to Cyberspace*. GSLIS (1998): 37–51.

Hendershot, Heather. "Sesame Street: Cognition and Communications Imperialism." In *Kids Media Culture*, ed. Marcia Kinder, 139–76. Durham, N.C.: Duke University Press, 1999.

Hesse, Hermann. *The Fairy Tales of Hermann Hesse*. Trans. Jack Zipes. New York: Bantam, 1995.

Higonnet, Anne. *Pictures of Innocence: The History and Crisis of Ideal Childhood*. London: Thames & Hudson, 1998.

Hoffmann, Heinrich. *Slovenly Peter's Story Book*. New York: McLoughlin Brothers, 1860.

————. *Lebenserinnerungen*. Frankfurt am Main: Insel, 1985.

————. *Slovenly Peter, or Cheerful Stories and Funny Pictures*. From the twenty-third edition of Dr. Henry Hoffmann. Philadelphia: Henry T. Coates & Co., c. 1900.

————. *Slovenly Peter, or Cheerful Stories and Funny Pictures for Good Little Folks*. Philadelphia: Winson, 1915.

————. *Struwwelpeter: Fearful Stories & Vile Pictures to Instruct Good Little Folks*. Illustr. Sarita Vendetta. Intro. Jack Zipes. Venice, Calif.: Feral House, 1999.

————. *Der ultimative Struwwelpeter oder Horrorgeschichten und grässliche Bilder. The Ultimate Shockheaded Peter or Horrible Stories and Noisy Pictures. A Junk Opera*. Adapt. Martyn Jacques of the Tiger Lilies. Illustr. Ralf Alex Fichtner. Berlin: Autorenhaus-Verlag, 1999.

Hoyle, Karen Nelson. *Wanda Gág*. New York: Twayne, 1994.

Hunt, Peter, ed. *Children's Literature: The Development of Criticism*. London: Routledge, 1990.

————. *Criticism, Theory, and Children's Literature*. London: Blackwell, 1991.

————, ed. *Literature for Children: Contemporary Criticism*. London: Routledge, 1992.

————. *An Introduction to Children's Literature*. Oxford: Oxford University Press, 1994.

————, ed. *International Companion Encyclopedia of Children's Literature*. London: Routledge, 1996.

————, ed. *Understanding Children's Literature*. London: Routledge, 1999.

Jacobs, A. J. *Fractured Fairy Tales*. New York: Bantam, 1997.

James, A., and A. Prout, eds. *Constructing and Reconstructing Childhood: Contemporary Issues in the Sociological Study of Childhood*. London: Falmer, 1997.

Jan, Isabelle. *La Littérature enfantine*. Paris: Editions Ouvrières, 1969. (*On Children's Literature*. London: Allen Lane, 1973.)

Janosch. *Janosch erzählt Grimm's Märchen*. Weinheim: Beltz & Gelberg, 1972.

————. *Not Quite as Grimm*. Trans. Patricia Crampton. London: Abelard-Schuman, 1974.

————. *Janosch erzählt Grimm's Märchen*. Rev. ed. Weinheim: Beltz & Gelberg, 1991.

Jenkins, Henry, ed. *The Children's Culture Reader*. New York: New York University Press, 1998.

————. "Professor Jenkins Goes to Washington." *Harper's Magazine* (July 1999): 19–23.

Jones, Terry. *Fairy Tales*. Illustr. Michael Foreman. London: Pavilion, 1981.

Karp, Stan. "Of Mickey Mouse and Monopolies." *Rethinking Schools* 14 (Winter 1999/2000): 19–20.

Kilbourne, Jean. *Deadly Persuasion: Why Women and Girls Must Fight the Addictive Power of Advertising*. New York: The Free Press, 1999.

Kincaid, James. *Child-Loving: The Erotic Child and Victorian Culture*. New York: Routledge, 1992.

Kinder, Marsha. *Playing with Power in Movies, Television, and Video Games: From Muppet Babies to Teenage Mutant Ninja Turtles*. Berkeley: University of California Press, 1993.

————. "Home Alone in the '90s: Generational War and Transgenerational Address in American Movies, Television, and Presidential Politics." In *In Front of the Children: Screen Entertainment and Young Audiences*, eds. Cary Bazalgette and David Buckingham, 75–91. London: British Film Institute, 1995.

————, ed. *Kids' Media Culture*. Durham, NC: Duke University Press, 1999.

Kline, Stephen. *Out of the Garden: Toys and Children's Culture in the Age of TV Marketing*. London: Verso, 1993.

Knowles, Murray, and Kirsten Malmkjaer. *Language and Control in Children's Literature*. London: Routledge, 1996.

Könneker, Marie-Luise. *Dr. Heinrich Hoffmanns "Struwwelpeter": Untersuchungen zur Entstehungs- und Funktionsgeschichte eines bürgerlichen Bilderbuchs*. Stuttgart: Metzler, 1977.

Kohl, Herbert. *The Discipline of Hope: Learning from a Lifetime of Teaching*. New York: Simon & Schuster, 1998.

Kohn, Alfie. *The Schools Our Children Deserve: Moving beyond Traditional Classrooms and "Tougher Standards."* Boston: Houghton Mifflin, 1999.

Kroeber, Karl. *Retelling / Rereading: The Fate of Storytelling in Modern Times*. New Brunswick, N.J.: Rutgers University Press, 1990.

Kutzer, Daphne M. *Writers of Multicultural Fiction for Young Adults*. Westport, Conn.: Greenwood, 1996.

_____. *Empire's Children: Empire and Imperialism in Classic British Children's Books*. New York: Garland, 2000.

Kuznets, Lois. *When Toys Come Alive: Narratives of Animation, Metamorphosis, and Development*. New Haven: Yale University Press, 1994.

Lanes, Selma. *Down the Rabbit Hole: Adventures and Misadventures in the Realm of Children's Literature*. New York: Atheneum, 1971.

Langfeldt, Johannes. "Märchen und Pädagogik." *Pädagogische Rundschau* 2 (1948): 521–25.

Lankshear, Colin, and Peter McLaren. *Critical Literacy: Politics, Praxis, and the Postmodern*. Albany: State University of New York Press, 1993.

Lasch, Christopher. *The Culture of Narcissism: American Life in an Age of Diminishing Expectations*. New York: Norton, 1979.

Leach, Penelope. *Children First*. New York: Knopf, 1994.

Lee, Tanith. *Red as Blood, or Tales from the Sisters Grimmer*. New York: Daw, 1983.

Lenartz, Werner. "Von der erzieherischen Kraft des Märchens." *Pädagogische Rundschau* 2 (1948): 330–36.

Lesnik-Oberstein, Karín. *Children's Literature: Criticism and the Fictional Child*. Oxford: Clarendon Press, 1994.

_____. "Essentials: What Is Children's Literature? What Is Childhood?" In *Understanding Children's Literature*, ed. Peter Hunt, 15–29. London: Routledge, 1999.

Lipman, Doug. *The Storytelling Coach: How to Listen, Praise, and Bring Out People's Best*. Little Rock: August House, 1995.

Llosa, Mario Vargas. *The Storyteller*. Trans. Helen Lane. New York: Farrar, Straus and Giroux, 1989.

Logan, Mawuena Kossi. *Narrating Africa: George Henty and the Fiction of Empire*. New York: Garland, 1999.

Lurie, Alison. *Don't Tell the Grown-Ups: Subversive Children's Literature*. Boston: Little, Brown, 1990.

_____. "Not for Muggles." *New York Review of Books* (December 16, 1999): 6, 8.

MacCann, Donnarae. *White Supremacy in Children's Literature: Characterizations of African Americans, 1830–1900*. New York: Garland, 1997.

Mackey, Margaret. *The Case of Peter Rabbit: Changing Conditions of Literature for Children*. New York: Garland, 1999.

MacLeod, Anne Scott. *American Childhood: Essays on Children's Literature of the 19th and 20th Centuries*. Athens: University of Georgia Press, 1994.

Maguire, Jack. *The Power of Personal Storytelling: Spinning Tales to Connect with Others*. New York: Putnam, 1998.

Maltin, Leonard. *Of Mice and Magic: A History of American Animated Cartoons*. New York: New American Library, 1980.

Manning, Steven. "Channel One Enters the Media Literacy Movement." *Rethinking Schools* 14 (Winter 1999/2000): 15, 17.

Maslin, Janet. "At Last, The Wizard Gets Back to School." The *New York Times* (July 10, 2000): B1, 6.

May, Jill. *Children's Literature and Critical Theory: Reading and Writing for Understanding*. New York: Oxford University Press, 1995.

McCallum, Robyn. *Ideologies of Identity in Adolescent Fiction: The Dialogic Construction of Subjectivity*. New York: Garland, 1999.

McChesney, Robert W. *Rich Media, Poor Democracy: Communication Politics in Dubious Times*. Urbana: University of Illinois Press, 1999.

McGillis, Roderick. *The Nimble Reader: Literary Theory and Children's Literature*. New York: Twayne, 1996.

_____, ed. *Voices of the Other: Children's Literature and the Postcolonial Context*. New York: Garland, 1999.

_____. "The Delights of Impossibility: No Children, No Books, Only Theory." *Children's Literature Association Quarterly* 23 (Winter 1998–1999): 202–8.

Meek, Margaret, "Introduction." In *International Companion Encyclopedia of Children's Literature*, ed. Peter Hunt, 1–13. London: Routledge, 1996.

Meigs, Cornelia, ed. *A Critical History of Children's Literature: A Survey of Children's Literature from the Earliest Times to the Present*. New York: Macmillan, 1953.

Miller, Alice. *The Drama of the Gifted Child*. Trans. Ruth Ward. New York: Basic Books, 1981.

_____. *For Your Own Good: Hidden Cruelty in Child-Rearing and the Roots of Violence*. Trans. Hildegarde and Hunt Hannum. New York: 1983.

_____. *Thou Shalt Not Be Aware: Society's Betrayal of the Child*. Trans. Hildegarde and Hunt Hannum. New York: Farrar, Straus and Giroux, 1986.

Miller, G. Wayne. *Toy Wars: The Epic Struggle between G. I. Joe, Barbie, and the Companies that Make Them*. Holbrook, Mass.: Adams Media Corporation, 1998.

Miller, Mark Crispin. "The Crushing Power of Big Publishing." *The Nation* (March 17, 1997): 11–18.

Molnar, Alex. *Giving Kids the Business: The Commercialization of America's Schools*. Boulder, Colo.: Westview Press, 1996.

Moore, Sharon. *We Love Harry Potter! We'll Tell You Why*. New York: St. Martin's Griffin, 1999.

Morris, Tim. *You're Only Young Twice: Children's Literature and Film.* Urbana: University of Illinois Press, 1999.

Murray, Gail. *American Children's Literature and the Construction of Childhood.* New York: Twayne, 1998.

Myers, Mitzi. "Missed Opportunities and Critical Malpractice: New Historicism and Children's Literature." *Children's Literature Association Quarterly* 13 (1988): 41–43.

Napoli, Donna Jo. *The Prince of the Pond: Otherwise Known as De Fawg Pin.* Illustr. Judith Byron Schachner. New York: Dutton, 1992.

_____. *The Magic Circle.* New York: Dutton, 1993.

_____. *Jimmy: The Pickpocket of the Palace.* Illustr. Judith Byron Schachner. New York: Dutton, 1995.

_____. *Zel.* New York: Dutton, 1996.

_____. *Sirena.* New York: Scholastic, 1998.

_____. *Crazy Jack.* New York: Delacorte, 1999.

Napoli, Donna Jo, and Richard Tchen. *Spinners.* New York: Dutton, 1999.

Nelson, Claudia, and Lynne Vallone, eds. *The Girl's Own: Cultural Histories of the Anglo-American Girl, 1830–1915.* Athens: University of Georgia Press, 1994.

Nikolejeva, Maria. *Children's Literature Comes of Age: Toward a New Aesthetics.* New York: Garland, 1995.

Nodelman, Perry. *Words about Pictures: The Narrative Art of Children's Picture Books.* Athens: University of Georgia Press, 1988.

_____. *The Pleasures of Children's Literature.* New York: Longman, 1990.

Oittinen, Riitta. *Translating for Children.* New York: Garland, 2000.

Paley, Vivian Gussin. *The Girl with the Brown Crayon: How Children Use Stories to Shape Their Lives.* Cambridge: Harvard University Press, 1997.

Palladino, Grace. *Teenagers: An American History.* New York: Basic Books, 1996.

Paul, Lissa. *Reading Otherways.* South Woodchester: Thimble Press, 1998.

Pellowski, Anne. *The World of Storytelling.* Rev. ed. Bronx: H. W. Wilson, 1990.

Petzet, Wolfgang. "Verteidigung des Märchens gegen seine Verleumder." *Prisma* 1 (1947): 3, 11.

Pipher, Mary. *Retrieving Ophelia: Saving the Selves of Adolescent Girls.* New York: G. P. Putnam's Sons, 1994.

Rahn, Suzanne. *Rediscoveries in Children's Literature.* New York: Garland, 1995.

Rölleke, Heinz. "Märchentheorien der Brüder Jacob und Wilhelm Grimm." *Märchenspiegel* 9 (August 1998): 67–69.

Rose, Jacqueline. *The Case of Peter Pan, or the Impossibility of Children's Fiction.* London: Macmillan, 1984.

Rowling, J. K. *Harry Potter and the Sorcerer's Stone*. New York: Scholastic, 1998.

———. *Harry Potter and the Chamber of Secrets*. New York: Scholastic, 1999.

———. *Harry Potter and the Prisoner of Azkaban*. New York: Scholastic, 1999.

———. *Harry Potter and the Goblet of Fire*. New York: Scholastic, 2000.

Rubright, Lynn. *Beyond the Beanstalk: Interdisciplinary Learning through Storytelling*. Portsmouth, N.H.: Heinemann, 1996.

Rustin, Margaret, and Michael Rustin. *Narratives of Love and Loss: Studies in Modern Children's Fiction*. London: Verso, 1987.

Schoefer, Christine. "Harry Potter's Girl Trouble." *Salon.com* (January 23, 2000): 1–4.

Scieszka, Jon. *The Frog Prince Continued*. Illustr. Steve Johnson. New York: Viking, 1991.

Scott, Alma. *Wanda Gág: The Story of an Artist*. Minneapolis: University of Minnesota Press, 1949.

Segal, Lore, and Maurice Sendak, eds. *The Juniper Tree and Other Tales from Grimm*. Trans. Lore Segal and Randall Jarrell. 2 vols. New York: Farrar, Straus and Giroux, 1973.

Seiter, Ellen. *Sold Separately: Parents & Children in Consumer Culture*. New Brunswick, N.J.: Rutgers University Press, 1995.

Shavit, Zohar. *The Poetics of Children's Literature*. Athens: University of Georgia Press, 1986.

Sheehan, John. "Why I Said No to Coca-Cola." *Rethinking Schools* 14 (Winter 1999/2000): 15.

Silko, Leslie Marmon. *Storyteller*. New York: Arcade, 1981.

Silvey, Anita, ed. *Children's Books and Their Creators*. Boston: Houghton Mifflin, 1995.

Smetanka, Mary Jane. "Once Upon a Time." *Star Tribune* (April 2, 2000): Section E, 1, 4.

Smith, Barbara Herrnstein. *Contingencies of Value: Alternative Perspectives for Critical Theory*. Cambridge: Harvard University Press, 1988.

Smith, Lillian. *The Unreluctant Years: A Critical Approach to Children's Literature*. Chicago: American Library Association, 1953.

Snow, Misti. "The Value of Virtue." *Star Tribune* (January 9, 1997): E1–2.

Sobol, Joseph Daniel. *The Storytellers' Journey: An American Revival*. Urbana: University of Illinois Press, 1999.

Stainton Rogers, Rex, and Wendy Stainton Rogers. *Stories of Childhood: Shifting Agendas of Child Concern*. London: Harvester Wheatsheaf, 1992.

Steinberg, Shirley R., and Joel L. Kincheloe, eds. *Kinderculture: The Corporate Construction of Childhood*. Boulder, Colo.: Westview Press, 1997.

Staples, Terry. *All Pals Together: The Story of Children's Cinema*. Edinburgh: Edinburgh University Press, 1997.

Stephens, John. *Language and Ideology in Children's Fiction*. London: Longman, 1992.

Stephens, John, and Robyn McCallum. *Retelling Stories, Framing Culture: Traditional Story and Metanarratives in Children's Literature*. New York: Garland, 1998.

Steward, John. *The New Child: British Art and the Origins of Modern Childhood, 1730–1830*. Berkeley: University of California Press, 1995.

Stone, Kay F. *Burning Brightly: New Light on Old Tales Told Today*. Peterborough, Ontario: Broadview, 1998.

Sutton, Roger. "Potter's Field." *The Horn Book* 75 (September/October 1999): 500–1.

Thacker, Deborah. "Disdain or Ignorance? Literary Theory and the Absence of Children's Literature." *The Lion and the Unicorn* 24 (January 2000): 1–17.

Tucker, Nicholas. *The Child and the Book: A Psychological and Literary Exploration*. Cambridge: Cambridge University Press, 1981.

Vallone, Lynne. *Disciplines of Virtue: Girls' Culture in the Eighteenth and Nineteenth Centuries*. New Haven: Yale University Press, 1995.

Vandergrift, Kay E. *Ways of Knowing: Literature and the Intellectual Life of Children*. Lanham, Md.: Scarecrow Press, 1996.

Velde, Vivian Vande. *Tales from the Brothers Grimm and the Sisters Weird*. New York: Harcourt Brace, 1995.

Watts, Steven. *The Magic Kingdom: Walt Disney and the American Way of Life*. Boston: Houghton Mifflin, 1997.

Wells, Joel. *Grimm Fairy Tales for Adults*. Illustr. Marilyn Fitschen. New York: Macmillan, 1967.

Williams, Geoffrey. "Children Becoming Readers: Readers and Literacy." In *Understanding Children's Literature*, ed. Peter Hunt, 151–62. London: Routledge, 1999.

Wilson, Michael. *Performance and Practice: Oral Narrative Traditions among Teenagers in Britain and Ireland*. Aldershot: Ashgate, 1997.

Winerip, Michael. "Harry Potter and the Sorcerer's Stone." *New York Times Book Review* (February 14, 1999): 26.

Wojik-Andrews, Ian. *Children's Films: History, Ideology, Pedagogy, Theory*. New York: Garland, 2000.

Wolf, Shelby Anne, and Shirley Brice Heath. *The Braid of Literature: Children's Worlds of Reading*. Cambridge: Harvard University Press, 1992.

Zelinsky, Paul O. *Rumpelstiltskin*. New York: Dutton, 1986.

Zipes, Jack, ed. *Don't Bet on the Prince: Contemporary Feminist Fairy Tales in North America and England*. New York: Methuen, 1986.

_____. *Fairy Tale as Myth / Myth as Fairy Tale*. Lexington: University Press of Kentucky, 1994.

_____. *Creative Storytelling: Building Community, Changing Lives*. New York: Routledge, 1995.

_____. *Happily Ever After: Fairy Tales, Children, and the Culture Industry*. New York: Routledge, 1997.

_____, ed. *The Oxford Companion to Fairy Tales: The Western Fairy Tale Tradition from Medieval to Modern*. Oxford: Oxford University Press, 2000.

Index

ABC books, 46, 56
activists, against culture industry, xii
Adorno, Theodor, x–xi, 12–13, 73
*The Adventures of Rocky and Bullwinkle and
     Friends*, 106
advertising
     effects on children, 11–12
     subliminal, 23(n24)
African Americans
     illiteracy among children of, 32
     storytelling traditions of, 137, 138
Agrippa, 162, 165, 168(n12)
AIDS, 20
Aiken, Joan, 186–187
Aladdin, 56, 175

Alderson, Brian, 186–187
Alexander, Lloyd, 174
Alger, Horatio, 175
Allen, Steve, x–xi
alternative educational systems, effects on
     consumerism, 21
American Association of Librarians, 54
Americanization of the Grimm's Fairy Tales,
     81–98
American Library Association, 72
Andersen, Hans Christian, 42, 85, 100, 154,
     182
Anmerkungen (Notes), of the *Children's and
     Household Tales* (Grimm & Grimm),
     103–104

Anno, Mitsumasa, 107, 114, 115–116
Anno's Twice-Told Tales by the Brothers Grimm & Mr. Fox, 107, 114
Antelope Valley (California), teenage cultural study of, 26, 28, 30–31, 32, 33, 34–35
Anthony, Edward, 106
Anthony, Joseph, 106
antiviolence societies, effects on consumerism, 21
Antony, 165
Apple, marketing by, 19
Arbuthnot, May Hill, 29
Ariès, Philippe, 40, 65
Audacious Kids: Coming of Age in America's Classic Children's Books (Griswold), 29
Augustus, 165
Avery, Gillian, 29

Babbitt, Natalie, 174
Baby-Sitters Club, 7
Bacchilega, Cristina, 123
Bakhtin, Mikhail, 29, 73, 166
Bakhtinian analysis, of children's books, 55
Barbie dolls, 58, 62, 84, 172
Barrymore, Drew, 124
Barthelme, Donald, 114
Barthes, Roland, 29, 129
Basile, Giambattista, 103
basketball games, commercialism in, 16–17
Baudrillard, Jean, 73
Baum, L. Frank, 182, 188(n4)
Bazalgette, Cary, 14
Beauty and the Beast, 56
"Beauty and the Beast", 113
Beckett, Sandra, 29
Behold the Child: American Children and their Books (Avery), 29
Bell, Terrel, 17
Benjamin, Walter, 73, 129–131, 134
Bennett, William, 3, 11, 58
The Berenstain Bears, 7, 56
Bernstein, Richard, 183–184, 185
Beyond the Beanstalk: Interdisplinary Learning through Storytelling (Rubright), 140–141
the Bible
    for children, 46
    magic and folklore in, 188(n4)
"Biotech Industry Bets Its Future on Storytelling", 128
Birmingham School of cultural studies, xii
Block, Francesca Lia, 35, 174
Book List, 54
Books Children, and Men (Hazard), 28
bookstores
    for children, 4, 83
    children's books in, 36, 52–53, 67, 83

Bourdieu, Pierre, 64–65, 70–71
Boynton, Robert, 43, 47
Briar Rose (Coover), 114
Brooke, Leslie, 82
Brooks, Bruce, 35
Broumas, Olga, 113
Brown, Margaret Wise, 53
Bryn Mawr Elementary School (Minneapolis), storytelling session at, 31
Buffy the Vampire Slayer, 180
The Bulletin of the Center for Children's Books, 54
Burger King, marketing by, 19
"Buried Alive: Our Children and the Avalanche of Crud" (Denby), 9
Burning Brightly: New Light on Old Tales Told Today (Stone), 138
Butler, Francelia, 26

Caldecott medal, 56, 68
Canadian Children's Literature, 26, 54
Canadian Children's Literature Association, 72
capitalist market, effects on children, xi–xii
Carnegie prize, 68
Caroline, Antonie, 150
Carryl, Guy Whetmore, fairy tale satires of, 105–106
Carter, Angela, 113
The Case of Peter Pan; or The Impossibility of Children's Fiction (Rose), 65, 184
Centuries of Childhood (Ariès), 40, 65
The Century, 105
Chamberlain, Chris, 2
chapbooks, for children, 46
Charlotte's Web, 7
child abuse and neglect
    as fairy tale themes, 110–111, 122, 154, 184
    Struwwelpeter and, 153, 155–156, 162
    in 19th and 20th centuries, 154, 167–168
    U.S. cases of, 33
child-defense organizations, effects on consumerism, 21
childhood, definition of, 40, 59(n2;n8), 65
children
    bookstores for, 4
    as consumers, 3–4, 11, 34, 67, 78–79
    cultural homogenization of, xiii, 1–23, 33, 48
    definition of, 40, 59(n2;n8), 65
    literacy of, 32, 66, 188
    living in poverty, 30, 32, 35
    reading habits of, 35
    socialization of, x, xiii
    Websites produced by, 40
Children and Childhood in Western Society (Cunningham), 65

Children in Jeopardy: Can We Break the Cycle of Poverty? (Harris), 30
Children's and Household Tales (Grimm & Grimm), 82, 101, 103
Children's Books and Their Creators (Silvey), 30
Children's Books Too Good to Miss (Arbuthnot), 29
Children's Book Week, 83
The Children's Culture Reader, 27
Children's Literature, 26, 54, 72
children's literature
  children's response to, 57–58
  debates on, xiii
  definition of, 40
  designers for, 49, 50
  distribution of, 52–54
  editors for, 49, 51, 83–84
  evaluation of, 61–80
  fate of, in schools, 24–38
  genres of, 46–47
  Harry Potter books in, 170–189
  history of, 45–46, 155
  illustrators of, 49, 50, 86
  libraries' role in, 5, 68, 72
  literary agents for, 49–50
  literary criticism of, 25, 29, 36, 68, 183–184
  nonexistence of, 39–60
  profitability of, 67, 68, 187, 188
  publishing of, 5, 7–8, 48, 49–52, 59
  reception of, 54–59
  reviewers of, 57
  teachers of, 50–54, 68, 69–70, 72–75
  workshops and programs on, 41–42, 72–73
  writers of, 43–45, 49, 50
Children's Literature: Criticism and the Fictional Child (Lesnick-Oberstein), 29, 65
Children's Literature and Culture, 26
Children's Literature Association (ChLA), 26, 54, 72
Children's Literature Association Quarterly, 26
Children's Literature Comes of Age: Toward a New Aesthetics (Nikolejeva), 29
Children's Literature in Education, 26, 54, 72
Children's Literature Quarterly, 54, 72
Children's Theatre of Minneapolis, 143
Cinderella, in *Ever After*, 123–124
"Cinderella" (Grimm/Cole), 116
Civilization and Its Discontents (Freud), 144
Clark, Beverly, 29
Cleopatra, 165
Close, Glenn, 14
Coca-Cola, marketing by, 19
Cole, Babette, 107, 116–117

Cole, Brock, 35
colleges and universities, children's literature courses in, 54
comics, for children, 46
consumerism, in children, 34
consumer protection organizations, 21
consumption bug (CB), 20
contamination
  definition of, 102–103
  of fairy tales, 99–125
"The Contamination of the Fairy Tale" (Zipes), xiv
Contingencies of Value: Alternative Perspectives for Critical Theory (Smith), 63
Coover, Robert, 114
Cormier, Robert, 5, 35
Cornell University, children's literature course at, 27
corporal punishment, of children, 155–156
Crane, Walter, 82
A Critical History of Children's Literature (Meigs), 29
critical theory, of children's literature, 29
Criticism, Theory, and Children's Literature (Hunt), 29
Crouch, Julian, 148, 159, 166, 167
Cruikshank, George, 82
"The Crushing Power of Big Publishing" (Miller), 50–51
Crutcher, Chris, 35
"The Cultural Homogenization of American Culture" (Zipes), xiii, 1–23
cultural pedagogy, of corporations, 33–34
culture industry, 148, 158
  effects on children, xi, xii, 10–11, 48, 57
Cunningham, Hugh, 65

Danesi, Marcel, 36
d'Aulnoy, Marie-Catherine, 103
David, 175
Deadly Persuasion: Why Women and Girls Must Fight the Addictive Power of Advertising (Kilbourne), 11
deconstructionist analysis, of children's books, 55
"De Gaudeif un sien Meester", 95
Denby, David, 4, 9–12
Derrida, Jacques, 29, 73
"Der Waldmensch", 131
Dialectic of the Enlightenment (Adorno & Horkheimer), x
"Di Bocca in Bocca", 142
didactic stories, for children, 46
Discover Card, 19
"Disdain or Ignorance? Literary Theory and the Absence of Children's Literature" (Thacker), 27

Disney Corporation, 182
    as book publishers, 56, 92
    fairy-tale films of, 84–85, 172
    marketing by, 13–14
"Doctorknowitall" (Janosch), 110
dolls, books accompanying, 58
Donner, Therese, marriage to Heinrich
        Hoffmann, 150
Donoghue, Emma, 107, 121–122
Doyle, Richard, 82
"Do You Know What We Are Doing to Your
        Books?" (Zipes), xiii
The Drama of the Gifted Child (Miller), 167
Dubrow, ___, 49

Eagleton, Terry, 73
editors, for children's books, 49, 51, 83–84
eighteenth century, children's literature
        in, 46
"The Elves" (Grimm/Sendak), 112
*The End of Victory: Cold War America and
        the Disillusioning of a Generation*
        (Engelhardt), 4
Engelhardt, Tom, 4–9, 12
Erfahrung, 130
Erziehungsbuch, 102
ethnic minority themes, in small-press
        books, 51
Eulalie, 83
Ever After [film], 123
Exxon, marketing by, 18, 19

fables, for children, 46, 56
The Fairies Up-To-Date (Anthony &
        Anthony), 106
fairy tales
    Americanization of, 81–98
    animated, 97(n5)
    for children, 46, 56, 83, 85, 87
    contamination of, 99–125
    "feminist", 42
    as a genre, 116
family, role in upbringing of children, 78
family associations, stand against culture
        industry, xii
feminist analyses
    of children's literature, 29, 55
    of Grimms' tales, 113, 114, 121, 125(n10)
feminist organizations, stand against culture
        industry, xii
feminist themes, in small-press books, 51
Ferguson, Andres, 15
fetal alcohol syndrome, 42
Fetscher, Iring, radical reversion of Grimms'
        tales by, 125(n9)
Fine, Anne, 35
Finnegan, William, 25–26
"The Fisherman and His Wife"
        (Grimm/Anno), 114
The Five Owls, 54

food companies, advertising by, 28–29
Foreman, Michael, 116
"The Forest Dweller", 131
*For Your Own Good: Hidden Cruelty in
        Child-Rearing and the Roots of
        Violence* (Miller), 167
Foucault, Michel, 29
"The Four Clever Brothers" (Grimm/Anno),
        114
"The Four Clever Sons" (Grimm/Anno),
        115–116
"The Four Skillful Brothers" (Grimm/Anno),
        114
Fractured Fairy Tales (Jacobs), 106
Freemasons, 149
"Free Time" (Adorno), 12
Freud, Sigmund, 29, 73, 144
Freudian analysis, of children's books, 55
"The Frog King" (Grimm/Cole), 113–116
"The Frog King" (Grimm/Lee), 113–114
"The Frog King" (Grimm/Napoli), 117/118
"The Frog King" (Grimm/Sendak), 110
The Frog Prince Continued (Scieszka), 117
The Frog Prince (Scieszka), 107
"From Mouth to Mouth", 142

Gág, Flavia, 87
Gág, Wanda, 81–98
    profile of, 85–97
Galloway, Priscilla, 107, 119
Gannon, Sue, summary of children's
        literature studies by, 37(n2)
Gardner, Lyn, 158
Garland Publishing, new book series of, 26
Garner, James Finn, 106
Gemeinschaft, decline of, 131
General Mills, marketing by, 19
Germany, purification of Grimms' tales in, 85
ghostwriters, 49, 50
Giannetti, Ryan, 2
*The Girl's Own: Cultural Histories of the
        Anglo-American Girls* (Nelson &
        Vallone), 29
The Girl with the Brown Crayon (Paley),
        77, 142
*Giving Kids the Business: The Commercial-
        ization of American Schools*
        (Molnar), 17
globalization, of capitalist conglomerates,
        xii, 21
"The Goblins" (Grimm/Sendak), 111, 112
Goethe, Johann Wolfgang von, 101
"The Golden Rope" (Lee), 113
Goluke, Ulrich, 128
Goodnight Moon (Brown), 53
Goosebumps series (Stine), 4, 8, 19, 42, 58
*Great Books: My Adventures with Homer,
        Rousseau, Woolf, and Other
        Indestructible Writers of the Western
        World* (Denby), 9

The Great Excluded, 26
Greenway prize, 68
Grimm, Jacob, 82, 85, 101, 103, 110, 112,
    114, 115, 117, 118, 182
Grimm, Wilhelm, 82, 85, 101, 103–104, 110,
    112, 114, 115, 117, 118, 182
Grimm brothers, 101–102, 112, 123
Grimm Fairy Tales for Adults (Wells), 106
Grimms' Fairy Tales
    Americanization by Wanda Gág, 81–98
    illustrations for, 110–111, 114, 116
    Indo-Germanic roots of, 104
    Kleine Ausgabe of, 109
    pre-texts of, 108, 109, 113, 114, 116
    satires and parodies of, 105–107, 116
Grimms' Fairy Tales (Kredel), 89
Grimms' tales, 84, 86, 100
    as Germanic, 99–102, 103
Grimm Tales Made Coy (Carryl), 105
Griswold, Jerome, 29
Gruelle, Johnny, 83, 89
Guy, Rosa, 5, 35

habitus, in learning, 64, 74, 75, 76
hablador, as Indian spiritual teacher, 127
Hamilton, Virginia, 5, 35
"Hansel and Gretel", 184
    Gág's illustration of, 86
"Hans My Hedgehog" (Janosch), 109
Harris, Irving, 32–33
Harry Potter and the Chamber of Secrets
    (Rowling), 176, 178
Harry Potter and the Goblet of Fire
    (Rowling), 176, 177, 178–179, 183,
    188(n1)
Harry Potter and the Prisoner of Azkaban
    (Rowling), 176, 178, 187
Harry Potter and the Sorcerer's Stone
    (Rowling), 173, 176, 186
Harry Potter books (Rowling), xiii, 4, 19,
    170–189
    children's response to, 185–186
    critiques of, 179, 183–184
    formulas for, 176–177
    phenomenon of, 170–172
"Harry Potter's Simplicity Lures Kids of All
    Ages" [article], 186
Hazard, Paul, 28
Hearne, Betsy, 59(n8)
"The Hedgehog and the Rabbit" (Gág), 91
Heidenbach, Nikolaus, 116
Hesse, Herman, 131, 132
Hirsch, E. D., 49, 58
The History of Goody Twoshoes (Newberry),
    7
The Hobbit (Tolkien), 85
Hoffmann, Antonie, 150
Hoffmann, Carl, 150
Hoffmann, E. T. A., 159
Hoffmann, Eduard, 150, 151

Hoffmann, Heinrich, *Der Struwwelpeter* of,
    148–157, 161, 162–164
Hoffmann, Philipp Jacob, 149
Hoffmann, Therese Donner, 150
Hollins College, children's literature
    program of, 73
"The Hollywood Way" (Boynton), 47
homogenization, of children, xiii
Hook, 14
Horkheimer, Max, x
The Horn Book, 26, 54, 83, 92, 94, 186, 187
Howker, Janni, 187
Hoyle, Karen Nelson, 82, 83, 92
Huckleberry Finn, 14
Humphreys, Earle, 82, 87, 94
Hundt, Reed, 11
Hunt, Margaret, 89
Hunt, Peter, 29, 30, 44–45, 49, 65, 73–74
Hyman, Trina Shart, 116

IBM, marketing by, 19
Ideologies of Identity in Adolescent Fiction
    (McCallum), 29
"I Like Fairy Tales" (Gág), 94
imperialism, in children's literature, 66
Improbable Theatre, 148
inner-city schools, poor funding of, 32
*International Companion Encyclopedia of
    Children's Literature* (Hunt), 30
International Research Society of Children's
    Literature, 26
*International Review of Children's Literature
    an Librarianship*, 72
Internet
    as advocacy group source, 23(n24)
    children's writers on, 53
Iwerks, Ub, 84

Jack the Giant Killer, 175
Jacobs, A. J., 106
Jacques, Martyn, 158, 159, 160, 164, 166
Jameson, Frederic, 73
Jan, Isabelle, 28
Janosch, 107, 109
Janosch erzählt Grimm's Marchen (Janosch),
    107, 109
Jenkins, Henry, 27, 34
Jimmy, the Pickpocket of the Palace (Napoli),
    118
Johnson, Steve, 117
Johnson Wax, marketing by, 19
Jones, Diana Wynne, 174
Jungian analysis, of children's books, 55
Jungian therapists, storytelling use by, 139
*The Juniper Tree and Other Tales from
    Grimm* (Segal & Sendak), 107, 110,
    111, 113

Kent, Clark, 175
Kilbourne, Jean, 11

Kincheloe, Joel L., 33–34
Kinder, Marsha, 34
Kinderculture: The Corporate Construction of Childhood (Steinberg & Kincheloe), 30
Kinderlieb, Heinrich, as Heinrich Hoffmann pseudonym, 151
Kinderlieb, Reimerich, as Heinrich Hoffmann pseudonym, 151
Kinder und Hausmärchen (Grimm & Grimm), *see also Children's and Household Tales*, 82, 101, 112.
"King Thrushbeard" (Grimm/Cole), 116
Kissing the Witch: Old Tales in New Skins (Donoghue), 107, 121–122
Klein, Melanie, 29
Kline, Stephen, 3, 27
Knoepflmacher, U. C., 27
Knowles, Murray, 29
Kredel, Fritz, 83, 89
Kroeber, Karl, 108, 130–131, 133, 134, 146(n5)
Kutzer, Daphne, 30
Kuznets, Lois, 29

Lacan, Jacques, 29, 73
Language and Control in Children's Literature (Knowles & Malmkjaer), 29
Language and Ideology in Children's Fiction (Stephens), 29
Lasch, Christopher, 138
Leach, Penelope, 21
Lee, Tanith, 107, 113, 114
legends, for children, 46
LeGuin, Ursula, 187
L'Engle, Madeleine, 43
Lesnik-Oberstein, Karín, 29, 65, 92
Lhéritier, Marie-Jeanne, 103
librarians, as readers of children's books, 55–56
libraries, economic deterioration of, 5, 67–68
Life magazine, 105
Lindgren, Astrid, 86–87
The Lion and the Unicorn, 26, 54, 72
The Lion King, 182
Lionni, Leo, 77, 142
Lipman, Doug, 141
literacy
    of children, 32, 66, 188
    as U.S. problem, 31–32
literary agents, 49–50
literary criticism, of children's literature, 25, 29, 36
"Little Jacob, and How He Became Fat", 156–158
"Little Red Riding Hood" (Carryl), 105
"Little Red Riding Hood" (Grimm & Grimm), 113
"Little Red Shoes", 154
Little Women (Alcott), 14
The London Tattler, 105
Lucas, George, 82

Lurie, Alison, 27
Lynton, Michael, 43
Lyotard, Jean-François, 73

MacDonald, George, 182
Machiguenga Indians (Amazon Jungle), storytelling of, 127
The Magic Circle (Grimm/Napoli), 107, 118
Malmkjaer, Kristen, 29
Manning, Stephen, 18
Marshall, James, 116
Marx, Karl, 73
Marxism, children's literature and, 29, 55
Mary Ann and Too Many Boys, 7
Mary Poppins (Travers), 86
Maslin, Janet, 188(n1)
Massee, May, 83–84
mass media, effects on children, 19–20
Mathiews, Frank K., 83
Mayer, Mercer, 116
Mayne, William, 187
Mazier, Norma Fox, 35
McCallum, Robyn, 29, 107–108
McDermott, Phelim, 148, 159, 166, 167
McGillis, Rod, 29, 65
media watch groups, effects on consumerism, xii, 21
Meek, Margaret, 30–31
Meigs, Cornelia, 29
Microsoft, marketing by, 19
Miller, Alice, 167
Miller, Mark, 51
Millions of Cats (Gág), 86
minority young men, unemployment among, 33
Modern Language Association, 54, 72–73
Molnar, Alex, 17–18
Monsanto Company, 128
"Monthly Forum for Young Writers" [*Star Tribune*], 2
Moore, Anne Carroll, 87, 92, 96
More, Thomas, 124
Moreau, Jeanne, 123
More Tales from Grimm (Gág), 82
Morris, Michael, 148, 158, 159
Morris, Tim, 27
movies, effect on children, 9, 13–15, 19
multiculturalism, use of term, 37
murder, in inner-city projects, 33
Myers, Mitzi, 77

"The Name" (Galloway), 119
Napoli, Donna Jo, 107, 117, 118, 119, 174
The Nation, article on publishing in, 50–51
National Association for the Preservation and Perpetuation of Storytelling (NAPPS), 138
National Council for the Teaching of English, 72
National Council of Teachers of English, 54

National Storytelling Association (NSA), 138
Nation of Risk, 17
Native Americans
   depiction in children's books, 42
   storytelling traditions of, 136–137, 138
"Neighborhood Bridges", 143
Nelson, Claudia, 29
New Age themes, in small-press books, 51
New American Dolls, stories with, 58
Newberry, John, 7
Newbery medal, 56, 68
New Historicism, in children's literature, 77
New Kids on the Block, 7
New Yorker, 25
New York Herald Tribune Books, 92
New York Times Book Review, 36, 72
Nielsen, Kay, 83
Nikolejeva, Maria, 29
The Nimble Reader: Literary Theory and
   Children's Literature (McGillis), 29
nineteenth century, children's literature
   in, 47
Nodelman, Perry, 29
nursery rhymes, for children, 46

On Children's Literature (Jan), 28
101 Dalmations, 13–14
oral tradition, storytellers in, 132–133
Out of the Garden: Toys and Children's
   Culture in the Age of TV Marketing
   (Kline), 3, 27

Paley, Vivian Gussin, 77, 142
Palladino, Grace, 36
parents, as readers of children's books, 56, 58
Penguin Books, children's books of, 43
penny novels, for children, 46
Perrault, Charles, 85, 100, 103
The Perverse Delight of "Shockheaded Peter"
   (Zipes), xiv
phenomenon, definitions of, 173
"The Phenomenon of Harry Potter, or Why
   All the Talk?" (Zipes), xiv, 170–189
picture books, for children, 46, 56, 117,
   155–156
Pippi Longstocking (Lindgren), 83
The Pleasures of Children's Literature
   (Nodelman), 29
Pocahontas, 56
poetry, for children, 46, 59
Politically Correct Bedtime Stories
   (Garner), 106
pop culture, effects on children, 9, 10
Postmodern Fairy Tales: Gender and
   Narrative Strategies (Bacchilega), 123
poststructuralist theory, of children's
   literature, 29, 37
Potter, Beatrice, 53
poverty, feminization of, 32, 35
The Power Rangers, 180

Pricksongs and Descants (Coover), 114
primers, for children, 46, 68
Prince Cinders (Cole), 107, 116–117
The Prince of Egypt [film], 43
The Prince of the Pond: Otherwise Known as
   De Fawg Pin (Napoli), 117
"The Princess and Her Future" (Lee),
   113–114
Princess Smartypants (Cole), 107, 116
Princeton University, children's literature
   course at, 27
Project TELL—Teaching English through
   Living Language, 140
Publishers Weekly, 83
publishing
   of children's books, 5, 7–8, 48
   megacorporations in, 51, 52
Pullman, Philip, 174

"Rabbit's Bride" (Grimm/Sendak), 111, 112
"Rabbit's Tale (Grimm/Sendak), 111
Rabelais, François, 166
racism
   in children's literature, 66, 162
   in mass media, 23(n24)
"Rapunzel" (Grimm & Grimm), 110, 113, 118
"Reading May Be Harmful to Your Kids: In
   the Nadirland of Today's Children's
   Books" (Engelhardt), 4
Reagan Administration, 17
realists, view of culture industry, xii
reception theory, of children's literature, 29
Red as Blood or Tales from the Sisters
   Grimmer (Lee), 107, 113
Reflections of Change: Children's Literature
   (Beckett), 29
Regendering the School Story: Sassy Sissies
   and Tattling Tomboys (Clark), 29
Reggio Emilia preschool movement, effects
   on consumerism, 21
"Reimerich Kinderlieb", as pseudonym of
   Heinrich Hoffmann, 151
religious institutions
   effects on children's literature, 188(n4)
   effects on consumerism, xii, 21
religious right, role in childhood regulation,
   79
religious themes, in small-press books, 51
The Reluctant Years (Smith), 29
"Rereading Wanda Gág", xiv
Retelling / Rereading (Kroeber), 130
Retelling Stories, Framing Culture: Story &
   Metanarratives in Children's Litera-
   ture (Stephens & McCallum), 107
Rhead, Louis John, 83
Rifkin, Jeremy, 128
Rölleke, Heinz, 101
romances, for children, 46
Rose, Jacqueline, 65, 184
Rosen, Michael, 35

Rowling, J. K., as Harry Potter author, 4, 171, 172, 173, 174, 175, 176, 178, 181, 182, 183, 184, 186

Rubright, Lynn, 140–141, 143

"Rumpelstiltskin" (Grimm/Donoghue), 121–123

"Rumpelstiltskin" (Grimm/Galloway), 119–120

"Rumpelstiltskin" (Grimm & Grimm), 118, 121

St. Nicholas, 165, 168(n12)

The Sandman (Hoffmann), 159

The Saturday Evening Post, 105

Schiano, Marisa, 142

Schoefer, Christine, 179, 180

Scholastic Inc.
    Harry Potter books of, 173, 187, 188
    marketing efforts of, 8, 19

schools, commercialization in, 17–22

Scieszka, Jon, 107, 117

Scott, Alma, 86

Seaman, Louise, 83

secret societies, purpose of, 145

Segal, Lore, 107, 110–114

Seiter, Ellen, 3, 27, 34

semiotics, of children's literature, 29

Sendak, Maurice, 107, 110–114

"The Seven Swabians" (Gág), 91

sexism
    in children's literature, 66
    in mass media, 23(n24)

Sexton, Anne, 113

Shockheaded Peter: A Junk Opera, 147–169

Signal, 26, 54

The Signs and Meanings of Adolescence (Danesi), 36

Silent Majority, role in childhood regulation, 79

Silvey, Anita, 30

Simmons College, children's literature program of, 73

"The Six Swans" (Gág), 91

Slovenly Peter, 148. *See also* Der *Struwwelpeter*

Slovenly Peter's Story Book, 156

Slovenly Peter (Zipes), xiii

Smetanka, Mary Jane, 171

Smith, Barbara Herrnstein, 63

Smith, Lillian, 29

Snow White and the Seven Dwarfs [film], 84–85, 93, 94, 97(n4)

Snow White and the Seven Dwarfs (Gág), 82, 91, 92

"Snow White and the Seven Dwarfs" (Grimm & Grimm), 110

Snow White (Barthelme), 114

Snow White (Gruelle), 89–90

Sobol, Joseph Daniel, 137, 139

Society for Children's Literature, 41

"The Soldier and his Magic Helpers" (Gág), 91

Sold Separately: Parents and Children in Consumer Culture (Seiter), 3, 27

Soper, George, 83

"The Sorcerer's Apprentice" (Gág), 94, 95–96

Sowerby, Millicent, 83

Spinelli, Jerry, 35

Spinners (Napoli & Tchen), 107, 118–119

sports, for children, 15–17, 19

sports stars, books on, 49

Staples, Terry, 14

Star Tribune (Minneapolis), x, 2

Star Wars, 180

Steinberg, Shirley, 33–34

Stephens, John, 29, 107–108

Stine, R. L., 4, 42

Stone, Kay, 138

"The Story about Fidgety Phillip" (Hoffmann), 151

"The Story about Flying Robert" (Hoffmann), 151

"The Story about Hans Who Never Looked Where He Was Going" (Hoffmann), 151

"The Story about Naughty Frederick" (Hoffmann), 151

"The Story about the Black Boys" (Hoffmann), 151

"The Story about the Soupy Caspar" (Hoffmann), 151

"The Story about the Thumbsucker" (Hoffmann), 151

"The Story about the Wild Hunter" (Hoffmann), 151, 161–162

The Story of the Bully-Boys (Jacques), 162, 164–165, 166

"The Story of the Inky Boys" (Hoffmann), 162–164

"The Story of the Man That Went Out Shooting" (Jacques), 160

"The Storyteller" (Benjamin), 129

The Storyteller (Vargas Llosa), 126–127

storytelling, 126–146, 185
    American revival of, 137–139, 144
    benefits to children, 31, 136, 142–143
    genuine, 133–135
    German documentary on, 144–145
    modern forms of, 128
    subjects of, 133
    threats to, 130–131
    use by teachers, 140–144

The Storytelling Coach: How to Listen, Praise, and Bring Out People's Best (Lipman), 141

Straparola, Giovan Francesco, 103

"Straw into Gold" (Velde), 120–121

Struwwelpeter: Fearful Stories & Vile Pictures to Instruct Good Little Folks (House), xiv

"Struwwelpeter and the Comical Crucifixion

of the Child" (Zipes), xiv
Der Struwwelpeter (Hoffmann), 85, 148–157, 158, 161, 166, 167
Struwwelpeter (Zipes), xiii
suffragette movement, fairy tale satires of, 106
Sutcliff, Rosemary, 187
Sutton, Roger, 187, 188(n2)
Sweet Valley Twins, 58, 62

"The Tale of the Spinster" (Donoghue), 107, 121–123
Tales from Grimm (Gág), 81–82, 87–88
Tales from the Brothers Grimm and the Sisters Weird (Velde), 107, 120
Tchen, Richard, 107, 118, 119
teachers, of children's literature, 55
Teenage Mutant Ninja Turtles, 7
teenagers, books for, 44–45
Teenagers: An American History (Palladino), 36
television, effects on children, x, 2–3, 9
Thacker, Deborah, 27–28
Theater Magazine, xiv
Three Gay Tales from Grimm (Gág), 82
Tiger Lillies, 148, 151, 158
Time Magazine, 15
Tolkien, J. R. R., 85
Tom Thumb, 175
toybooks, for children, 46
toys, commodification of children by, 4, 22(n4)
Toy Story, 14
Toy Story 2, 14
Transcending Boundaries: Writing for a Dual Audience of Children and Adults (Beckett), 29
Travers, P. L., 86
Truly Grim Tales (Galloway), 107, 119
Turner, Mindy, cultural study of, 26, 28, 30–31, 32, 33, 34–36, 37
"Tutti Frutti" [club], 150

unions, effects on consumerism, 21
University of Texas (Arlington), children's literature course at, 27
university presses, children's literature studies by, 27
USA Today, Harry Potter article in, 186
Utopia (More), 124

Vallone, Lynne, 29
"The Value of Evaluating the Value of Children's Literature" (Zipes), xiv
Vandergrift, Kay E., 36
Vargas Llosa, Mario, 126, 130, 131, 134
Velde, Vivian Vande, 107, 120, 121
"The Very Sad Story about the Matches" (Hoffmann), 151
violence

on mass media, 9
in New York subways, 33
in schools, 79

"Wanda Gág's Americanization of the Grimms' Fairy Tales" (Zipes), xiv
Warshow, Robert, 9
Ways of Knowing: Literature and the Intellectual Life of Children (Vandergrift), 36
Websites, for children's literature, 40, 53–54, 68, 174
Weil, Kurt, 158
Wells, Joel, 106
Wengert, Martha, 34–35
When Toys Come Alive: Narratives of Animation, Metamorphosis, and Development (Kuznets), 29
Where's Waldo, 7, 56
Where The Wild Things Are (Sendak), 7
Whitney, Bertha, 83
Whitney, Elinor, 83
"Why Children's Literature Does Not Exist" (Zipes), xiii
Williams, Geoffrey, 58
Wilson, Michael, 141–142
Winnicott, D.W., 29
"The Wisdom and Folly of Storytelling " (Zipes), xiv
"The Wishing Table, The Gold Donkey, and The Cudgel-in-the-Sack" (Gág), 91
The Wizard of Oz, 91
"Wolfland" (Lee), 113
women
    advertising effects on, 11–12
    images in mass media, 23(n24)
    living in poverty, 32, 35
    as professors of children's literature, 55, 59(n8)
    as writers for children, 83
women's movement, fairy tale satires of, 106
World Business Council for Sustainable Development, 128
Writers of Multicultural Fiction for Young Adults (Kutzer), 30

X-Men , 180

Yolen, Jane, 174
You've Got Mail [film], 52

Zel (Grimm/Napoli), 118
Zelinsky, Paul O., 116
Zigrosser, Carl, 87
Zipes, Hanna, 61–62
Zipes, Jack, xiii–xiv
Zisla, Lloyd, 2
Zuratas, Saul, 127
Zwerger, Lisbeth, 116